I've led a bunch of companies, wribooks, given countless speeches leadership to MBA's in over a dozen leadership book I've given to my ch way through their own diverse care advice, digital marketing, mental wellness connectivity, teaching and homecare. Why? Because it's written for all of them (and for me too). So reach in, reset and reach out. You may find it's for you too.

Kevin Roberts
Founder Red Rose Consulting
Former Chairman and CEO of
Saatchi & Saatchi Worldwide

Archana Mohan's *The Through Line* is like a conversation with a mentor or coach who calls you out – but in the best way. She brings warmth, wit and wisdom to the table, reminding us that true leadership – the kind that moves, strengthens and genuinely cares for others – is about knowing ourselves and listening closely to and challenging the inner narratives that guide us. If you want to connect who you are with how you lead, this book offers the clarity and heart to get you there.

Hélène Biandudi Hofer
Journalist and Co-Founder of Good Conflict

Archana has done an extremely rare thing of writing a book about leadership that challenges your preconceptions and allows you the space and a framework to think expansively about what kind of leader you want to be. Archana fully embraces nuance and complexity but uses empiricism and compelling storytelling to make sense of the through line. A must read for anyone looking to be the best they can be in all aspects of their life.

Emily Bushby
Deputy Chief Executive Officer, NESTA

When I met Archana I knew I touched 'genuine'. You can't miss it. Her book is a great guide to rediscover, renew and celebrate the genuine. Can we be servant leaders for this moment in history? Read this book and love life and leadership. Be thoroughly you, through and through.

Ruth Dearnley OBE
President and Founder, STOP THE TRAFFIK

Archana shares a deeply personal and gripping journey of self-discovery on her path to leadership. Leadership success is often measured by outward success. Title. Influence. Wealth. Yet this story, beautifully written, shows that the real power to lead comes from within. By identifying your through line – you unlock your true potential. Be inspired and prepare to inspire.

Caroline Stokell
CEO, investment management

Profoundly inspiring and deeply through-provoking. A book that will stay with you for a long time.

Musidora Jorgensen

the through line

How understanding who you are **empowers** how you lead

Archana Mohan

First published in Great Britain by Practical Inspiration Publishing, 2025

© Text Archana Mohan and illustrations Ash Lamb, 2025

Photography: Stephanie Belton 2025

The moral rights of the author have been asserted

ISBN   9781788606820   (hardback)
       9781788606837   (paperback)
       9781788606851   (epub)
       9781788606844   (Kindle)

All rights reserved. This book, or any portion thereof, may not be reproduced without the express written permission of the author.

Every effort has been made to trace copyright holders and to obtain their permission for the use of copyright material. The publisher apologizes for any errors or omissions and would be grateful if notified of any corrections that should be incorporated in future reprints or editions of this book.

Want to bulk-buy copies of this book for your team and colleagues? We can customize the content and co-brand *The Through Line* to suit your business's needs.

Please email info@practicalinspiration.com for more details.

Contents

Dedication ix

About the author xi

Introduction 1
    Why read this book? 1
    Finding a through line 4
    Uncertainty is the system 7
    If you don't, who will? 9
    To lose your way is to learn the way 10
    Let's begin 15

Chapter 1: Crossing lines 17
    In a nutshell 17
    Hidden in plain sight 18
    See it to name it 19
    Use it 21
    Caring to notice 23
    Hope in uncertainty 27
    True colours 30
    Unearthing a truth 31
    Your turn 35

Chapter 2: The through line: a blueprint for leadership 37

　In a nutshell 37

　All the world's a stage 38

　Avoid flat packing 41

　Leadership structures and categories 43

　Know yourself 46

　Be consistent 47

　Storytelling with intent 48

　Integrate the stories 50

　Complicate the narrative: experience is not a prerequisite for impact 53

　One person, one story, six words 56

　Your turn 58

Chapter 3: A line to understand: reach in 61

　In a nutshell 61

　Daring to feel 62

　Some questions to ask 63

　Decision-making in uncertainty 64

　An inside job 67

　How to tune out the static 69

　Excavate your lines 73

　Inner mastery 76

　Outer impact 77

　Your turn 79

Chapter 4: A line to change: reset 85

    In a nutshell 85

    Sick and tired 86

    Surrender as a reset 88

    Change leadership 90

    Free solo 95

    Ease or discomfort 96

    The courage to keep revising 100

    Generative conversations 103

    A blank sheet of paper 105

    Your turn 107

Chapter 5: A line to care: reach out 111

    In a nutshell 111

    A duty to care 112

    Company means connection 115

    An outside job 118

    Deep care 120

    The empty chair 127

    Caring innovation 130

    Design thinking 132

    Complicate the narrative: not every caring encounter is a resounding success 135

    Leadership is reaching out 136

    Your turn 138

Chapter 6: A line to inspire: if you don't who will? 143

    In a nutshell 143

    What is inspiration? 144

    If you don't inspire, who will? 145

    Training and development 148

    Mastery over success 149

    The Queasy Eagle 150

    From through line to inspiration 151

    Inspiration to change the world 153

    Your turn 155

Chapter 7: A line to go further: what is next? 157

    Rewilding 157

    What is next? 158

Notes 161

Bibliography 179

Acknowledgements 193

Index 197

Dedication

You can't go back and change the beginning. But you can start where you are and change the ending.[1]

To my mother who showed me that reaching in had to be the foundation for reaching out. While she can no longer read this, I hope she would be proud.

About the author

Archana Mohan is a leader, teacher and author who believes that authentic leadership starts from within. Growing up in a multicultural environment, Archana witnessed first-hand how strong leadership could build relationships, bridge cultural divides and foster collaboration. She brings a unique perspective to her work, drawing on her experiences as both a teacher and a leader to drive innovation. Her journey, shaped by paradox and fuelled by curiosity, has taught her that leadership isn't about ticking boxes or chasing external validation – it's about embracing complexity, leaning into discomfort and crafting your through line. As Chief Operations and Technology Officer within the finance sector,

Archana has a passion for unlocking human potential. She has built teams, led through uncertainty and empowered others to find their path forward.

Archana's academic qualifications include a BA in French Literature from Brown University, an MA in Education from Columbia University, and an MBA in Finance from Yale University. When she is not helping others lead from their core, Archana can be found learning from life's twists and turns, and reminding everyone that the most important question is: *if you don't, who will?*

You can connect with Archana at www.linkedin.com/in/archana-mohan-3b40b83.

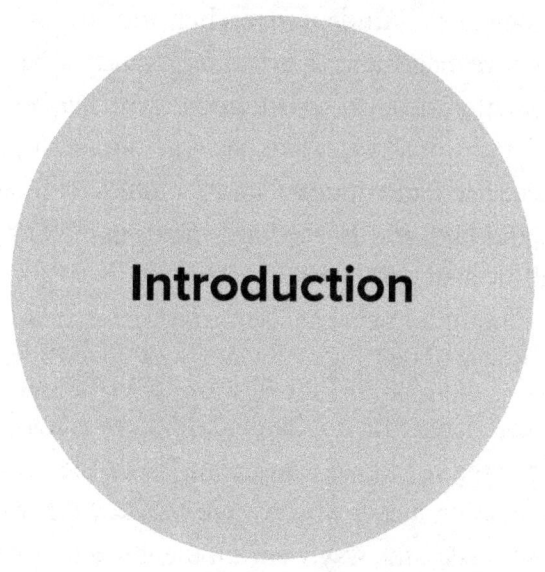

Introduction

Some journeys are direct, and some are circuitous; some are heroic, and some are fearful and muddled. But every journey, honestly undertaken, stands a chance of taking us toward the place where our deep gladness meets the world's deep need.[2]

Why read this book?

We've all had our share of bosses. The ones who inspire and uplift, the ones who focus on their own performance, and those who fall somewhere in the messy middle. The kind who have moments of greatness and moments of uncertainty.

The ones who aren't afraid to show their humanity, who own their missteps, and who somehow bring out the best in the team, making the whole greater than the sum of its parts.

Over the past three decades, I've been on teams, built teams and led them. From student to teacher, and now as a leader in investment management, I've walked the same path as you. I'm not smarter, stronger or better than you. I've been scared, confused and worried just like you. I've been clear, calm and proud too. I've had triumphs and stumbles, exhibited both courage and fear, and learned a thing or two along the way. We've all walked these lines: business lines, reporting lines and those bottom lines that seem to define success.

But there's a line that matters more than all the others. A line only we can define. It's not handed down by a boss, nor does it appear in the corporate handbook. This is the through line. The line that connects who we are to the work we do, the choices we make, the way we lead, the impact we have.

A through line connects who you are with how you lead. It offers insight into your psychological core. It roots you in your values, principles and goals while adapting to new information. It unifies your choices, experiences, highs and lows. Once you recognize it, the way you lead changes. Leadership becomes lighter. Less forced. More you. As author Luvvie Ajayi Jones says, 'The intersection of our personal and professional lives is continuously blurred, because wherever we go, there we are.'[3]

This book is about uncovering that line. It's about reaching in, resetting and reaching out. Each step links to the next. Each is interdependent. Each requires time and patience. It's not easy. But neither is the alternative – rumination, stagnation, disconnection. You already lead. Now it's time to lead as you.

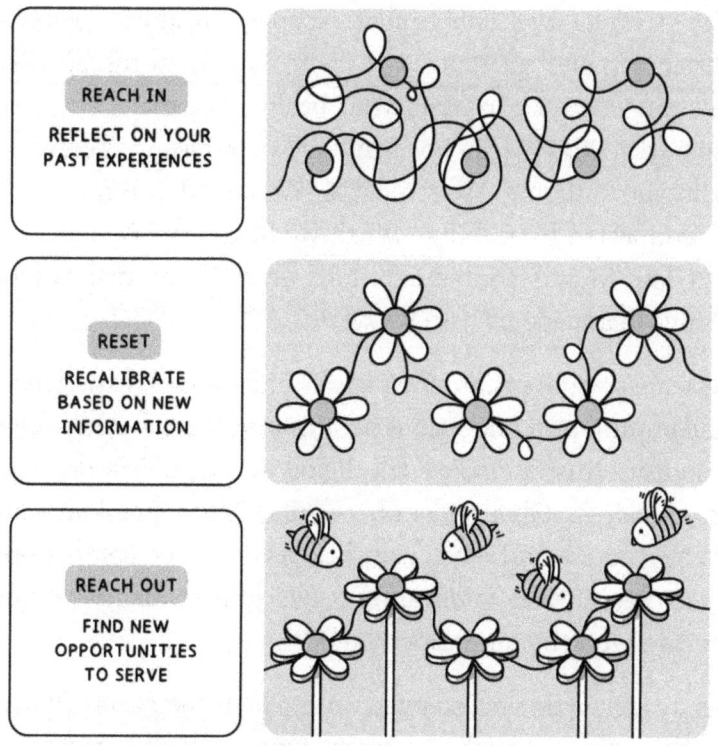

Figure 1: Reach in, reset, reach out

A word of warning: this may seem simple, but it will not be easy. We will wrestle with paradoxes. In the complex landscape of leadership you already do it. You have had to embrace new and sometimes uncomfortable ways of working. You have had to wrestle with being focused while being agile. You have had to move with urgency while remaining thoughtful. You have drilled down into the unsaid despite feeling awkward. As one of my bosses loves to tell me, chaos is normal. Leadership asks us to step up anyway.

Finding a through line

The pandemic reminded us about the importance of stepping up. COVID-19, subsequent school closures, physical distancing and quarantine challenged us. It turns out that avoiding a virus can harm your health. The pandemic sped up our feelings of fear. For many the virus meant discomfort, pain and suffering. We struggled. We ranted. We raved. We disconnected from things which we held dear. We retreated into family units, for better or for worse. We lost many of the things that made us who we were.

As teams withdrew into their family units, shared experiences and impromptu connections became rare. We saw exhaustion. We heard frustration. We felt digital overload. Fear drove us to retreat. As Olympic gold medallist Missy Franklin said, 'Who you are and what you do outside of the competition space can have a significantly bigger impact than what you do and who you are inside of it'.[4]

As we locked down, I stepped up as Chief Operations Officer. In the quiet, while the incessant hum of doubt persisted, I felt the weight of responsibility. I knew that my team was depending on me. I wanted to live up to those expectations. But I felt out of my depth.[5] When you are on the razor's edge between fear and courage it is tempting to tap out. The fear was real. So was the courage. But there was no playbook. We scrambled to react. We rushed to get home, learn the joys of Zoom or Teams and focus on the metrics.

Constrained by circumstance, I started asking different questions. What if leadership was about more than managing metrics? What if it was about making room for others? What if we could ensure that our relationships continued to grow in a world where opportunities for connection had become virtual or virtually non-existent? What if we engaged more actively in a world where we seemed constantly on mute, speaking words but rarely listening? What if we encouraged connection in a world where disconnection was leaving an indelible mark on our collective experience?

We longed for normal. But we had to face the truth. Normal was gone. And perhaps because of that, I remembered the power of a through line.

In 1985, my father took a transformational role in Egypt. It was the opportunity of a lifetime, to lead a cross-cultural team and build a business from the ground up. I was entering adolescence, pushing boundaries and driving my folks crazy. Most of my memories of that time are like ageing snapshots, moments in time captured in small squares, colours blurring and details sparse. But one thing is etched in my memory – the power of storytelling.

At the end of most months, my father would come home carrying several VHS tapes from the company's head office in the US. The tapes were like gold dust. They contained endless spools of potential advertisements that the company was testing. On Sundays, after lunch, my father would sit down and watch those ads. Initially, I had no understanding of what these tapes were. But over time, I started to look forward to seeing stories of products I had never encountered: peanut butter that was hard to beat, cleaning products that cut grease and made rooms shine, laundry detergent that made everything spanking new. Everyday products came alive, simply and concisely, with one through line. I fell in love.

I fell in love with the idea that a through line could anchor us to an idea. I fell in love with the idea that when it was clear, a through line had a mystical power – to connect you to something that you had yet to understand. To engage your senses. To pull at your heartstrings. To make you act.

So, as I faced the challenges in front of me, I did the only thing I could think of: I searched for our through line. I threw everything out. My judgement. My expectations. My baggage. I improvised. I pulled out a blank sheet of paper and I started engaging, listening, writing. I dug deep to figure out what truly motivated me. I sought to figure what motivated others. I asked questions. I listened. I stepped out of competition and comparison. I started from truth – my truth, our truth. I identified the psychological core of my leadership story; the golden thread that connected who I am with how I lead. I showed up, warts and all. And I encouraged others to do the same.

Something fundamental shifted. It was as if a light had been switched on. Where once tasks had felt insurmountable, I witnessed the power of action. We faced the small tasks first and then bigger ones without fear. We abandoned excuses. We chose to act.

With time, creative solutions emerged. Our behaviour shifted. Our questions evolved. We tested. We learned. We connected the seemingly unconnected. We listened to how caring, curiosity and hope fuelled us. We built on the strengths of the team and gathered to uncover our collective purpose. We contributed to a toolkit of strategies: educational sessions to learn, regular surveys to build on each other, and time for rest and recovery.

Identifying our through lines changed the tenor of our interactions. We created an environment in which people had both personal agency and collective meaning. We identified with what we had done. But we learned that we would also be identified by what we had yet to do, outside of competition, comparison and scarcity. We wanted to find the value in enough. Our through lines got us there.

Over two years, we gave each other permission to reach in so that we could reach out. The result? Our self-assessed levels of commitment doubled. We regained space and time. And we reconnected as a result.

Uncertainty is the system

> As new technologies, chronic uncertainty, and ever-shifting markets continue to reshape industries and redefine the future of work, we need to develop skill sets, mindsets, toolsets and systems to support feedback cultures, reward critical and anticipatory thinking and foster deep collaboration and inclusivity.[6]

Uncertainty is not a bug in the system. It is the system. As leaders, we must steer into uncertainty, not away from it. Amy Webb, futurist, author and founder of the Future Today Institute, likens leading through uncertainty to driving on ice. Our instincts tell us to swerve out of the way, but physics demands that we steer into the slide. '[Y]ou are slowing down time and you are reducing uncertainty by making a ton of tiny decisions while remaining as calm as you possibly can.'[7] The future isn't smooth. It's filled with ice patches. And when we hit them, we will want to swerve out of the way. We are wired to resist it, but that resistance drains us.

Persistent uncertainty is metabolically expensive.[8] Our brains wire themselves to these uncertainties, causing a metabolic drag which makes us vulnerable to physical and mental struggle. According to a survey conducted by Deloitte in 2018, 77% of executives reported feeling burnout at their current job.[9] And poor employee mental health costs UK employers £51 billion a year.[10] Leaders often burn out because they try to control the uncontrollable. They swerve out of the way.

What can we do instead? We can steer into the slide. We can reach in, reset, reach out.

When the pandemic subsided and it was safe to return to the office, our team gathered in shiny, new offices. It had been a challenging time. We had weathered a significant storm. I wanted to find a way to continue the work that had begun during lockdown. To bring joy into the (virtual) rooms. And so I started writing a newsletter which I named 'Above the Bottom Line', not as a solution but as an experiment. Each month I shared a simple story, something practical, something that made us stop and think. I offered one through line each month, practicable through three actions: reach in (an opportunity to look inwards), reset (an opportunity to think again), reach out (an opportunity to serve). What started as an experiment became a habit. Little by little, we found our way. We showed up. We focused. We acted with intention and consistency. We didn't fight uncertainty. We danced with it. And ultimately, we answered that most critical of questions: if you don't, who will?

If you don't, who will?

On a crisp May morning in Cambridge, Massachusetts, with a bright sky that signalled new beginnings, Tom Hanks stepped onto the Harvard stage. He wasn't just Tom Hanks, the actor we know. He was Tom Hanks, the storyteller, the author, the human being who's made a career out of connection.

More than 9,000 graduating students, parents and friends gathered for the commencement, their excitement palpable. Draped in Harvard's crimson robes, Hanks walked the procession. Somehow, he seemed small, almost vulnerable in the sea of graduates. The crowd roared, 'Tom Hanks, we love you.' 'Run Forrest, Run!' The familiar shouts rang out, but Hanks didn't let the spotlight stay on him for long. He stopped here and there, offering a fist bump, sharing a quick laugh, responding to questions. Always, though, he turned the focus back to the students. He wove their names, their stories, into his remarks, reminding everyone that this moment wasn't about him, it was about them. About the future they were about to create, and the stories they were about to tell. He 'refracted [attention] into pure joy and shared humanity… a healing energy in a sorry time'.[11]

As he approached the podium, he stopped and stared out at the crowd. Waiting for the cheers to die down, Hanks would go on to deliver a speech that took my breath away. A speech that was an expression of hope. A call to action. One which had themes of individual responsibility, connection and authenticity. He kept returning to one idea. That truth is fragile and beautiful. It requires all of us to step up. We must take care of the work that remains. The work that has no expiry. The work of making the world a better place.

Of keeping the promises of those who came before us; the promises to those who will come after us. He exuded decency, honesty and grace.

> Would you respect the law and the rights of all? Because if you don't, who will? When your food is brought to you, will you thank the server? Because if you don't, who will? Would you pick up the litter that has missed the recycling bin? Because if you don't, who will? Will you vote your conscience and make sure your neighbour [can] do the same? Because if you don't, who will?[12]

Five words. If you don't, who will? The call was clear.

What was it about the call that resonated with me? I have come to believe that it was the paradox of the moment. The fact that in a time of constraints, fear and outrage, Hanks was able to construct a solid through line. The power of his words rang true. As leaders or aspiring leaders, we are faced with that simple question every day – if you don't, who will? One through line to help us all find answers. Recontextualized for leadership. Reimagined for purpose. Repurposed for insight.

To lose your way is to learn the way

Born about a century earlier, Sally Clark came from humble beginnings. Growing up in Wales, times were hard. There was no electricity, no running water. But that did not stifle her spirit. She experienced the Blitz, watched dogfights in the air and ran to air-raid shelters with her sister. She found inner strength. At the age of seven, she appeared on the radio, offering a message of hope in dark times. That little girl grew up to be known as singer, songwriter and actor, Petula Clark. And 50 years after her birth, Petula Clark would help my father on the day I was born.[13]

It was a cold, wet November day. My mother had gone into labour. My father drove her to the *Bois Gentil* (the gentle wood) maternity clinic. She jumped out. He rushed to find a parking space. Realizing that, in the rush, he had inadvertently left his wallet at home, he parked the car, racing into the clinic to get help. A lovely woman called out, 'Do you need help?' 'Yes,' he answered, 'my wife has gone into labour with our first born and I forgot my wallet at home. It is too far to go back, and I am not sure what to do.' 'Don't worry,' she answered, 'here is some change. Put it into the parking meter and go be with your wife.' Thanking her in his usual manner, my father gratefully accepted the change, shoved it into the parking meter and raced off. It was only when he was safely inside the clinic that he realized. That woman was Petula Clark.

I often heard the story of my arrival into the world while growing up. It was a small moment, but one that echoed through my life. The way my parents told it, the universe conspired to ensure that everything went smoothly. And yet, I often wondered – how could one innocuous act change the course of so many lives? Why had Petula helped my dad? Why does anyone step in when they don't have to? Maybe it's because they see what truly matters: connection, humanity, leadership.

I grew up surrounded by love. My parents raised my sister and me to believe in goodness. They were not blind to the difficulties of life. But no matter how tough things became, I saw them give. They gave their time, their knowledge, and the little money they had to others. Constantly. They made sure that those they loved flourished. It's not that they ever said the words, but as a child, I heard their actions speak. Loudly.

I grew up a third-culture kid[14] who, when I finally learned how to speak, did so haltingly and with care. I remember walking around with a blanket stuffed into my mouth for comfort. A self-imposed gag order drove me to stay silent. My stammering ended as suddenly and inexplicably as it began.

I soaked up language. The languages of my family, Malayalam, Telegu, Hindi and English, and the language of my host country, French. I spent hours speaking into the bright orange receiver of my plastic Fisher-Price telephone, repeating a single phrase over and over, 'Parce que le'. Because. Looking back, my need to understand and to be understood was ever present. It foreshadowed my drive to listen, learn and contribute.

School changed things. Home felt like my safe space, but the outside world seemed scary. I felt uncomfortable, sensing things that others seemed blind to. I read rooms. I understood what others valued. I integrated their priorities. I listened to what they needed. The bells tolled. Loudly.

My values repeatedly collided with the labels others placed on me: the Indian, the immigrant, the foreigner, the singer, the piano player, the joker, the connector, the student, the achiever, the teacher, the leader. Not every label was bad, untrue or painful, but each one felt limiting. Each addressed only a part of my identity and failed to appreciate the whole. No one ever asked me what I thought or gave me a chance to weigh in. They didn't ask, they just told.

To escape the discomfort, I ran. Mostly, I ran from myself. I wanted to be someone else, to live up to expectations, to get the grades, the degrees, the job, to belong. I ran without ever questioning whether that was what I wanted. I ran to keep moving, from one classroom to another, from one conversation to another, from one job to another. The love that surrounded me as a child dissipated. The world felt cold. Love rarely felt unconditional, but while I ran, I didn't notice. So I kept running.

The world had boxes, and I didn't fit into any of them. I kept moving, thinking that achievement would bring fulfilment. But it didn't. No degree or job title filled the gap. I still didn't belong. The shiny trappings of success didn't lead to my happiness. Instead, scarcity and discomfort persisted.

Life limited my ability to be myself. I never questioned what I wanted. I measured myself by someone else's yardstick. The distance between external expectations and my achievements created my level of judgement. That judgement felt heavy. I morphed into someone I believed the world wanted to see. The change was slow; like gaining weight it happened gradually. As singer and songwriter Alicia Keys describes in her memoir, *More Myself*:[15] 'We shift ourselves not in sweeping pivots but in movements so tiny that they are hardly perceptible even in our own view. Years can pass before we finally discover that after handing over our power, piece by small piece—we no longer even look like ourselves.'

Minuscule steps led me somewhere I never intended to go. I opened a map, knew where I wanted to go, but the others on my journey showed me a new place. Like a magpie with a shiny new toy, I went willingly. No one forced me to change; I allowed change to happen. Frantic led to more frantic. The quest for more distracted me from the beauty of enough. The constraints tightened around me.

Yet, as the Swahili proverb says, '*Kupotea njia ndio kujua njia*' (To lose the way is to learn the way). As I lost my way, I learned the way. The very constraints I was fighting enhanced my problem-solving skills, my focus and my creativity. They narrowed the problem space. I wanted to show up, so I focused on how to do that. The constraints focused my mind on one aspect of a problem. If I wanted to show up, I needed to accept myself. That led to deeper exploration and creative solutions. I listened, I tested, I learned. I let my fear go. And slowly, the constraints allowed me to connect unrelated concepts. Acceptance allowed me to see that I could be more than one thing. The need to overcome my limitations pushed me to expand the boundaries of my thinking.[16] By leaning into discomfort, by letting the constraints push me to grow in new ways, I slowly recognized that the very limits I was fighting were the ones that would set me free.

Discomfort taught me to have compassion for the many whom society treated as 'other'. I developed a deep interest in anyone who was either forced into a box or told they didn't belong. Perhaps that's why I chose to educate neurodiverse children. I wanted them to see their potential beyond the tests, the labels and the expectations. Perhaps that's why I went back to school after a decade of teaching – to figure out what service meant. Fundamentally, I kept searching for a way to belong and to help others do the same. That exploration ultimately led me into leadership.

Let's begin

This isn't a book of quick fixes. There is no magic formula or secret sauce here. Instead, this book is an invitation to discover something that's already within you. To offer you a simple blueprint that could drive your leadership impact.[17] That could empower it. That could enlarge it. That could multiply it.

Leadership isn't about being perfect. It's about showing up. Even when we may not want to. It's about accepting that we are all enough. It's about connecting who we are to how we lead, one step at a time. Much like a cento,[18] that indefatigable type of poetry that quilts together disparate lines into one coherent whole, leadership is made up of many pieces, stitched together by reflection, action and possibility. This is your chance to see those pieces differently, to pull them together in a way that's truly yours. To integrate emotions into mindset. To open a pathway to rethink previously formed conceptions. To call out possibilities. To connect what is to what could be. To apply these learnings to leadership and life.

Let's begin.

1

Crossing lines

Leadership as an area of intellectual inquiry remains thin, and little original thought has been given to what leader learning in the second decade of the 21st century should look like.[19]

In a nutshell

Leadership isn't about checking items off a to-do list or living up to external expectations. It's about digging deep, finding the essence of who you are, and letting that guide your choices. When you cut through the clutter, truth emerges. It's the foundation that steadies you through uncertainty and complexity. And here's the thing, it doesn't prescribe what you *should* do or who you *should* be. This through line is yours alone. Recognize it, and you unlock freedom. The freedom to lean into discomfort, to take bold steps, to lead with purpose. Perfection becomes irrelevant. What matters is awareness. That awareness is where your power lies.

Hidden in plain sight

Sandbars are impermanent. They are transitory, emerging at unexpected moments, disappearing as quickly as they arrived. As the ocean churns away, sandbars are subject to fluctuations. They are often filled with treasures – corals, seashells and even unexpected marine life. But just as they appear, they can disappear. They remain hidden in plain sight until the waters recede. And the next time the sandbar emerges, it will look, feel and sound unique. Completely different.

As leaders, our through lines are like these sandbars, lines that weave themselves through the experiences, relationships and jobs in our lives. The lines that connect the starting line to what will inevitably come – the finish line. The through line links them together much like a sandbar. Emerging when others need to see it, disappearing until next time.

In our busy and noisy world, we are afraid to embrace the quiet. But during the lockdowns that affected us all, quiet seemed the only thing we had. I found it scary and lonely. So I started reading, voraciously, in a way I had never done before. I also started writing. Writing without a filter. It felt like remembering that there are two sides to a veil. Gradually I realized that much like these sandbars, answers can sometimes be hidden in plain sight. That if I understood myself, I could better understand others. That I had the power to identify patterns. That if I understood where I came from, I might uncover where I wanted to go.

Slowly and painstakingly the truth emerged. Blurry at first. And then clearer. It's not just about finding the way forward, it's also about understanding what came before. The past matters. Someone said history is your story, and I believe that to be true. Understanding your story makes you stronger. Because it informs you. It teaches you what truly matters. And it enables the whispers of your true self to emerge.

Through lines are fundamental to who we are. If we do not understand them, we do not understand ourselves. If we do not understand ourselves, much of our work life may feel like we are on the receiving end of externalities. Our through lines create space between what we experience – the disappointing email, the challenging question from a colleague at a meeting, the behaviours that we do not understand – and our response to those moments. They empower us to act with intention rather than instinct. They ground us on the inside and empower us to act with intention on the outside.

We spend a third of our lives working, and during this time we navigate all sorts of change. Change of careers. Change of roles. Change of teams. Change of circumstances. Change of location. Change of salary. Change of problems to solve. To manage those changes, at times we draw on lived experience. At others, we draw on the thinking of others. When that does not work, we resort to trial and error. And each time, whether it works or it does not, when we reflect, we learn. We grow. And we develop new skills. This is the springboard from which we learn, about ourselves and each other.

See it to name it

At the Berkeley graduation in 2003, writer Anne Lamott advised students that the secret to success was simple. 'Ignore your parents' expectations, give money to the ACLU, and find out the truth about who you are.'[20] The through line is one illustration of that truth. It integrates your experiences and forms your psychological core. It is the internal command centre that enables you to lead yourself, the bedrock upon which effective leadership is constructed. Understanding it empowers you. Understanding it teaches you. Understanding it unlocks your potential. As Anne puts it, 'You can see the underlying essence only when you strip away the business, and then some surprising connections appear'.[21] Understanding your cohesive narrative and learning how to use it can help align what you most value with how you act and what you aim to achieve. Then you can lead, as '[w]hen purpose and profession align, we breathe lighter'.[22]

Our through lines offer possibility. They connect the mysteries of who we are with how we choose to lead. They answer the central question of where we came from. The through line does not tell you what you must do. It does not tell you who you need to be. It does not compare you using anyone else's ruler. Instead it is the purest representation of you. It represents the shape of you, what identifies you, makes you and defines you. Each of these representations is unique, significant and beautiful. Each of these representations leads to a centrality of you. To a whole picture of you. Like the portraits of artist Chuck Close, the through line pans outward from a series of individual pixels to the whole of you.

Think of your life as a quilt. Each piece a reflection of what you value, what you've experienced and what you stand for. When you step back and see the whole, that's your thread. Confucius once said, 'I weave it all together into a single thread'.[23] That's what we do when we stop drifting and start acting with purpose.

The through line, that single thread, is the space of highest potential within you. In most cases, this through line reflects the purest part of who you are and your noblest intentions. When you operate from this core, you can free yourself from blinding beliefs, limiting habits and insecurities.

Finding that core and sticking to it is not easy. If you are like me, sometimes you operate from this core, sometimes you drift away from it. But you can always begin again. Because once you identify that core, it is always there for you to come back to and connect with. Once you see it, you can name it. Once you name it, you can use it. Then you, too, can find the courage to steer into discomfort.

Use it

We live in a complex reality. The through line offers a practical way to embrace nuance, rupture and disconnection. It goes beyond what you can see. We will always be riveted by what is dramatic. We are conditioned to look for the 'right' answers. Yet, the quality of our questions can determine the quality of our leadership. Living in questions and embracing who we are is a generative way to further our leadership. And generative creation can calm us down, infusing our leadership with a sense of the truest of us.

Our through lines form the foundation of our character. Character comes from the ancient Greek word meaning the imprint left on a coin after its manufacture. Character is like a unique fingerprint that defines who you are, what you believe and what you value. While talent sets the floor, character sets the ceiling on what we can accomplish. 'Character, like a photograph, develops in darkness.'[24] Our through lines clarify, strengthen and expound what we know and what we still need to learn. They allow us to rethink meaning. We literally re-cognize. Our through lines form a language and vocabulary that binds us together. They challenge our belief system forcing us to rethink as we move through the world. They quilt our thoughts, experiences and behaviours into the coherence of who we are. They clarify the horizon, allowing us to see where we wish to go. When the going gets tough, they align heart, body and mind. And once we identify them, we can walk through life lightly. Never clinging to the line, rather holding space, gently, for it to recalibrate as we learn. As CEO of pension provider and investment firm TIAA, Thasunda Duckett, likes to say, we rent our titles, but we own our character.[25] Our through lines give us clarity on that.

The beauty of knowing this line is that it can help make the unexplainable, explainable. It resonates within us, resounding, gentle and yet solid. Like the foundation of a home, the through line ensures that what is built above it stays steady. It welcomes the power of the elements – those extrinsic factors that will ebb and flow and will undoubtedly come as we move through life. Uncertainty and change will hit. Struggles will continue. And yet, so too joy will come again. So too contentment, that state of equanimity, will rise again. We will finally understand that our success is not a goal to be achieved or a checklist that needs ticking off. The journey towards mastery[26] will mean that we are guided by our through line. Like the compass that always points to true north, so too our through line will point to our true core. And once we find it, it will give us answers to that ultimate of leadership questions – if you don't, who will?

Caring to notice

The people who change the world are the ones who care. We want more evidence, more data, more science. We could also use more care. When we see it, we feel it. And it energizes everyone to do the same. Author Seth Godin said it best: 'Each one of us can show up in our own way, but the choice is the same: to lead, to create work that matters, and to find the magic that happens when we are lucky enough to cocreate with people who care.'[27] Knowing and using your through line allows you to care for others.

The *caffè sospeso* is Italian for a suspended coffee. This a coffee paid for in advance as an anonymous act of kindness. The tradition began in the working-class cafes of Naples. Someone who had experienced good luck would order a *sospeso*, paying the price of two coffees but receiving and consuming only one. Anyone who enquired if a *sospeso* was available would then be served a coffee for free. This small, anonymous act of kindness illustrates how caring can become a powerful, contagious force.

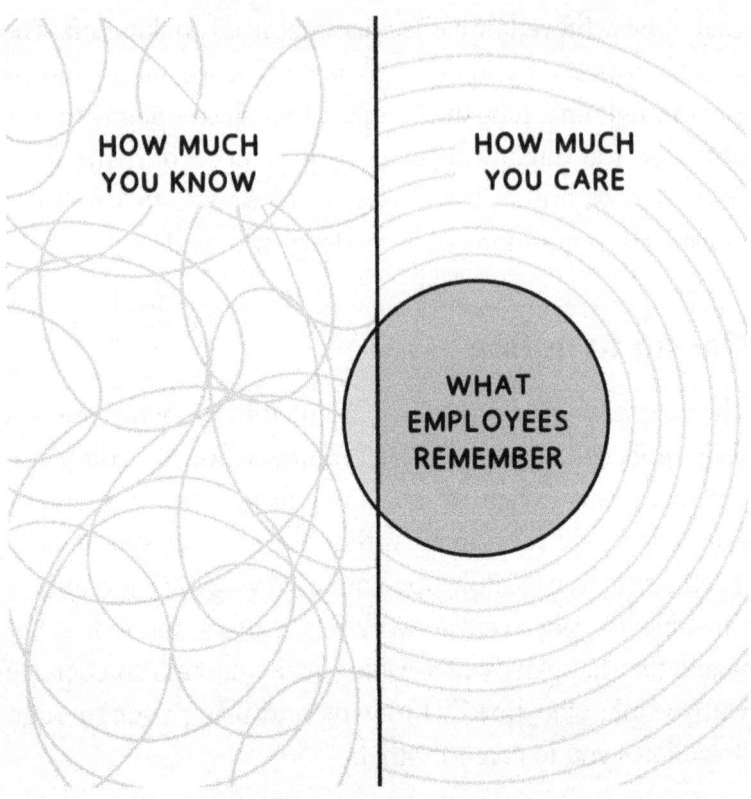

Figure 2: What employees remember

'Leadership is not about titles, positions, or flow charts. It is about one life influencing another.'[28] Leadership is never one thing exercised by one person. It is an activity carried out by people at all levels of an organization. We are not born leaders. But we can learn to become one. I propose that to guide and impact outcomes, leadership should seek to answer one question – if you don't, who will? That question can frame our objectives, frame the coaching of our teams, and frame our search for mastery. And to answer that question – you must care.

As leaders, we are asked to care. To see things that others do not see. It's easy to undervalue what you don't see. But when you care enough, you start to notice things that others do not. You make the familiar unfamiliar, and you counter the in-built tendency to habituate. You change the way you see as you change the way you think. That is when the magic happens.

Leaders work in an ecosystem with others who supply vital information. 'Whether you're talking about an executive, manager, sports coach, or schoolteacher, leadership is about guiding and impacting outcomes, enabling groups of people to work together to accomplish what they couldn't do working individually.'[29] As leaders, we are prone to emotions, biases and blind spots. So leadership should not be a solo endeavour but a collaborative effort that seeks to build on diverse perspectives and talents. Peter Michael Senge, an American systems scientist and a senior lecturer at the MIT Sloan School of Management, writes: 'It cannot be stressed too much that team learning is a team skill. A group of talented individual learners will not necessarily produce a learning team any more than a group of talented athletes will produce a great sports team. Learning teams learn how to learn together.'[30]

Leaders should encourage divergent thinking, create environments where people can thrive, and navigate complexity with grace and skill. Many focus on the heroic acts that exemplify leadership. 'These smart and successful executives are masters at leading with their heads.'[31] But often, leadership requires the non-heroic, painstaking work that involves paying attention and being able to learn quickly, in real time. To care to notice. To make sense of the context in which we operate, build relationships across our organizations, create a compelling picture of the future, and develop new ways of achieving that vision. 'We have to do the hard work and the heart work.'[32]

Leadership spans the heart and the head, the intellectual and the interpersonal, the rational and the intuitive and the conceptual and creative. We must accept that we will rarely have all these skills all the time. We will naturally be incomplete. But that does not mean we are incompetent. When we care, we understand what we are good at and what we need help with. When we care, we learn how we can work with others to build on our attributes.

Much of leadership development focuses on externalities. What we need to do, what we need to learn, what we need to say. We come to believe that the perfect leader exists. And we integrate that this perfect leader is not us. Our discomfort naturally leads us to look for simple solutions to the ongoing uncertainty: quick fixes, hacks, short cuts. We develop value statements. We take courses. We engage in learning new techniques. We separate who we are from how we lead. We forget that '[l]ife begins at the edge of your comfort zone'.[33]

Nowhere is this more evident than in the classroom. I began my career as a teacher, working with and advocating for neurodiverse children. During this time, my role was often to ease discomfort. We rarely taught children that healthy struggle is part of any learning process. Yet as Susan David states, 'Discomfort is the price of admission to a meaningful life'.[34] Leaders must remember this. Conflating ease with wellbeing can, paradoxically, make our teams less resilient, less capable, less confident and more fragile.

Caring to notice may not require more. It may in fact require less. You already have a lot of information. It lies within you. So instead of slamming on the brakes, what if you steered into discomfort? What if you paused to explore your values, beliefs and aspirations? Then you might discover how to cross lines, connect lines, and bridge divides. By remaining grounded in your through lines, you could lead without limits. Indeed, you could edgewalk[35] through leadership.

Hope in uncertainty

While most of us fear uncertainty, Rebecca Solnit sees hope in it. Solnit has long been known for her interdisciplinary and wandering writing style. Credited with first coining the term 'mansplaining' in 2003, her ability to refract politics, history, personal experience and critique through the lens of a poet is unparalleled. She finds connections between the disparate. 'I try to look for alternatives and the overlooked entrances and exits.'[36] She believes that our cultures repeatedly limit the range of our humanity and goads us to take note. She looks for near and far adjacencies. Her voice, shaped through her experiences, has become a voice of the resistance. One which fights for those less fortunate. One which points out injustices. One which highlights missing links.

Her journey was fraught. She grew up north of San Francisco in a violent home. So she took refuge in the local public library and the great wide-open spaces surrounding her home. Adolescence remained challenging. She was ignored during her parents' difficult divorce and experienced 'outsider-ness' in high school. She dropped out at 15, got her GED and enrolled in university. She then moved to Paris, to escape it all. After a year, she returned to the US and earned an English degree. She attended Berkeley's school of journalism yet the feeling of not fitting in continued. She was drawn to the punk scene which she described as 'wonderful, because it was for nerds and misfits and weirdos and people who were willing to embrace something that was for outsiders not insiders'.[37]

After publishing a few pieces in her early 20s, Solnit began to understand the power of stories. And it is here that the power of her through line shines through. 'We think we tell stories, but stories often tell us, tell us to love or to hate, to see or to be blind', she writes in *The Faraway Nearby*.

> Often, too often, stories saddle us, ride us, whip us onward, tell us what to do, and we do it without questioning. The task of learning to be free requires learning to hear them, to question them, to pause and hear silence, to name them, and then to become the storyteller.[38]

The power in understanding who you are can inform what you are doing and why. This can also mean you steer towards your destination with more intention while inspiring those around you to do the same.

We think we see life as it is. Instead, we see life as we are. We describe and move through the world as it appears to us. This is the great paradox. Should we pause and first understand ourselves? Should we identify our deeply held and sometimes hidden assumptions, the daily actions that matter, the repeated stories we tell ourselves, the symbols and rituals that we care about and the reinforcing processes that we are a part of?

Engaging in self-discovery allows us to understand the consistent themes that have shaped our lives, encouraging self-awareness without self-centredness.

I came upon Solnit in 2019, when she adapted the well-loved fairytale, *Cinderella* and transformed the protagonist into a self-determined leader. 'Cinderella Liberator' put Cinderella, armed with agency, front and centre. Princess status was never the endgame. Instead, reaching in, resetting and reaching out drove Cinderella to set the terms of her own life. I was captivated by the relevance of this ideation. One in which we each need to recognize our worth and gifts to resist rules that might limit our potential.

Solnit pushed gently against categorization and labels. What if the evil stepmother was a metaphor for the societal forces of scarcity? What if the stepsisters were simply conditioned by their environment to believe their only value was beauty? 'If you think of a kind of ecology of ideas, there are more than enough people telling us how horrific and terrible and bad everything is, and I do not really need to join that project,' she said. 'There's a whole other project of trying to counterbalance that – sometimes we do win, and this is how it worked in the past.' She continued, 'Change is often unpredictable and indirect. We do not know the future. We have changed the world many times, and remembering that, that history, is really a source of power to continue and it does not get talked about nearly enough.'[39]

When asked to define her through line, she replied, 'They told her to shut up. So she got louder.'[40] Unlike the snow globes that comedian Mae Martin humorously describes as mere showpieces,[41] the through lines are uniquely ours. Whether we choose to share them or not, the value lies in understanding them. The beauty isn't in displaying them for everyone to see; it is in holding them lightly. Without clasping. Ready to let them shift if experiences tell us more. Ready to embrace them when that is what we need. Ready to focus on others, as we recognize that we are all interconnected.

True colours

As I embarked on learning about through lines, I found that many cultures give them colour. Colour encodes and classifies. Colour unites. Colour orders chaos. In fact, the word 'cosmetic' (or the colours we put on our faces) derives from the Greek word 'cosmos' meaning to order. Decking ourselves out in colour can order our world, or simply others' perceptions of us. So cultures have attributed colour to through lines. These colourful lines symbolize connection. They remind us of good fortune. They ward off evil spirits. They allow us to find purpose: they help us steer into the paradoxes of life and to lead from our core.

Our (his)stories are filled with through lines. When Theseus escaped the minotaur's grasp, he did so with a red ball of yarn which Ariadne gave him. That thread led him out of harm's way and back to freedom. In *Wahlverwandschaften*, Goethe's red thread illustrated the divine or poetic thread of life, thought and art, invisible and unbroken. Admiral Nelson ordered that a scarlet thread be woven into every one of the Naval Service's ropes (Rogue's Yarn). From the smallest heaving line to the largest cord, this identified the ropes which belonged to the British Navy, making them harder to steal. In Eastern traditions, a red thread is the connective tissue that binds two individuals to each other. In Hinduism, the red thread is a symbol of strength, resilience and unity. My father wore this red thread (*Molathadu*) around his waist to ward off evil. When my sister struggled to sleep as a child, a *Molathadu* was tied around her waist too. It symbolized the interconnectedness of life and the acceptance of life's opposing forces (the paradoxes). In Sweden, '*rod trad*' or in France, '*le fil rouge*', are used describe something that follows a theme and connects disparate events or ideas. Jim Collins and Jerry Porras wrote about the unifying power of the 'golden thread' when they linked a business's core ideology with its envisioned future.[42] These threads were representations of common themes, brought to life in living colour.

Unearthing a truth

My interest in the connective thread began before I could speak. I felt a deep need to understand who I was, where I came from and where I fit in. I wondered why some ties were strengthened because of the struggle, while others frayed for no apparent reason. Understanding my threads gave me the power to change things. It is not like anyone told me I needed to find my through line. But I knew, in my bones, that understanding it was fundamental to understanding who I was and who I wanted to be.

When you start excavating the unsaid and the unconscious roots of who you are, you stumble upon discoveries that you do not immediately comprehend. I started seeing how my through line started even before I was born; that it was linked to my parents and grandparents, to the freedom fighters who stood up to power, to the people who left home with nothing and built something. It called me to stop measuring myself by someone else's yardstick. It asked me to hold opposing thoughts, ideas and feelings lightly. To see beauty in challenge, vulnerability in courage, order in chaos.

My through line was crafted, sometimes uncomfortably through the experiences of my life. The past was no excuse. But it offered one explanation. It began with a childhood of opposites – a world celebrating India and a world choosing to ignore it, a world of English and one of French, a world of the culinary explosions of spices and the world of unpasteurized creamy white cheeses. It continued with the push and pull of culture – one which valued mastery, generosity and inner strength, and one which prized success, money and material things. It evolved into norms and labels – one which called me to categorize myself as one thing and one which encouraged me to be many things. It captured the paradoxes of life and death, the grief of loss and the joy of birth. It morphed into an inquiry of leadership – what it means and what it could be.

Slowly, my values clarified. Community and family centred me. Home was where the heart was. A delicious meal had the power to unite. Everyone was welcome no matter the time or the place. There was never a substitute for hard work. Learning was everywhere and opened paths that seemed unthinkable. It had never been about knowing it all. It had always been about learning it all.

My act of revolution was the acceptance of my past. As writer and a leading voice in the US civil rights movement, James Baldwin said so beautifully, 'To accept one's past – one's history – is not the same thing as drowning in it; it is learning how to use it.'[43] And that acceptance unlocked discoveries. I was built to break a mould. All I needed to do was to look up. And suddenly, I saw that even running was a privilege. I used to run to escape. Now I run to come home.

I found community. I found people who cared to learn. For business and society we did more. The through line clarified. I wanted to let it guide me and define my path. Every time I veered off course, the line remained present. Reminding me to stay focused. To ask more questions. To stay true to my values. To let my behaviours align to my objectives. And to refuse to let others define me. I listened to those who chose to teach. I built a network of those who chose to support and challenge me. And I contributed to those who needed me.

This exploration led me to a through line that now guides my work – paradox is the lifeblood of every individual, encounter, and opportunity for growth – embrace it. I am so many things. I don't have to be just one thing. That is the ultimate paradox. I am scared and I am courageous. I am vulnerable and I am strong. I am uncertain and I am bold. All those things are true. None of those things stand alone. Without paradox, life would be dull. With paradox, we are better able to embrace the imperfections in the world of work. As I learned from my mother, embracing the darkness helps you appreciate the light.

My through line, or what I have come to call a truth line, reminds me of what centred looks like. Speaking my truth is not easy. It is often uncomfortable, raw and emotional. Yet as a leader, I am called to do this every day. The days of placing myself on mute are over. I now hold my line, gently. I understand that I am responsible for the stories I tell myself and the stories I share with others. I hold the power to change those stories, if I so choose.

For the past ten years that through line has become more indelible. It has allowed me to be part of teams, to build teams and to lead teams. And today I stand here glancing around at what lies before me. I know that there is more to do. That the greatest act of revolution remains a quiet one. One which requires that I accept myself repeatedly. One which calls me to look out at the possibilities and integrate the lessons to be learned. To make it through one twist and turn at a time. Always maintaining focus and awareness that the through line will give me both the perspective and the strength to stay the course and to reach for the inevitable finish line. However challenging that may be.

Through discomfort, I started to see that once we understand who we are, we can define how we wish to lead. We have choice. We build agency. The lines that surround us become information, not directives. The lines provide order. The chaos no longer seems scary. Moral courage[44] becomes fundamental. And gradually, we navigate each hurdle with intention, because we understand our core – we understand that our through lines afford us an anchor during any storm. That this core sits in our souls. And that, as Beyonce says, our souls are what make us beautiful and strong.

> Soul has no colour, no shape, no form. Just like all your work, it goes far beyond what the eye can see.

You have the power to change perception, to inspire and empower, and to show people how to embrace their complications, and see the flaws, and the true beauty and strength that is inside all of us.[45]

Your turn

Throughout this book, you will be asked to try things out. You should feel free to dip in and out of the exercises as you see fit. The process of introspection can sometimes feel daunting. Our histories are filled with moments that we don't necessarily want to relive. I would like to offer one suggestion as you move through these exercises. Instead of asking *why*, try asking *what*. I found this reframe powerful. 'Why' questions trap us in our past, leading to (unhelpful) rumination. Instead, 'what' questions can help us create propulsion and forward motion through our emotions. They can help us stay objective, future-focused and empowered to act. Here are some questions to get you started. I encourage you to craft your own.

- What am I feeling right now?
- What are the situations that make me feel this way? What are the situations that make me feel differently?
- What do I not understand? What do I understand?
- What is another explanation for what I am seeing?
- What are the steps I could take to do things differently?

2

The through line: a blueprint for leadership

Remember: there are no small parts, only small actors.[46]

LIFE EXPERIENCES   LEADERSHIP

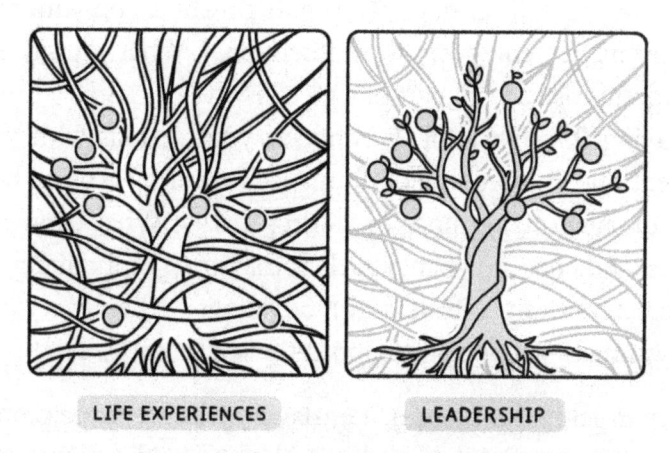

Figure 3: Life experiences for leadership

In a nutshell

We are storytellers. Understanding the stories we tell helps us craft a blueprint of who we are, what matters to us and where we want to go. These experiences, challenges and lessons create a through line that informs how we lead. Embracing the complexity

> of our through lines makes work meaningful. By understanding our stories, we in turn create environments where everyone has clarity, believes they matter and is driven by a shared sense of purpose. The through line serves as a bridge between who we are and how we lead.

All the world's a stage

Picture yourself on stage. The spotlight shines on your face. Every movement, every word intentional. What you say isn't random. Instead, it's part of a greater whole. There's a thread weaving through it all. It connects your actions with your intentions. It drives the performance forward. It's never been about memorizing lines or hitting marks. What captivates your audience is when you live the story, embodying the character's desires, fears and motivations. When everything flows, that's when magic happens.

Born in 1863, Konstantin Stanislavsky was deeply passionate about theatre. From an early age, he attended performances with his family and participated in amateur productions. Though he initially pursued a career in business, his love for the stage never waned, and he eventually devoted himself fully to acting and theatre.

Born with a weak voice and small stature, Stanislavsky felt limited. His voice lacked the power and resonance of seasoned actors. His diminutive stature made it difficult for him to command attention on stage. Recognizing the importance of vocal projection and physical presence, he worked tirelessly to develop his voice and improve his stage presence.

He sought to understand what made performances truly impactful, beyond mere technical proficiency. His work was rooted in observation, intuition and introspection. Through years of studying, acting and directing, he began to recognize a common thread running through the most compelling performances – the through line. His journey to understanding its importance was one of exploration, experimentation and a relentless pursuit of authenticity on stage.

Stanislavsky realized that for a performance to truly resonate with audiences, it needed coherence and continuity. It was not enough for actors to simply recite lines or mimic emotions; they needed to embody a character's journey from start to finish, with a clear through line guiding their every action.

He experimented with various techniques, delving into the psychology of characters, exploring their motivations, and emphasizing the importance of emotional truth on stage. Through trial and error, he refined his approach, eventually codifying his insights into what became known as the Stanislavsky System.

With Stanislavsky's through line technique, actors delve deep into their characters, understanding their emotional arcs, their objectives, and the obstacles they face. It is about finding the through line that guides every beat of the performance, from the opening scene to the final curtain call. Each action is driven by the character's inner truth, creating a sense of authenticity that resonates with audiences.

Just as a skilled conductor leads an orchestra through a symphony, actors using Stanislavsky's through line technique lead viewers on an emotional journey, guiding them through highs and lows, twists and turns. Every gesture, every expression serves the through line, amplifying the narrative and drawing spectators into the world of the play.

Stanislavsky didn't just change the way people acted. He unlocked the potential for something deeper, more human. The through line wasn't just a theatrical technique; it became a way of living. By understanding the emotional truth behind every action, actors could connect with audiences on a visceral level, creating performances that transcended the stage.

In today's world, neuroscience might back up what Stanislavsky intuitively knew. Research on empathy, brain function and emotional processing would likely reinforce his belief in the power of emotional truth on stage. Mirror neurons, for example, could explain why we feel what the characters feel. The science behind storytelling supports his idea that a clear through line can captivate and engage people in profound ways.

But here's the real takeaway: Stanislavsky's through line isn't just for actors, it's for all of us. It's about aligning what's inside with what we show the world. It's about living authentically, with purpose and consistency. Whether you're leading a team or telling your own story, that thread, your through line, is what keeps everything together.

In leadership, just like on stage, authenticity matters. Authenticity is the alignment between what is going on inside yourself and how you express it. Employees are drawn to leaders who exhibit authenticity and a deep sense of purpose, as it resonates with their own need for meaningful work. Ninety-two per cent of Gen Z respondents [47] recently rated authenticity as their most important personal value. It's not just about telling people where to go; it's about showing them the way by living your values every day. When you understand your through line, you create a path that others want to follow.

Avoid flat packing

I appreciate the possibility that a flat-packed IKEA box presents. The instructions are ordered, simple, visualized. The pieces are counted out with precision and exactitude. If done correctly, every single piece fits together to create something brand new. My first IKEA desk was a delightful bright red, L-shaped desk. It would be my workspace for the next few years. I loved that desk. It symbolized new beginnings, possibility and potential. Its gleam reminded me of the joy I had had when building it.

As leaders, the demands placed on us are vast. The world is changing. Disruption seems everywhere. Businesses must adapt. Leaders are called to face existential threats and challenges while responding to increasing demands from stakeholders. We expect our leaders to have the intellect to make sense of complexity. We want them to paint a picture of the future that brings others along. We respect them when their operational know-how translates strategy into concrete plans. And all the while we require them to have the interpersonal skills to foster commitment to undertakings that could fail. No single person can live up to all those expectations. Yet the trend of hacking our way through leadership persists. We aim to flat pack the leadership experience like an IKEA desk. We barely notice it – the need to boil leadership and life down into sound bites is everywhere – it is integrated into our advertising, social media feeds, messaging and even language.

Figure 4: Hacks and quick fixes

Tidy narratives help us feel better. We are drawn to the simplicity of quick fixes. We search for ways to reduce the friction in our lives. We want to find order in chaos. We start out just trying to lead better. But it never quite works out. Like the magic tricks that fascinated us as children, after checking all the boxes, new boxes appear. Progress feels like quicksand. One step forward, two steps back. So we feel frustrated, guilty, lost and panicked.

When we try to boil everything down to hacks, we miss the nuance, authenticity and joy of leadership. We miss its beauty and complexity. Leadership cannot (and must not) be reduced to a set of atomistic traits, behaviours and skills. Leadership is inherently complex, nuanced and multi-faceted. It is impossible to summarize every part of leadership in sound bites or simple narratives. Leadership can be uncomfortable. Intractable problems or questions have imperfect information and no clear answers. Because the context changes. The challenges change. The shape of the systems in which we operate change. So, too, leadership must change.

We cannot separate ourselves from the systems we are part of. Teaching taught me about the double-edged sword of expectations. Corporate cultures often mirror school cultures, reinforcing early patterns of chasing external validation, striving to fit in, and fighting to be perceived positively. In the business world, success is often measured by key performance indicators, in much the same way that academic success is measured by standardized test scores. We measure our self-worth against external markers of success, competing for power and privilege under the assumption that more is always better.

Leadership structures and categories

Hierarchical structures perpetuate the notion that leadership is about telling people what to do. Promotions and rewards are tied to performance metrics set by others, reinforcing a cycle where power, higher salaries and bonuses are the ultimate prizes for conforming to these standards. Reviews force us into predefined categories, leaving little room for creative or unconventional contributions. The bell curve breeds competition, and individual differences in personality, maturity and leadership styles significantly impact learning, performance and wellbeing. Stress remains and it has an impact. In 2021, the National Bureau of Economic Research found that industry-wide downturns reduce CEOs' life expectancies by 1.5 years.[48] Most of the more than 1,600 CEOs in the study lived into their 80s, longer than average for the general population but shorter, in some cases, than they might have lived with less stress.

Stress permeates our lives. So, beaten down by our systems, we attend panels for advice and retreats to connect on a deeper level. We re-energize ourselves and feel like hope lives on. Then we return to the same cutthroat culture that demands immediate results. We hear calls to accelerate innovation, cultivate ethical leadership, address burnout and lead with compassion. Rinse and repeat.

Research carried out by Gallup shows that only one in ten people are hardwired for people leadership. And that only another two in ten have the capacity to do it well.[49] Yet companies spend a fortune investing in leadership training hoping that competency development produces the same outcome as awareness. There is clearly a need for a new way of leading. One that is holistic, with service at its core.

Sure we must keep things understandable and understood to maximize our opportunities for comprehension, innovation and growth. But by breaking everything down into chunks, what if what we are doing is creating an illusion of simplicity? What if we are encouraging black and white thinking?

Our brains adore categories. We are wired for it. The ability to sort through the reams of information that we ingest each day requires classifying what we encounter into categories.

But what if 'categories are where thoughts go to die'.[50] When we are confused, overwhelmed or stressed by information and expectations, what if that is the signal that we shouldn't categorize but rather question? As I observe the world, it feels like we are more prone to outrage. We are externally focused, externally motivated, and externally driven. Any challenge causes anger to rear its head. When we most need maturity, wisdom and reflection, we seem anchored to the simplistic, self-centred, power-over mindset.

This begs several questions. Is there is another way? Could we recover the space to build our own definitions of what empowered leadership could look like? Does it have to be difficult? What if one size does not have to fit all?

My experience tells me that we are all works in progress. Whether we are aspiring or experienced leaders, we are messy, flawed and human. We must stop trying to be all things to all people. We must accept our attributes and understand that they can show up as either strengths or weaknesses based on context. Because, when we do, we naturally find others to fill in the gaps. We widen the lens. We question to understand people's motivations. We listen better. We find the courage to steer into discomfort. Then, much like musical compositions and unlike that red IKEA desk, our businesses will no longer be a simple sum of the parts. They will be more. As cellist Yo-Yo Ma says, 'A composition is always more than the sum of its parts. In other words, a good piece of music is more than itself. It is like a prism, which you can see from each facet a single totality.'[51]

Know yourself

> Knowing yourself is the beginning of all wisdom.[52]

'Know thyself' is a philosophical maxim inscribed on the Temple of Apollo in the ancient Greek precinct of Delphi. The first time I heard this, I wondered if I did. I had seen the models of what 'good leadership' was. I had sought, often in vain, to model exemplary behaviour. Leadership for me was aiming to reach someone else's standards. Yet trying to be someone else or something else was exhausting. It failed as a strategy. I could not sustain it. It felt untrue. I lacked authenticity when I tried. I lacked self-concept clarity.

Self-concept comprises self-knowledge, self-understanding and self-awareness. According to organizational psychologist, researcher and author Dr Tasha Eurich, 'We've found that even though most people believe they are self-aware, self-awareness is a truly rare quality: We estimate that only 10%–15% of the people we studied actually fit the criteria.'[53, 54]

Building self-concept clarity,[55] understanding the shape of our identity, underpins solid decision-making in the face of uncertainty. The degree to which we have a clear, well-defined and stable perception of who we are impacts the solidity of our self-concept. Knowing the content of one's identity is useful in leveraging our attributes and committing to a clear perspective. The through line is one representation of this self-concept.

Then questions like should I remain in my current job or move laterally in the same business, should I move to a new employer in a similar job or relocate, should I change careers or start my own business, no longer feel insurmountable. Of course, the answers to these questions will differ for each of us. They will depend on social, economic and personal choices and constraints. But they force us to confront our values and preferences. And understanding these can help navigate uncertainty. They help our decision-making.

Leaders with high self-concept clarity can more easily understand how new or unfolding events relate to their current circumstances. They have a more clearly held picture of their desired end-state and goals. They exhibit mental toughness, the resilience that is required in the face of change and challenge. They develop intrapersonal skills,[56] the internal abilities and behaviours that help manage emotions, cope with challenges and learn new information. They understand their character and motivations – with clarity. Self-concept clarity facilitates authenticity and consistency in behaviour which, in turn, fosters trust.[57]

Be consistent

Lacking self-concept clarity is a recipe for indecisive and inconsistent behaviour. Inconsistent leaders take up a lot of our resources. The boss who is always awful is easier to dismiss (he is just terrible, I don't need to worry, it is not about me). The one who is only frequently supportive but also often undermining (who will I get today, Dr Jekyll or Mr Hyde?) requires more emotional resources to deal with. When a leader's behaviour is hard to predict, it is next to impossible for teammates to develop even small levels of trust in them. Worse, the emotional labour required to manage them, significantly outpaces that required for consistently difficult leaders.

Consistency matters. Progress does not always come about by making a huge effort in a brief time. For example, exercising for seven hours for one day a week instead of one hour every day may have different effects. If our habits, practices, discipline and behaviours are consistent, we have internal process management and we are more likely to reach our goals.[58] Importantly, trust is founded on others' ability to understand and predict your behaviours, and therefore consistency fosters trust.

The research continues to grow. However, what we know so far is that self-concept clarity plays a key role in effective leadership. Leaders who understand themselves well are more confident, consistent and capable of making decisions that align with their values and organizational goals. Of course, there is no guarantee that even when you know yourself, your decisions will be faultless. But making decisions while standing rooted in your truest self will give you comfort that you have made them in good faith. And that is the best we can do.

Storytelling with intent

Great leadership is storytelling with intent. It's painting a picture of where you want to go and bringing people along on the journey. First, you must be clear on your own direction and your through line. When you've taken the time to listen to yourself, you're better equipped to listen to others. And that's where real connection happens.

For 60,000 years, humankind has told stories to inform, relate, connect and dream. We are constantly telling stories about where we think we are headed and what we need to focus on. Stories come in all shapes and sizes. They come to us through books, music, art and life. Stories change perspectives, offer hope and unite. When we lead, we are telling stories about who we think we are as leaders, projecting our vision of what we think is important, and where we want people to focus. We are always projecting a story, whether we mean to or not. So it is our responsibility to spend some time excavating our through lines – the themes of the stories we convey, to ensure they are what we want them to be.

Whether we recognize it or not, the world needs wise leaders. Leaders who encourage divergent thinking, create environments where people can thrive, and navigate complexity with grace and skill. We need leaders who can think in complex ways. We must understand our stories, go inwards, to reach outwards. We do not naturally spend enough time in reflection mostly because it is hard, painful and often uncomfortable. But it is essential. We must realize that we too are complex, nuanced and rarely fit into one category.

Understanding our stories allows us to start crafting a blueprint of who we are, where we have come from, what matters to us. Introspection is the bridge between us and those we lead. Once we know ourselves, we can help guide. In fact, the more we define our self-concept, the more we can rely on others to complete the picture. Taking action is rarely glamorous. It is often messy, flawed and awkward. But it is through action that we progress.

According to British poet and novelist Ben Okri: 'Stories are the secret reservoir of values: change the stories individuals or nations live by and tell themselves, and you change the individuals and nations.'[59]

The process of getting to know ourselves is ongoing. We are constantly shifting and changing based on the contours of our experience. And that is normal. Unpicking our through lines from all of this, starts by reaching inwards. We then reset based on new information, and ultimately reach out, to serve. Poet Courtney Peppernell says it so beautifully.

> You can't skip chapters, that's not how life works. You have to read every line, meet every character. You won't enjoy all of it. Hell, some chapters will make you cry for weeks. You will read things you don't want to read; you will have moments when you don't want the pages to end. But you have to keep going. Stories keep the world revolving. Live yours, don't miss out.[60]

Exploring your through line honours not only who you are, but also who you wish to be(come). It celebrates the rise and fall of life, the joy, the pain and everything in between. It enables action and reminds us that we are all more than enough. The pressing question is, if you don't, who will?

Integrate the stories

> 'Now pay attention. Because I am about to tell you the secret to life. Are you ready? The whole damn thing is about decisions. Little, insignificant decisions that clear the road for monster truck, life altering ones.

You see every path you take leads to another choice.
And some choices could change everything.'[61]

Our experiences shape who we are, and the unique paths we have walked carve out the through lines that guide us. Through lines are formed over time. They emerge from the integration of experiences, learnings and challenges across our careers. These lines guide our choices and actions. They can serve as a reference point for decision-making. And they adapt and evolve while remaining rooted in fundamental principles. These through lines, born from the tapestry of our lives, give depth and direction to our actions. Like the sandbars that offer navigational support, our through lines play crucial roles in the ecosystems in which we operate. They offer us scaffolding as we serve.

When we understand our personal narratives and the underlying themes of our experiences, we are better equipped to connect our work to a larger sense of purpose. Amy Wrzesniewski and her colleagues at Yale University explored how people view their work and found that those who see their jobs as intrinsically tied to their personal values and life stories experienced greater job satisfaction, engagement and resilience.[62] Put another way, when we can trace the threads of our past, recognize pivotal moments, and see how they converge, we gain clarity on our motivations and goals. We make sense of our past to inform our future. We find meaning.

In Viktor Frankl's seminal work, *Man's Search for Meaning*, he explored how finding meaning (which is made up of comprehension, mattering and purpose)[63] is crucial for overcoming life's challenges. When individuals find meaning in their experiences, they can endure and thrive despite hardships. Because meaning helps us make sense of the world. Leadership is no different. Organizational psychologist Karl Weick translated the concept of meaning into sensemaking in leadership. He likened sensemaking to cartography. Just as a cartographer decides where to look, which details to emphasize, and what features to include, our sensemaking depends on our focus, our choices and our perspectives.

Our through lines also illuminate our intrinsic motivations. In 1977, two young psychologists at the University of Rochester would meet and begin work to uncover what motivates us. Edward Deci and Richard Ryan posited that we feel motivated not when we are rewarded by extrinsic factors, but rather when we are driven by our intrinsic motivations. They demonstrated that when we feel autonomous, competent and connected, we thrive. Uncovering our through lines supports all three. You build autonomy when your actions are congruent with who you are. You feel competent when your actions are purposeful and well-directed. You connect with others as you share who you are with those around you and learn about them.

The through lines guide our focus, our choices and our perspectives. They help us feel autonomous, competent and connected. They uncover meaning. And all of this allows us to answer the profound question, why am I doing this? This understanding propels us forward. It transforms abstract purpose into tangible action. This understanding shapes us. It transcends mere analysis. It is an act of creativity,[64] requiring us to bring ourselves into the process, embracing both the complexity and the beauty of the landscapes we explore.

In organizational settings, leaders who understand and communicate their through lines can inspire their teams more effectively. Then, 'leaders articulate a picture of the future, a direction for their group to work towards'.[65] They make sense of information and provide a vision.[66] They act like sponges.[67] They filter and interpret their groups' circumstances and situations, helping to make sense of these while articulating a view of the future. According to a report by the *Harvard Business Review*, leaders who align their actions with a clear understanding of their personal and organizational values, create more engaged and productive workplaces.[68]

The contours of your experience form the bedrock of your through lines. By delving into your personal history and understanding these guiding threads, you unlock the ability to translate purpose into action. The question, 'Why am I doing this?' transforms from a daunting query into a quest, driving you forward with intention and clarity. This alignment not only enriches your fulfilment but also elevates the impact on those around you, fostering a culture of authenticity, purpose and commitment.

Complicate the narrative: experience is not a prerequisite for impact

Journalists and conflict mediators Amanda Ripley and Hélène Biandudi Hofer came into our business and shared a wonderful toolkit of strategies to navigate conflict productively. You can explore their work at www.thegoodconflict.com. One of the highlights of the discussion was something that Amanda referenced as 'complicating the narrative'. Through years of research, it turns out that we need complexity to understand (and be open to) nuance.

> The lesson for journalists (or anyone) working amidst intractable conflict: complicate the narrative. First, complexity leads to a fuller, more accurate story. Secondly, it boosts the odds that your work will matter – particularly if it is about a polarising issue. When people encounter complexity, they become more curious and less closed off to new information. They listen, in other words.[69]

In service of complicating this narrative, I thought it would be useful to offer a different perspective on how to identify your through lines. Narratives drive what our world looks like, however sometimes they are built on shoddy ground. Sometimes if they are overly broad or too simplistic, they can influence the way we work. If our through lines are built on shaky ground, could they drive our lives in the 'wrong' direction?

While the idea that individual experiences shape our purpose and actions is compelling, there is also a different argument, that suggests you don't need extensive experience to explore it.

When Deci and Ryan developed their Self-Determination Theory, they also posited that intrinsic motivation, driven by those innate psychological needs for competence, autonomy and connection, can provide sufficient grounding for individuals to find purpose and direction *without* relying heavily on past experiences. Instead, we can derive a sense of purpose from our natural curiosity, desire for mastery, and the inherent satisfaction of doing something well or contributing to something larger than ourselves.

Research on values-based living supports this view. Values are core beliefs that transcend specific situations and guide behaviour. There seems to be a growing body of research that suggests that when we clarify and act according to our core values, we report higher levels of life satisfaction. Values vary. They can be abstract, such as a commitment to justice, compassion or creativity, and do not necessarily stem from specific life experiences. Instead, they can be deeply ingrained from cultural, familial or educational influences.

Additionally, the concept of a 'beginner's mind' which is rooted in Zen Buddhism, suggests that approaching life with an open and eager mind can lead to profound insights. Think about the last time you felt intrinsically motivated independent of your experience. Imagine a five-year-old encountering a piano for the first time. The child might press random keys, fascinated by the different sounds. They have no preconceived notions of what is 'correct' or 'beautiful'; they simply approach the instrument with curiosity and a sense of wonder.

In the work context, innovative thinking and disruptive leadership also support the idea that extensive experience is not always required. Successful innovation can come from individuals who simply challenge the status quo and approach problems with fresh perspectives, rather than relying on experience. This suggests that purpose and direction can emerge from a forward-looking mindset and a willingness to explore new possibilities, rather than solely being anchored in experience.

The rise of young entrepreneurs and leaders who achieve significant impact early in their careers illustrates that a deep sense of purpose can emerge from vision and passion. Research by the Kauffman Foundation indicates that the average age of successful startup founders is around 40,[70] but there are notable exceptions where much younger individuals, driven by a powerful sense of mission and vision, have created highly successful ventures.

While first-hand experience can certainly inform and shape our through lines, they are not the only path to finding them. Intrinsic motivation, core values, a beginner's mindset and a forward-looking vision can all provide a powerful sense of purpose and direction. Extensive experience is not a prerequisite for understanding and articulating one's through line. We can do it without. So which is better: exploring a through line through the lens of your experience or exploring it without experience but from the perspective of a fresh start? Neither. Both. Either. The key is not which means you use, but rather that you start.

One person, one story, six words

Legend has it that one day, Ernest Hemingway was in the Algonquin Hotel with some writing buddies having lunch. The conversation led to a wager. Hemingway bet that he could draft an entire story in six words. After everyone put their money down, Hemingway jotted down a few words on a napkin. He then passed the napkin around the table. *'For sale: baby shoes, never worn.'* Though short, the writers could not deny that these words formed a full story. He won the bet.

It remains unclear who penned those six words. But in 2006, Larry Smith decided they had value. Larry had founded *SMITH* magazine focused on long-form, personal storytelling. Celebrating the chicken's view, the view from the ground up, he wanted to involve the magazine's community in a new and engaging way of storytelling. He threw down the gauntlet. Draft your story in six words. He shut down his computer for the night. When he logged back in the next morning, 10,000 people had responded. The six-word memoir was (re)born.

The paradoxical relationship between limitation and creativity that we saw previously highlights the adaptive nature of human cognition. As Larry described it, the constraint did not stop creativity, it fuelled it. By giving folks a place to share their story while limiting it to a few words, he gave everyone the ability to create. As the project branched off, folks began using it in their workplaces, communities, families and classrooms. It ranged from the bittersweet ('dementia caused unforgettable pain and sorrow') and poignant ('I still make coffee for two'), to the inspirational ('from migrant worker to NASA astronaut') and hilarious ('married by Elvis, divorced by Friday').[71]

Since then, the project has become a global phenomenon, it has generated a series of best-selling books, has featured in media outlets and was even renamed the 'American haiku'. More than 1.5 million people have shared their version. It continues to expand and gather momentum.

But with success, comes challenge. In 2008, a few days after launching the project as a separate entity from the magazine, the site crashed. Traffic, traction and an idea caused uncurbed enthusiasm, and a crash. So what did Larry do? He freaked out. Then he called his technology friend, Ted. Ted spoke to a guy and that guy did his magic. When he logged back in, six words greeted him: **Down for maintenance. Be back soon.** The community had rallied.

The site crashed again in 2024, and the stakes felt higher. The login feature stopped working. No one could share stories. The hundreds of stories that flowed through each day, stopped appearing. Larry fielded countless emails asking what had happened. The site went down for several weeks.

So what happened to the community? Well it regrouped, showed up and found other ways to connect. Community members created their own message threads while the site was down. When the site went back online, one of the first stories that greeted Larry was – '**The glitch left me without words**. For several weeks I could not log into the six-word memoirs. It was like I left a family gathering without being able to say goodbye.'[72] That was exactly how Larry felt. He had found his through line – **to create and sustain a community** – in six words.

Your turn

The six-word memoir is a way to enhance the excavation of your through line. Through the creation of an artificial constraint, word limitation, I hope to fuel your creativity. Have a think about six words that tell one story of who you are. You may have several ideas. Jot them all down. Your words can evolve and shift with time. But they will give you a first glimpse at a simple form of your through line.

If you want to access your six words by looking forward, you might start with these questions. What lights you up? What drains you? What enrages you? What gets you up in the morning, even without an alarm clock? Who do you call when things go well? Who do you call when things go badly? If you could only share one thing about yourself, what would it be? When was the last time you felt happy?

If you want to access your six words using your experiences as a springboard – you can try this. Draw your lifeline – the line that illustrates the time from your birth to your present moment. Then on this line, write down (without too much filtering) all the mountaintop moments, those that fill you with pride, and the canyon moments, those that reflect tough challenges or moments which drew you inward. Put the mountaintops on top of the line. The canyons on the bottom. Then step back. Look at your notes. Identify themes or trends that appear. And start jotting these down. Then try crafting six words that connect these ideas. See what emerges for you.

> My six words: Catch and release, embrace the paradox.

3

A line to understand: reach in

To be nobody-but-yourself in a world which is doing its best, night and day, to make you like everybody else, means to fight the hardest battle which any human being can fight; and never stop fighting.[73]

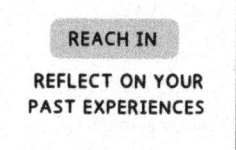

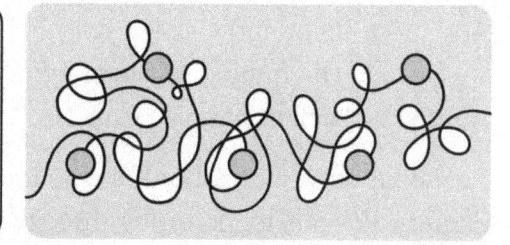

REACH IN
REFLECT ON YOUR
PAST EXPERIENCES

Figure 5: Reach in

In a nutshell

The journey to understanding oneself is a deeply personal and ongoing one. It involves excavating the through lines, the core principles, values and motivations that guide our decisions and actions. By reaching in, we learn to navigate life's complexities

> with clarity and purpose. We build emotional agility and enhance cognitive clarity. We can manage stress, make decisions, and lead effectively by aligning our internal compass with our external actions.

Daring to feel

Fear, stress, anxiety, grief. We felt all those things during the pandemic. We had likely felt these emotions before. But lockdown brought a torrent of emotions to the fore. We felt fear of the unknown. We felt the stress of juggling a multitude of responsibilities for our families, our friends, our communities. We felt anxiety as we navigated uncertainty. And most importantly we felt grief, a loss of everything that we prized. The number of times I heard the phrase, 'I just want to go back to normal', surprised me.

For some, this smörgåsbord of emotions forced a process of enquiry. For others, powering through was the only option. We navigated home life, work life, health concerns and losses. We did not realize that normal evolves, that our lives are constantly shifting, evolving, moving. That the ebb and flow of our lives is normal. Instead, a sense of loss caused grief. And in the throes of grief, our brains defaulted to judgement and punishment. And it was not necessarily of others. It was simply of ourselves. Thoughts like I did not do enough today. I will do more tomorrow. He did not help me with the project when I needed it. The next time she asks me for something, I will say no. We retreated.

Relationships shifted. Both the ones we constructed with others but importantly the one we had with ourselves. We understood that staying open and asking questions was important. Yet, as we sat with our grief, our loneliness and our fear, we struggled to find openness, curiosity and wonder. As Amanda Ripley says, 'It is impossible to feel curiosity and outrage at the same time.'[74] When we needed to stay open most of all, our instincts made us shut down, protect, withdraw and retreat.

But there is hope. We can train our brains to think differently, to steer into the slide. Somewhat like the muscle memory that we joke about when we talk about riding bikes (once you know how to ride a bike you can always ride a bike), we can teach our brains to remember. The trick (and I use that word lightly) is to practise when you are not under pressure, uncertain or afraid. Practise when things are calm, and you will recall what to do when things are not.

> **Some questions to ask**
>
> - What story am I telling myself?
> - What could the other perspective be?
> - What do I need to know?

From this reflection, we hold space for each other's grief, and we witness the collective sadness that does not necessarily have a solution. We may feel afraid while doing so. But we do so anyway. That is compassion. As American Buddhist nun Pema Chödrön writes, 'When we practice generating compassion, we can expect to experience our fear of pain. Compassion practice is daring. It involves learning to relax and allow ourselves to move gently toward what scares us.'[75]

Decision-making in uncertainty

> When everything outside feels incoherent, we need to reach in for coherence.[76]

As we have discussed, when moments of crisis occur, we rarely have time to consider alternatives in any depth. Job insecurity, technological advancements and increasing workloads have compounded stress over the last decade. Leaders navigate various dimensions of uncertainty constantly. They have had to learn how to navigate complex international landscapes, balancing risks and opportunities against a volatile geopolitical backdrop. Economic instability, influenced by factors such as trade tensions, financial crises and unpredictable market dynamics, requires leaders to constantly adapt their strategies. The rapid pace of technological change, including advancements in AI, automation and digital transformation, forces leaders to continuously innovate and adapt.

The COVID-19 pandemic exemplified the kind of unforeseen challenge that can disrupt businesses globally, requiring leaders to make rapid, high-stakes decisions in uncertain environments. Climate change and environmental sustainability are becoming increasingly important, adding another layer of uncertainty as businesses must adapt to regulatory changes and shifting consumer preferences. Geopolitical tensions, such as trade wars, Brexit and regional conflicts, contribute to an unpredictable business environment. As leaders, we must embrace what Scottish physicist, James Clerk Maxwell called thoroughly conscious ignorance.

The problem with stress and uncertainty is that they impact our ability to make decisions. In the 1970s, psychologists like Daniel Kahneman began to show that humans are subject to a variety of biases and illusions. 'We are influenced by completely automatic things that we have no control over, and we don't know we're doing it', Kahneman said.[77]

This phenomenon is well documented in neuroscientific research. Stress and uncertainty interfere with rational decision-making through multiple neurobiological mechanisms. These include neurochemical changes, the inhibition of the prefrontal cortex, amygdala hyperactivity, impairments in working memory, and disrupted neural networks. These mechanisms go some way to explaining why stressed and uncertain individuals often make less optimal decisions. They also provide a means to think about ways to protect against our instincts. Let us look at these in turn.

1. **Neurochemical changes**: Stress triggers the release of cortisol and alters dopamine levels, both of which play critical roles in decision-making. Elevated cortisol affects how we think, while altered dopamine-signalling affects our assessment of risk and reward. Acute stress changes dopamine levels in the brain, influencing risk-taking behaviour and reward sensitivity. These changes can lead to more impulsive and less rational decisions.[78]

2. **Inhibition of the prefrontal cortex**: The prefrontal cortex, a part of your brain located right behind

your forehead, is critical for executive functions such as decision-making, planning and regulating emotions. Under stress, the area's activity is often impaired, leading to decreased cognitive control and increased reliance on more primitive brain regions. Stress activates the amygdala, which in turn inhibits the prefrontal cortex. So we lose the ability to think clearly. We default to habitual, automatic responses over thoughtful decision-making.[79]

3. **Hyperactivity of the amygdala**: While all of this is going on in the prefrontal cortex, the amygdala (an almond shaped area in your brain sometimes called the reptilian brain), which processes emotions, becomes hyperactive. This heightened activity can overshadow rational thought processes, leading to decisions driven by emotional reactions rather than logical reasoning. Stress induces amygdala hyperactivity, which biases individuals towards immediate rewards and short-term outcomes, often at the expense of long-term goals.[80] Author and philosopher Charles Handy summarized the impact succinctly: 'Where there is no vision, there you find short-termism, for then there is no reason to compromise today for an unknown tomorrow.'[81]

4. **Impaired working memory**: Stress and uncertainty can also degrade working memory; a system used to hold and manipulate information temporarily. Impairments in working memory can hinder the ability to process information effectively and make informed decisions. Stress reduces the capacity of

working memory by affecting our prefrontal cortex, leading to poorer decision-making performance.[82]

5. **Disrupted decision-making**: Stress and uncertainty disrupt the neural networks involved in decision-making, including the connectivity between the prefrontal cortex and other brain regions. This disruption impairs the integration of cognitive and emotional information necessary for sound decision-making. It also hampers the functional connectivity within decision-making networks, resulting in compromised judgement and increased reliance on habitual responses.[83]

Things are not looking good for our decision-making abilities under stress and uncertainty. But as we have already seen, uncertainty is the system. So is there hope? Yes, there is.

An inside job

The advice industry bombards us with tips on how to feel better, perform better, lead better. Books, podcasts, documentaries, commentary surround us. The irony is not lost on me; this book may be no exception. However, before you adopt new strategies to become 'better', I suggest reaching in first.

With nuanced introspection, self-reflection builds internal self-awareness. Introspection alone isn't always effective. Most of us understand that we need to look inward. However, we must also mind the questions we ask ourselves and how we ask them. As you saw earlier, asking 'what' questions instead of 'why' questions, for example, can move us from backward-looking reflection to a forward-looking one. Then, once we conduct an audit of where we are, we can decide where we want to go. Reaching in with due consideration, uncovers our through lines as we go to a place 'within, down the hall past our defences, where we keep track of our reasons for being. That room is one we should always return to'.[84] This unlocks who we are.

Why should you care? At the end of the self-reflection rainbow, lies centred decision-making, adaptability, stress management and leadership.

Research shows that leaders with high self-awareness[85] are better equipped to handle the stress and ambiguity associated with uncertain environments. They better regulate their emotions to support their teams (emotional labour[86]). Self-aware leaders are more likely to make better decisions[87] because they are more attuned to their emotional response to uncertainty[88] and to how their feelings and thoughts influence their choices. In fact, self-awareness[89] builds emotional agility by regulating emotional responses, reducing stress and improving overall wellbeing in uncertain contexts. Then, leaders guide their teams through periods of uncertainty,[90] by managing their own reactions and supporting team members effectively.

Self-awareness[91] is also linked to greater cognitive clarity. This helps leaders make more deliberate and effective decisions when faced with uncertainty. They understand their attributes and biases, leading to more rational and objective decision-making. Self-awareness contributes to greater adaptability.[92] Leaders can adjust their strategies when navigating complex and uncertain business landscapes. They create more resilient and responsive organizations by demonstrating authenticity[93] and fostering a resilient culture.

Self-awareness leads to emotional agility, cognitive clarity and adaptability. It helps us counter our instincts. So, don't shy away from the work. Simply put, we need to understand our past to (re)imagine our future. Reach in. It is an inside job.

How to tune out the static

> A catastrophe is nothing but a puzzle with the volume of drama turned up very high.[94]

So how do we uncover our through lines? We must tune out the static and reach in.

When I was growing up, my father had a transistor radio. Each morning he would tune into the BBC World Service. Using his small radio, he would set the short-wave frequency to his favourite channel, turning a large dial to find just the right setting. He patiently tuned out as much static as he could. At the start of each hour, the familiar six beeps would echo through the kitchen as the newsreader's voice would roar to life. First heard on 5 February 1924, the six beeps were designed by John Reith, head of the BBC, and Frank Watson Dyson, the astronomer royal. They were controlled by two mechanical clocks at the Royal Greenwich Observatory – hence their name, the Greenwich time signal.

This morning ritual came to symbolize so much as I grew up. It signalled the beginning of a day, the start of the news, but perhaps most importantly the tuning out of noise and the tuning in of what was going on around the world, at a time when news was much harder to come by and when finding out what was happening was not just a click away. I am often reminded of the feelings associated with those pips when I try to reach in. Embodied awareness allows me to stop, metaphorically wait for the six beeps, tune out the static of my brain and tune in to what I feel, how I feel it and, importantly, why. It allows me to remember to reach in.

Writing is also a wonderful portal to tune out the static; to take stock, pause and reflect on what drives you. In 1986, the psychology professor James Pennebaker[95] conducted a series of experiments. He asked students to spend 15 minutes writing about the biggest trauma of their lives or, if they had not experienced a trauma, their most challenging time. They were told to let go of filters and to include their deepest thoughts, even if they had never shared these thoughts before. For four days running, they did the same thing. It was not easy. In fact, Pennebaker described how one in 20 students would end up crying as a result. But when asked whether they wanted to continue, they always did. Meanwhile a control group spent the same number of sessions writing a description of something neutral, such as a tree or their dorm room.

Then he waited for six months, monitoring how often the students visited the health centre. The day he saw the results, he left the lab, walked over to his friend who was waiting for him in a car and told him he had found something big. The students who had written about their feelings had made significantly fewer trips to the doctor in the subsequent months.

Pennebaker's research found that expressive writing could lead to several health benefits including reduced stress and anxiety, improved immune functions and mental health improvements. He proposed that there might be several mechanisms at play. Writing about experiences helped individuals process pent-up emotions. This helped them make sense of events, thereby reducing their emotional impact. And by organizing thoughts and feelings through writing, they developed coping strategies to make healthy choices. His work explored how writing about one's thoughts and feelings could be a powerful tool for emotional release, cognitive processing and behavioural change, leading to a healthier and more balanced life.[96]

Tuning out the static can take several forms. It can be as simple as jotting down your feelings on a note on your phone. Or carrying a notebook with you for those inklings that you wish to explore. Or taking photographs of the moments you want to remember so you can revisit them later. Or taking a walk in nature to breathe. The external world is out of your control; outside of yourself. You can only control your internal environment. I am often reminded of Apple's CEO, Tim Cook's fabulous phrase, 'National Parks are like palate cleansers for the mind'.[97] Nature can provide us perspective if we let it. Perspective stems from experience. Instead of blocking and tackling whatever life throws at us, we can train ourselves to tune out the static.

Let me repeat myself. I know that self-inquiry can be daunting. We do not want to explore the things that cause pain. Going back in time can often make things appear larger than they are. But remember that there is joy hiding there too. You will never eliminate all your scars. But you are in the driving seat from here on out. As you work to understand yourself, you will no longer be at the mercy of what happened. Instead, you will build connections. Think about your experiences like a stiff neck. You think that you need to fix your neck. So you head to a specialist. They tell you that the pain in your neck is caused by a problem in your foot. Sort your foot out and your neck will heal. Every part of your body is connected. And so too are your experiences. Your through lines can provide the link between distinct parts of your life. They provide context. Context for who you are and how you lead. They point out how to connect where you are with where you want to go.

Pennebaker's work continues to evolve, with recent studies exploring the nuances of how diverse types of writing and linguistic patterns affect health outcomes. Collaborations with researchers have expanded the applications of expressive writing to diverse populations and settings. But there is a thorny issue. I have learned that there is something which researchers prize, and that is replicability. This is the idea that a hypothesis is only evidenced if the study that first showed causation can be replicated. There have been many press articles about how few social psychology experiments are replicable. This has thrown into question the veracity of many claims. Pennebaker's studies are no exception to the rule. His discovery inspired a generation of researchers to conduct several hundred studies. However, subsequent studies have shown only a small relationship between expressive writing and healing.

However small the impact, leaders should take note. As a free intervention, it has the possibility to open critical and creative thinking, two skills sorely needed in any business environment. If expressive writing exercises could reduce stress and improve wellbeing even slightly, it is worth trying. It costs nothing and could offer benefits over time.

Excavate your lines

Excavating your through lines builds self-awareness. This can impact your ability to navigate personal and professional challenges with ease. A little like an artist's back-turned paintings, shielded from the external eye, our through lines are ours to hold first. These guiding principles inform our decisions, actions and goals, providing a coherent direction amid the complexities of leadership. And while this adaptability is vital for personal growth and resilience, it also allows us to pivot without losing sight of our core values and objectives when leading.

Your through line allows you to cross boundaries. Its flexibility fuels your resilience and agility in the face of complexity. By making the implicit explicit, you are better able to make clear and satisfying decisions.

A through line can identify our purpose. Individuals with a keen sense of purpose are better equipped to manage stress and adapt to change. Change is hard. This is because our brains are wired for the status quo – they are consuming endless pieces of data and want to make sense of this information by engaging in shortcuts that are not always accurate.

Second, our brains have limited capacity. One National Academy of Sciences study of more than 1,000 parole board hearings demonstrated this. According to the researchers, at the beginning of a day or after lunch, judges would grant parole in 65% of the cases. By the end of the morning or at the end of the day, favourable decisions decreased to zero.[98] In other words, the more tired our brains get, the more we decide no change is better than any change.

Finally, change is a pain. Thanks to fMRI technology, we now know that our brains react to change in the same way they react to physical pain.

Clarifying our through lines helps prioritize actions, filter out distractions and focus on what truly matters. They reduce the pressure on our brains! For example, someone whose through line is to foster community and connection might prioritize social interactions and community-building activities, leading to a more fulfilling and purpose-driven life. The through line makes our intrinsic motivations clear and our values explicit. When we can clearly understand our core beliefs and long-term goals, we make more satisfying and coherent decisions. A well-defined personal purpose contributes to psychological wellbeing and resilience.[99] By maintaining a clear through line, we can make sense of our experiences, align actions with our values, and pursue goals that are deeply meaningful to us.

Our through lines also clarify different facets of our identity. Seeing yourself as more than a single identity can offer freedom. In fact, self-complexity[100] has been linked to stronger wellbeing (think about complicating the narrative). When we understand that we can be more than one thing, we understand that we can dare, bounce back, and live to experience another day without concern for any labels that limit us.

At work a through line is equally essential. Leaders with a clear and compelling vision can inspire and guide their teams more effectively. Visionary companies, led by leaders with a powerful sense of purpose, are successful and resilient.[101] A leader's through line acts as a beacon, aligning the team's efforts and ensuring that everyone works towards a common goal.

Additionally, leaders who make their through line explicit, enhance understanding and decision-making within their teams. Understanding the corporate through line becomes easier. In practical terms, this can be seen in how leaders communicate the vision during times of change or uncertainty. A leader who consistently reinforces the organization's through line can help their team navigate challenges with confidence and coherence. For example, during a major organizational shift, a leader who emphasizes the core mission of innovation and customer focus can help the team stay aligned and motivated despite the disruptions. By clearly articulating the organization's core values and long-term vision, leaders create a sense of shared purpose and direction. This clarity helps team members understand how their individual roles contribute to the broader mission, leading to increased motivation, engagement and job satisfaction.

Whether from a personal or business perspective, a through line's adaptability and explicit nature enhances resilience, agility and decision-making. By embracing and articulating a through line, we can navigate boundaries and challenges with clarity and purpose, ensuring that our actions are aligned with our broader goals, values and purpose.

Inner mastery

In the past, leadership has been an outer game. You say, you decide, you act, and you are a leader. But ancient wisdom and modern science reveal a powerful truth: to get to our full potential in life and leadership, we need to first master our inner game. When we approach leadership in this way, from our inner core, we begin to align with what is truest and highest within us, and we free ourselves from habits of the past to achieve breakthroughs in our behaviour.[102]

Professor Hitendra Wadhwa teaches at Columbia Business School. He has spent his life studying the intersection of science and faith. He explores how ordinary people ascend to extraordinary leadership positions. What I love about his work is the power of his message: we need to be masters of ourselves *before* we try to be masters of the universe. His research supports the value of identifying our through lines to do so.

All manner of externalities can disrupt traditional (and even longstanding) business models. Think of Blockbuster and Netflix, hospitality and Airbnb, HMV and Spotify. Disruption can be better navigated together. We must resist the idea that leadership is the remit of a few. In fact, a Gartner survey of more than 6,500 employees and 100 CHROs found that the best businesses rely on their workforces, not executives, to lead change.[103] We each have a role. Who we are influences how we lead.

Many aim to deconstruct leadership into a series of atomistic traits. Perhaps that is because we can then teach leadership in the same way that we would teach learning our multiplication tables. Skills like having difficult conversations, setting priorities, giving feedback are teachable. And these are important skills. However, they do not fully capture the inner work.

Professor Wadhwa's work illustrates how every outward action begins with inner understanding. He believes that peak performance is a state, not a trait, one that each of us can cultivate by activating five energies: purpose, wisdom, growth, love and self-realization. He suggests that the relevant pathways already exist within us. That we are not just one personality, instead we have multiple personalities (see self-complexity) which adapt to the situations in which we find ourselves.

Discovering Professor Wadhwa's work has helped me rethink and enhance my framework. Reaching in helps us understand ourselves. We can then work on mastering our internal environments. And through that work, we can start taking actions externally which align with the ones we take internally. Then we lead.

Outer impact[104]

Food has always been a great connector in my life. From my childhood memories of huge extended family gatherings as my parents whipped up a culinary storm, to my joy in hosting dinners at home, I genuinely believe there is nothing like coming together over a good meal. I have lived in London for the last 20 years. And over that time, I have been wowed by the variety and quality of restaurants in this city. So when I heard Professor Wadhwa recount his experience at Hoppers, a Sri Lankan restaurant in the heart of Soho, I leaned in.

The restaurant's signature hoppers are bowl-shaped, fermented rice and coconut pancakes, crisp around the edges, soft and fluffy in the centre. These crispy, fluffy delights marry beautifully with the pungent and fiery spices of curries. For the foodies among you, the hopper originated in south India where it was known as an '*appam*'. British settlers struggled with the pronunciation and began referring to them as 'hoppers'. The name stuck. I encourage you to visit when you are next able.[105]

Professor Wadhwa was sitting alone, enjoying his meal. Around 9.30 pm, the staff announced that the kitchen would be closing and that last orders should be placed within five minutes. Feeling like he might enjoy one more hopper, Professor Wadhwa placed his order. The table next to him, ignored the warning and the two guests continued to engage in a heated debate. Ten minutes passed when the gentleman, realizing that he would like one more hopper, called the waiter over. The waiter apologized, telling him that the kitchen was now closed. The man asked if he might have some rice instead, and again the waiter repeated that last orders were done.

Feeling slightly smug that he had managed to order one more hopper in time, Professor Wadhwa moved into judgement. 'What an idiot', he thought. Why had the man not paid better attention to the warnings that the kitchen was closing. Almost immediately, a different part of him (and some might argue the kinder part) argued that the couple were in conversation. That is why they did not hear the warning. He reflected on the times he missed warnings because his focus was elsewhere. So, lifting the veil of judgement and embracing his kinder self, he leant over and offered the gentleman his hopper. When he described the story, he talked about that inner fight – the one between the part of himself that wanted to keep the hopper for himself smug in the knowledge that he 'had listened when it mattered'; and the part of him that believed in sharing with a full heart, in living into the values that his mother had instilled in him. These two parts of him were in conflict. As Abraham Lincoln once said, 'A house divided against itself cannot stand'.

The gentleman smiled, politely refused, and Wadhwa finished his meal. He rose to pay his bill. It was then that the waiter informed him that the couple had paid his bill. He reflected, 'Without any need for recompense, the couple had paid. I realized that I was the one who had been silly. I was the one who had judged. They had done a good deed and left without a trace.'[106] Inner mastery for outer impact, a powerful phrase that we would be wise to remember.

Your turn

> You cannot grow without an accurate understanding of who you are and where you're starting from, and there is no app for that.[107]

Accessing your through line requires thought. As I embarked on excavating mine, I went through several exercises that helped me consolidate my thoughts. I present three of my favourites below. I take credit for none of these. In fact, I encourage you to gather more information directly from the sources (these are listed below). I hope these thought prompts will kick start your process. Revise. Revisit. Explore. See what you discover.

1. **Value cards – Paul Ingram**

    Columbia Business School professor Paul Ingram has been studying what connects us. He believes that values are our internal control system. And understanding these explains so much about why we react in the way that we do. In fact, in moments of crisis, our core values often guide us most profoundly. By knowing and understanding them explicitly we will be better able to make decisions which feel right.

    Pull out a piece of paper and write down eight values that you prize. Most of us aren't aware of what we value until we are asked. Even then it can be difficult to identify those that are most important to us. These are essential to uncover, as they will point you in the direction of what matters most to you. If you're looking for a guide and further exercises on values, have a look at Brené Brown's handy list of 100 values.[108]

    Some questions that might prompt your identification are: In what situations, in work and elsewhere, do you feel true to yourself, so that what you think, feel, say, and do are in perfect harmony? When do you not feel this way? What limits you in those situations?

2. **Would you recognize your soul in the dark? – John Amaechi**

    The story of NBA basketball player and organizational psychologist, John Amaechi, inspired me. His leadership lessons fuelled my learning and created space in my otherwise hectic days. John shares a question that his mother, Wendy Amaechi, posed when he announced that he wanted to play basketball in the NBA. 'Would you recognize your soul in the dark?'[109]

    Wendy goes on to explain that those who want to achieve ordinary things can let external circumstances push them along. However, those who choose extraordinary destinations cannot rely on fate to get them there. Instead, they need to know themselves – fully. This requires an understanding of the self. This is what she describes as a soul in the dark; when all visible distinguishing physical factors are taken away – who are we?

    I have come back to this question often. It helps me reach in. Importantly, it helps me navigate to my core when life throws me curved balls. Some questions that you might consider include: What is your most common state or mood? What happens when you experience extreme emotions? When do you feel peace, and how often does that occur? What agitates you? What inspires joy and lifts your spirits? What types of interactions do you look for? What types of interactions do you avoid? My only advice: start simple, start small, but please start.

    ·

3. **Purpose on a page – Kevin Roberts**

   Former ad man, international business leader, founder, consultant and educator Kevin Roberts came into our business in 2022 to help us work through our purpose. As we emerged from the pandemic, we wanted to work on naming our purpose to set a cohesive direction. For integrity, we wanted our purpose to derive from the ecosystem that we inhabited – the full diversity of employees, customers, neighbours, partners and leaders touched by our work. Kevin's model for 'purposing' was one which encouraged discomfort, creative thinking and consensus building. It clarified the work that we had already done and set the stage for the path we wanted to explore. It allowed us to refine what we prized in pursuit of mastery. The result was a purpose that held authority and impact, creativity and authenticity, aspirations and truth.

   Kevin breaks down 'purposing' into five parts – identifying beliefs, defining spirit, character and focus and elaborating on an inspirational dream. The work applies to each of us too. This framework can challenge the stories that saddle us. It can allow us the space to listen, question and name what we value as we reach in. Then we can define how we want to show up.

I encourage you to contact Kevin directly for more information on his programmes (https://redrose.consulting/). Here, I have aimed to summarize the work we undertook to get to know ourselves. This is filtered through the lens of my understanding, so any errors or omissions are my own.

1. **Explore your character**: pick eight attributes of your character that drive who you are. Start (at the bottom) with who you are internally and end (at the top) with how this manifests externally. Be intentional, authentic and aspirational. Think of your character like a ladder towards your spirit.

2. **Name your beliefs**: what are the eight beliefs (values in action) that drive your leadership style. What do you stand for? Ask yourself what makes you inspirational, credible, memorable and true. We must hold these lightly as it's important to remember that beliefs can change as we do.

3. **Describe your spirit**: what is the superpower that helps you show up?

4. **Define your focus**: what determines your direction and your priorities? What aligns your everyday actions with your through line? Your focus should be action-based, memorable and simple.

5. **Craft your inspirational dream**: this is your reason for being, your through line. It clarifies the meaning, intent and direction of your work. It explains how you create value and make a difference. This is the touchstone through which all your endeavours are assessed. It is unique, imaginative, simple and compelling. You may not be able to measure it, but you know it is true.

I offer you my purpose on a page below as an example. I look forward to seeing what this exercise unlocks for you.

Inspirational dream	
To transform plumbing into poetry	
Spirit	
There's no place like home.	
Beliefs	**Character**
Reach in, reset, reach out: feel well to do well.	Imaginative
Share the purple crayon: draw what you dream.	Gritty
Don't hide the cheese: honour others by honouring yourself.	Bold
	Aware
Find the right shoes: use the right tools, in the right way, at the right time.	Nomadic
	Whacky
Splash in puddles: share the wonder, bring someone with you.	Kind
	Family
Clarify the melody: bring the funk and soul into conversations.	
Uplift, nourish, catalyse: care costs nothing but means a lot.	
Do hard better: stay open and rethink.	
Focus	
Unleash remarkable.	

4

A line to change: reset

We need courage to take ourselves seriously, to look closely without flinching, to regard the things that frighten us in life and art with wonder.[110]

RESET
RECALIBRATE BASED ON NEW INFORMATION

Figure 6: Reset

In a nutshell

In today's rapidly evolving landscape, intrinsic well-being, generative conversations and the blank page offer a helping hand to overcome complex challenges. Embracing intrinsic rewards, such as personal growth and purpose, helps individuals and organizations reset and thrive amid external pressures and fears. Generative conversations, where diverse perspectives are integrated, foster innovative solutions and dynamic problem-solving. Together, these concepts advocate for a reset. They support a shift from traditional, top-down approaches to more collaborative and adaptive strategies. They highlight the importance of integrating internal motivations, diverse viewpoints and creative freedom to achieve sustainable resilience.

Sick and tired[111]

Gabby Thomas became the second-fastest woman ever when she ran the 200 m in 21.61 seconds at the 2021 US Olympic Team Trials. She then won two medals at the Tokyo Olympics and a further three in Paris. However, her relationship with running was not always straightforward. Gabby's diverse interests made her question whether running was the right path for her. Her reset forced a reckoning.

Soccer was Gabby's first love. Running wasn't something she wanted to pursue. When her mom encouraged her to join the track and field team, she discovered speed. Soon expectations set in. People congratulated her, expressed their pride and happiness at having her on the team. She felt pressure to succeed and others' potential disappointment if she didn't. Eager to be successful, she neglected her own happiness so as not to squander her talent.

Gabby sought ways to teach herself to love running. She worked hard, stayed focused and challenged herself to find the joy in the sport. Yet, the pull of other interests persisted. She wanted to explore neurobiology, study abroad, work part-time in a lab, socialize. She walked the tightrope between exploration and expectation.

During her freshman year at Harvard, Gabby took a course on the history of health disparities in the US entitled, *Sick and Tired of Being Sick and Tired*. She learned about the Tuskegee Syphilis Study and Henrietta Lacks, examples of medical advancements made at the expense of black bodies. These lessons prompted Gabby to reach in. She began exploring her upbringing, her mother's sacrifices and courage. Still running continued to intrude. She felt stuck, her potential obscured by uncertainty and perhaps a reluctance to embrace it. Resentment and grief set in.

Sophomore year, an Olympic year, saw Gabby achieve sixth place in the 200 m trials. She ruminated in all that running was taking away. The internal tussle between gratitude and resentment proved challenging. So, at a crossroads, she chose to step away. She spent eight weeks in Senegal. She reset. She immersed herself in the country's religion and culture with a cohort of likeminded individuals. She stopped training and started living. Far from home, expectations, judgement, social media and digital connections, Gabby found space. She gave herself permission to be. The reset provided new perspective. Returning to Boston with a refreshed mindset, she let go of the anxiety and embraced clarity.

Junior year evolved into a breakout year. She excelled both in the classroom and on the field, breaking the collegiate record and winning the NCAA championship. Nothing changed in the workouts, the commitment or what it took. However,

Senegal served as a reminder to live life on her terms. She stopped being pigeonholed. Nothing was out of bounds. Though she still listened to the advice, she made her own decisions and took calculated risks, thoroughly enjoying the process. Balancing coursework, a part-time job and training invigorated her. She loved every aspect of the work. Her passion for each element enhanced all the others. The reset proved fundamental.

Surrender as a reset

Accepting who we are and acknowledging that we are works in progress go hand in hand. Our through lines support resilience and wellbeing because they allow us to lead from our core. However, they should also evolve.

You already understand that this work has no final product. This is because every input adds information into the mix. Revising your through line will be essential. It will be a source of power. That is the beauty of a reset: it lets you see change as an opportunity to evolve and grow. It allows you to recalibrate your through line. It builds external self-awareness, an understanding of how others view you.[112] When we see ourselves as others do, we tend to have better relationships. We are constantly seeing, feeling, hearing new things. This information is data. When your reaction to that information feels misaligned with your values, something might feel off. You might feel out of sorts. You might become angry. And often those feelings point directly to the part of yourself that is being challenged. And that is when you most need to reset.

Resetting is prominent in parenthood. We are constantly confronting beliefs about ourselves. The challenge is to rethink why emotions arise. And sometimes they point to baggage we need to leave behind (surrender). I recently gave my daughter her birthday gift. One of my values is gratitude. I have always believed that we are owed nothing. When someone shows us kindness, we must name it, recognize it, and value it. That evening, my daughter opened her present and her first comment was, 'Why did you get me this? I don't need it'. Instead of pausing and taking a breath – I immediately felt the anger rising. 'What do you mean why did I get this for you? It's a present?' And I promptly stormed out of the room.

The next day, we discussed my reaction (and hers). It became clear. When my values were threatened, when my daughter did not behave in a way I expected her to, I felt anger, disappointment, sadness. She experienced the moment completely differently – she was simply asking a question and did not understand the volume of my response. We think the louder we speak the more we will be heard. But often we are not even having the same conversation. In that moment, I was unable to disaggregate feedback as information rather than judgement. And that was a signpost to my values being pushed. Parenting involves a lifelong commitment to learning and growing on a moment-by-moment basis. I swiftly relearned that lesson.

Emotions serve as data; these signposts contain valuable information. Reflecting on them allows you to reset your through line. The through line affords us a line into our character, that mixture of values, behaviours and beliefs. Strong emotions often signpost that something needs resetting.

We don't lead in a vacuum. We don't live on a mountaintop, free from the messiness of daily life. We have multiple through lines that interconnect with others and these can also shift, extend and evolve over time. That is why the reset is so essential. It allows us to embrace the paradox of leadership. 'Each skill makes requisite its opposite.'[113] While we need to build grit, we must also know when to quit. While we experience the wins, we must integrate the losses. While we pursue goals, we must understand when we should surrender. Similarly, after we reach in, we must accept that we also must reset.

The archer's paradox shows that to hit a target you sometimes must aim slightly askew. Our through lines are akin to that. To achieve our most empowered leadership, we sometimes must reset to move closer to the target.

So the question is why?

Change leadership

Think back to a time where you felt like change was all around you. Did you feel like you had to run to adapt? Did you feel like you were never quite meeting deadlines, objectives, aspirations? I know I have. We often move to categorize change within binaries: positive or negative, vital or unnecessary, easy or difficult. Often, it encompasses all the above.

Every year businesses spend millions on change management. Change is the only constant and we pay for it. We want to win. To win we need to change. For decades, businesses tried to adapt technology. Change was slow. Operational hurdles got in the way. Legacy systems and sunk costs made change psychologically hard. And the interdependence of systems made upgrading them unwieldy. Then the pandemic happened and for the first time, digital transformation became necessary.

A typical organization has undertaken five major firmwide changes in the past three years – and nearly 75% expect to multiply the types of major change initiatives they will undertake in the next three. Yet half of change initiatives fail, and only 34% are a clear success.[114]

As we have already observed, our brains hate change because it hurts. Many leadership articles seek to offer tools to manage change. The language we use is telling. Steer through change. Navigate change. Embrace change. Change is felt all around us – up, down and around. What if instead of building strategies to navigate change, we saw change as an opportunity to learn? What if we saw change as an opportunity to sustain, stretch and transform? What if instead of change management, we explored change leadership? What if we used change as the springboard to reset?

To manage change, we are bombarded with advice. Do more, be more, achieve more. Productivity becomes our focus – how to measure it, enhance it, maintain it. Our systems reinforce the belief that unless we measure up, we are not enough. We cultivate a mindset of scarcity. Implicitly or explicitly we reinforce these assumptions in our teams.

Leadership at high speed has a shelf life. 'People are often moving fast and working with the first ideas that come to mind, they end up accepting additive solutions without considering subtraction at all.'[115] Could it be that the traditional leadership model, driven by relentless demands and an 'always on' mentality jeopardizes our abilities? Frantic causes more frantic. Pushing through is not a strategy.

What if, when change hit, we took small steps to substitute feelings of scarcity and fear with feelings of being enough. A through line can help us to do just that. It allows us to fine tune our leadership muscles, to draw on the courage and to choose among imperfect options and unexpected demands. We must recognize that with leadership comes responsibility. It is not enough to just revert to the status quo. We must step away, take stock and build perspective. We must reset.

The people in Bengal live with tigers. How do they live with tigers without killing them? At first, they added. They built fences, went out in groups, crafted scarecrows, installed electric wires. They tried to 'navigate' change. But it didn't work. One villager took a step back. They made a simple yet striking observation. Tigers often attack from behind. The solution: wear a mask on the back of your head. They reset.[116]

Recalibrating our through line resets us. It allows us to spring forward after setbacks. By zooming out, we gain perspective. The through line then shifts and evolves. It is impacted by the internal and external circumstances that collide during moments of change. When we reset, we integrate new information into the rich collage that originally created it. It does not remain static or fixed. Instead, it evolves, grows, shape shifts and adapts. Change is the opportunity.

Change teaches us about what we love and who we are in the face of it. Every time I have faced change it has scared me at first. Perhaps, change scares us because it threatens some part of our identity. We confront irrelevance. We worry that if we fail to navigate change, we may no longer be needed. We may no longer belong. We all have beliefs about our identities. So we will protect those at all costs. It's our defence. So the treadmill continues – we seek perfection in the face of change. We convince ourselves that we must never fail; because if we do, we may not be leaders. The fallacy lies in believing that leaders are perfect. 'Perfectionism is the belief that something is broken – you. So you dress up your brokenness with degrees, achievements, accolades, pieces of paper, none of which can fix what you think you are fixing.'[117]

What if instead we started from our core? Instead of letting externalities dictate our actions, what if we reset expectations by reevaluating our through lines? By asking what leadership means to us. By identifying the features of leadership that make us come back to it day after day.

Most of us don't do the job for the power, recognition, or the money. We recognize that those things are transient, and that the happiness they bring wears off. The hedonic treadmill never fails to disappoint. The hedonic treadmill describes our tendency to return to our steady state after positive or negative events. Comedian Trevor Noah says it beautifully, 'If you're not careful in life, you can see everything as a given once you've experienced it for too long.'[118]

We do the job for deeper reasons. We wish to serve. We value learning. We see problems to solve. We see a need. So we read, practise, modify and continue showing up. We reset. And by doing so, we amplify our impact.

It is a cognitive fallacy to believe that when faced with change, everything will stay the same. Conditions change, circumstances change, we change and leadership changes as a result. Just like the changing world, our through lines change too. They adapt and evolve in the face of these changes. We build the ability to adapt more proactively too. Change does not have to be black and white. It can be nuanced.

We are part of complex ecosystems. We cannot forecast what will happen. But we can get into shape to accept that change will happen. It is not a matter of if, but when. When the change hits, it can be disorienting and even upsetting. But our through lines remind us that we have encountered change before. Not in this exact moment, but in similar moments. Practice tunes our mental muscles to recognize our emotional response. Our minds remember that we can navigate change. In fact, our hearts know we are built for it. We may feel intimidated by its scale, but how we respond matters.

Our through lines hold the psychological strategies that have worked previously. They offer a toolkit to inform the navigation of recent changes. Referring to our through lines provides perspective. By stepping away from the detail and widening the lens, we can gain perspective. And that perspective allows us to recruit an inner strength when we need it most. We know what matters to us. We know what drives us. We know the attributes that will be most valuable to us. So we prepare, connect, collaborate, and we build a path through the change most suited to the circumstances. Our through lines deliver choice when we need it most.

This is the moment where research ends, and personal experience starts. Reading about what works is one strategy. It is one I have often relied on. If I can understand what others do in these moments, I can deploy similar tools myself. It feels safe. The reality is no one-size-fits-all solution exists in those most challenging moments of change. What works for you, what feels right to you, will differ for each of us. But you have the information to proceed. You just need to remember.

I do not want to extrapolate my experience as the rule. There is no footnote for that. But I know one thing. That if you have the courage to use your through line when you feel most afraid, you return to your core. This calms the emotions. This keeps you grounded. And from that place, with whatever added information presents itself, you reset, and you make decisions. When every fibre in your being tells you to steer away from the slide, in that moment, you steer into it. And magic happens.

Free solo

Free soloing vividly illustrates the power of embracing change. It shows how change can lead to collaboration and perspective-taking. In 2017, Alex Honnold ascended the face of El Capitan in Yosemite National Park in three hours and 56 minutes, without ropes. With imagination and thorough practice, he desensitized himself to the most fearful situations, showcasing the crucial role of mental preparation and adaptability in extreme conditions. He reached in and reset using a through line.

Then in 2023, Honnold undertook the ascent of Ingmikortilaq (meaning 'the separate one' in Greenlandic), a remote 3,750-foot cliff rising from a fjord on Greenland's east coast. This granite and gneiss monolith, formed over three million years ago, had never been climbed. The purpose of this climb was unique; it was constructed as a science-based mission focused on climate change. By braving the elements, the team aimed to collect unprecedented information about the impact of melting Greenlandic glaciers on the world.

The expedition highlighted two critical points: change happens, *and* progress remains possible. Honnold partnered with Heidi Sevestre, a scientist working at the Arctic Monitoring and Assessment Program. Alongside 12 research institutes, including NASA, the team gathered crucial data on glaciers and the surrounding ocean. Over six weeks, they traversed a large part of the fjords, installing instruments on the cliffs to measure water salinity and temperature. Each leg of the trip provided valuable data on glaciers and assessed the wider impacts of climate change.

As a non-scientist, Honnold found Greenland's scale, beauty and potential awe-inspiring. He learned about the interdependencies between our countries and Greenland's essential role in our climate. He appreciated how a reset is required, when faced with new information and challenges. He revised his through line to navigate treacherous circumstances. Through it all, he demonstrated how persistence, collaboration and resets can build knowledge for good.

Ease or discomfort

> 'Smooth seas do not make skillful sailors.' African Proverb

In the 1920s, an industrial management professor, Elton Mayo, and his protégé, Fritz Roethlisberger, at Harvard Business School, began a series of large-scale studies on employee productivity. They studied the needs and wants of workers on performance. Not surprisingly, lighting influenced output. But a sense of community and a sense of responsibility to that community – what we now call purpose – had an even greater effect.

Fast forward 100 years, and the work has shifted. The essence of the work that began a century ago remains. But today it is about purpose powering performance rather than the other way around. Businesses are called to put people and planet before, or at least alongside, profit. For decades (stemming in large part from Frederik Taylor's work in the early 1900s) people separated their work and personal identities. Increasingly, this separation is no longer a prerequisite. Empathy plays a critical role. As Microsoft's CEO Satya Nadella famously said, 'Empathy makes you a better innovator'.

Yet an inconvenient truth persists: a subset of the world's most transformational companies find success relying on short-term performance. This brings up a core issue – is this sustainable? Is this what we want?

COVID-19 shook, took and reshaped lives everywhere. As the biggest health crisis in more than a century, with unmatched global reach and duration, tectonic shifts were at play. We faced an unprecedented opportunity. For the first time in a long while, governments, businesses and individuals collaborated to ensure that we stayed safe and resilient. The crisis highlighted the importance of resetting.

We returned to what really matters. We looked at ourselves and each other. We accepted that business models needed to shift to include head, heart and guts. The pandemic spurred a re-thinking of how and what we mean by wellbeing.

Yet, in our search for wellbeing have we prioritized ease over discomfort? And in so doing have we lost our ability to learn? To grow? To debate?

The Finnish trait *sisu* translates to grim determination in the face of hardships. The Finns get comfortable with discomfort. As the Finns endured harsh weather conditions and earned their hard-won freedom from Russia following the devastation of the Second World War, they integrated comfort into discomfort.

Each of us strives as hard as everyone else to be the person we intend to be. Read the news, scroll through social media or simply listen to the political rhetoric and it's easy to become discouraged or to feel hopeless. Our lives, full of digital speed and devotion to productivity or growth may leave us overwhelmed or depleted. We long for quick fixes or one-size-fits-all solutions. We look for heroes who will save us from ourselves. When our heroes falter, we give up, become cynical, despair. We decide that we are doomed.

But what if what makes us heroic is not that we power through, boldly. Instead, it is the unique human ability to simultaneously hold more than one truth to be true. Leadership comes from boldness and vulnerability. We find that by resetting when challenges arise.

Over time, I have made my goals more visible, more public and more audacious, clearly codifying my intent while inviting others to join me. When people join in a quest, they need to see where they can add value and help. If you cannot be vulnerable, people cannot join you. If they cannot join you, they cannot follow you.

As we explored previously, the path to wellbeing is found in embracing intrinsic rewards and motivations. While we often think that extrinsic rewards such as money, status and external validation will lead to fulfilment, research finds that intrinsic rewards are much more powerful. Extrinsic rewards, such as salary increases, bonuses and promotions, are often most visible at work. However, extrinsic rewards can sometimes undermine intrinsic motivation, particularly when these rewards are contingent on performance.[119] While extrinsic rewards might boost short-term performance, they can diminish long-term interest and intrinsic motivation.

Scarcity and fear play a powerful role here. They can severely hinder our professional development. Scarcity captures our mind, reducing our cognitive capacity and decision-making ability.[120] This creates tunnel vision that focuses our minds on immediate deficits. We neglect our long-term goals and growth. Fear, particularly in the workplace, leads to stress and anxiety, impacting our productivity and job satisfaction.[121]

To cultivate intrinsic wellbeing, it is essential to focus on activities and goals that align with our intrinsic motivators. Our through lines expose those intrinsic motivators, enabling us to reset and adapt during choppy times. By prioritizing intrinsic rewards over extrinsic ones, we foster a deeper sense of fulfilment and resilience.

Intrinsic motivators such as personal growth, mastery and a sense of purpose are crucial for sustained fulfilment. Three fundamental psychological needs – autonomy, competence and connection – are powerful motivators.[122] Meeting these needs fosters intrinsic motivation, enhancing wellbeing and performance. When we perceive our work as a calling, an activity deeply connected to our identity and purpose, we tend to report higher levels of job satisfaction and personal fulfilment.[123] This sense of calling acts as an intrinsic motivator, providing a stable through line that guides us through professional and personal challenges. Meeting our intrinsic needs results in higher levels of satisfaction, engagement and overall wellbeing. By understanding and prioritizing these intrinsic factors, we can overcome feelings of scarcity and fear. We can reset and thrive in the face of challenge (and change).

Moreover, intrinsic motivators contribute to resilience. When we pursue goals driven by intrinsic motivators, we are more likely to exhibit resilience in the face of setbacks.[124] Our inner drive to achieve personal growth and mastery helps us persevere, adapt and thrive, even when external circumstances are unfavourable. It helps us reset. The through line's foundation in intrinsic motivators serves as a continuous thread that can guide us through challenges.

The courage to keep revising

> Rather than attempting to reach the final draft of ourselves, we should find the courage to keep revising.[125]

A through line integrates new experiences when you reset, enabling you to lead with stability and purpose amid change, aligning actions with your core values and goals. We are constantly building a past, and each experience matters. The work is never finished, yet there is joy in getting stronger while doing it.

We are complex creatures, filled with intricacies and challenges. Complexity can offer hope, energy and possibility. But to appreciate that complexity – we must reset. Solutions to thorny problems are often not simple or straightforward. They are not merely puzzles to solve. Most complex problems are a result of a multitude of entangled systems, dependent and thorny. When we step back – we may first see chaos. And often we determine that chaos is bad. But what if chaos is the natural order of things? What if chaos is a call to disrupt the status quo? What if it is required for new conditions to emerge?

Dissolution could bring forth new meaning.

> I will not let my blindness build a brick wall around me. I would give my eyes one hundred times again to have the chance to do the things I have done, and the things I can still do.[126]

Brad Snyder, a retired Navy explosives ordnance disposal officer in Iraq and Afghanistan, has won five gold medals and two silver medals in swimming at the Paralympic Games. His journey is a testament to the power of resetting in the face of change.[127]

Snyder grew up eager to continue his family's tradition of service. He graduated from the US Naval Academy in 2006 and deployed to Iraq and Afghanistan. In an unfortunate accident, Snyder stepped on an IED in 2011. Shrapnel shot into his face and caused permanent damage to his eyes.

Despite this loss, Snyder redefined his life – he found the strength to reset. After moving back to Florida, his old swimming coach offered him a chance to return to the sport, a childhood passion. He found solace in swimming's sensory experience rather than the visual cues he previously relished. The water became a sanctuary where he could reconnect with his inner strength and grace, crucial for his emotional healing amid the never-ending physical challenges.

Snyder embarked on an intense training regimen, swiftly adapting to blind swimming techniques. He overcame his instinctive independence and accepted help. This profound shift contrasted with his military background. He recognized the necessity of guidance and support, crucial amid change. Despite initial doubts and fears, Snyder's determination solidified as he trained rigorously to compete at the highest level. His journey fused physical prowess and emotional resilience, navigating challenges with a newfound humility and openness to support.

Qualifying for the Paralympics represented a triumph over adversity, marking a milestone in Snyder's post-injury life. Exactly one year after losing his sight, Brad went on to compete in the 2012 Paralympics in London. The race was not just a physical test but a testament to Snyder's unwavering spirit and to the supportive network that fuelled his journey. Winning a gold medal amplified the celebration. Snyder's focus shifted to acknowledging the countless individuals who contributed to his success. From fellow service members in Afghanistan to family, coaches and friends, Snyder celebrated the profound impact of collective support on his path to the podium.

Brad Snyder's story encapsulates the transformative power of resetting as a path to fulfilment. He inspires me with his perseverance, courage to adapt, and acceptance of the connections that sustain us through life's most challenging chapters. He lives the courage of a reset.

Generative conversations

As we have explored so far, leading through complex and paradoxical problems is no small feat. Often, these require innovative thinking and collective action, rather than the command-and-control leadership style of old. Instead, generative conversations are essential to resetting. Folks with different perspectives, experiences, skills and knowledge come together to explore an issue from different angles and to excavate new ways to move forward. As researchers and leadership experts Marcus Buckingham and Ashley Goodall state, 'We have treated organizations like increasingly complex machines in which the humans are but component parts and in which the solutions to any ills involve tweaking the system from the top — by addressing culture broadly — or by upgrading the individual components, the humans, themselves.'[128] But we have forgotten that the magic is found not in the individuals or the culture alone – rather it is found in the power of their integration, the collective, the team.

Founded in 1856, Stockholm's Enskilda Bank (SEB) was the first private bank and one of the first commercial banks in Sweden. The family-owned business was built on long-term relationships, entrepreneurship and innovation. It evolved from different perspectives.

But in 2018, a changing business environment, growth and increasing complexity meant the culture was shifting. A fear of risk-taking had led to inward focus. This lack of perspective made everyone fearful. Managers were controlling – if their teams made a mistake, it would escalate upwards. Employees worried that if they made a wrong decision, they would be blamed. Meetings were endless, with fundamental mistrust across teams. Everyone came to speak, but never to listen. The decision-making process was slow and arduous. Culture was eroding while collaboration and commitment declined.

Determined to break the cycle, Per Hugander, the bank's Head of Leadership and Organizational Development at the time, decided to launch a skills-based framework to (re)teach perspective. The team wanted to create an environment, 'where it was okay to show who you are and what you think'.[129] They wanted to foster perspective-taking. To create connection through exploration. To reset.

Hugander used jazz to teach an explorative approach. In each introductory session, he played a big band, jazz tune. Here, the musicians focused on delivering their rehearsed contributions until everyone got it right. He contrasted this with Miles Davis' 'So What'. This song was recorded in one take, with no script and no notes. Mistakes were incorporated as part of the process. What emerged was kept. Hugander adopted this 'first take' attitude and applied it to perspective-taking. The lessons were simple: listen more, play less; build on each other; contribute to what is about to emerge. He widened the lens.

Over five years, the results were remarkable. The blame culture dissipated. Meetings were shorter. The decision-making process and its quality improved. Strategic challenges progressed. During the COVID-19 pandemic, instead of calling in debt, SEB negotiated with perspective. The bank did not lose a single dollar in the process. The company's through line had been reset. New information had been incorporated to adapt to change.

A blank sheet of paper

> I like the fact that the blank page is truly a blank page. I like, when I write the next book, that I get to burn it all down and start again.[130]

In 1995, I began my career as a teacher at a girls' school in Manhattan. I was beyond excited that I had managed to unlock this opportunity. The head teacher was supportive, the staff were lovely, and the girls embraced me. I began as an assistant in a Kindergarten classroom. My first mentor, Bettina, was an articulate and dedicated teacher. She would arrive every morning, holding her wheatgrass juice, smiling and ready to take on anything. She believed, before it may have been fashionable to think so, that 'Having a world that is bigger than the world you see is critical.'[131] Through the stories she would share, Bettina offered all students hope.

Every afternoon, we would gather on the story mat and read. I don't know if you've ever been witness to what happens in a Kindergarten classroom, but for me, that was the first time I experienced the power of boundless curiosity and wonder.[132] Those five-year-olds were open; open to learning, open to listening, open to growing, open to trying. Every story Bettina shared, allowed them to glimpse new worlds and learn new perspectives. She would engage them with questions. Ask them to write new endings. Get them to share their perspectives. Each day was a masterclass in what it means to embrace the beginner's mindset. They would explore, innovate, develop and build on each other.

After a year of working as an assistant, I moved on to take over my first classroom. They say leadership is something you (l)earn. I believe it could not be truer in a classroom. You only earn trust in a classroom when you build consensus. You only earn trust when you take risks. You only earn trust if you share your stories and your through line. So to say I worked hard, would be an understatement. It was never for external validation. My world focused on each child. I wanted every single student to feel seen and heard. So I continued with the tradition that Bettina had started. Every afternoon we read.

Harold and the Purple Crayon[133] was one of my favourites. Published in 1955, the story reflected its time. Consumerism was on the rise. We wanted things to be identical. Coca-Cola was first produced in cans and the business had discovered the power of distribution. McDonalds was innovating to give customers the same set of flavours in every location. Disneyland opened its gates to provide automated, assembly-line experiences. Conformity was prized over individuality. Yet, in becoming like everyone else, we were losing a part of ourselves. Harold offered a different way. There are many examples of the influence the book had on the world, but one of my favourite stories is how singer and songwriter Prince fell in love with the colour purple after his mother read him the book ('Purple Rain' was not purple by chance.)[134]

One evening, after thinking it over for some time, Harold picks up his purple crayon and goes for a walk in the moonlight. He draws a forest, an apple tree, and a dragon to guard it. He gets scared so his crayon trembles and he falls into an ocean but rescues himself by drawing a sailboat. He lands on a deserted island, has a picnic and makes new friends. He climbs a mountain to look out over the horizon, slips and falls, but quickly draws a hot air balloon into which he clambers. He lands in the big city, searching for home. But then he remembers, his bedroom window always frames the moon on clear nights. So he looks up at the moon, draws his window, his house, his room, climbs into bed and falls asleep.

Every time I read the story it transported the children to the different worlds they saw pictured on each page. What started with a blank sheet of paper was soon filled with the trials, tribulations and ultimate problem-solving skills of a five-year-old. The thing that always impressed me was how, when seen through the eyes of a child, no problem was too thorny. No adventure too big. No encounter too small. And home was always the place that they rested, safe in the knowledge that this was where the heart was. The place where one could finally lie down and rest and reset. The story resonated with every kid. And I still return to it often.

Your turn

What if you could draw the world you wanted to see? What if you had the power to use your through line to reset expectations? What if you had a blank sheet of paper?

There was a time before we knew that we had to turn the volume down. I'm sure you remember a time when you just were. When you let wonder guide you. As we grow up, we start censoring our actions and our thoughts soon follow.

We get stuck. And often we think we have no energy left to get unstuck. But what if you just did not go deeper? What if you simply stayed where you are? What if you asked for help? What if you simply reminded yourself that this feels hard because it is? The demons trapped behind doors and pacing in the dark only get stronger when you resist. The only way to subdue them is to let them out into the light, name them, accept them and then conquer them. The blank sheet of paper offers you a portal through which to do just that. Wonder is a renewable resource. We should remember to draw on it.

Resetting our lives feels risky. But it is also the way to imagine what the future could look like. Opening ourselves up to possibility is both essential and existential. It requires time and patience. It requires courage. And then it requires consideration for how you will achieve those dreams. Because ambition and dreams without a plan are simply wishes. After all, a plan is what brings dreams to life.

Here's an example. Born in the birthplace of hip hop, Alicia Keys dreamed big dreams. Magic and music transformed her. The empire state of mind reflected who she was.[135] And on 9 October 2016, one of the busiest intersections in the world, Times Square, slowed to a halt for her music.

Do you want to be good, or do you want to be great? That was the question she asked her team moments before she started singing. Surrounded by the towers and people who raised her, Keys went on to deliver a concert that reflected on the issues of the time. No topic was off limits. And Alicia didn't hold back. She poured her heart and her soul into the music. She collaborated, improvised and inspired. Alicia dreamed up the world she wanted to see. And then she made it happen. She closed the concert with John Lennon's 'Imagine', a call to the possibilities that we can dream up, if only we are willing to try.

Here is my challenge. Pull out a blank sheet of paper. In the context of your leadership, draw what you dream. Think about your through line and all it affords you. Then input all the new learnings you may have acquired along your journey. Remember this is not an exercise about how well you draw. This is simply an exercise on what you could do if the world was your canvas; if you could reset and draw what you dream. Hidden within a humble sheet of paper lies a power waiting to be unleashed.

5

A line to care: reach out

Never doubt that a small group of thoughtful, committed citizens can change the world; indeed, it's the only thing that ever has.[136]

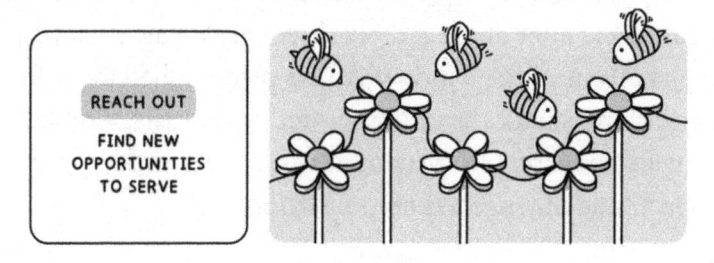

REACH OUT
FIND NEW OPPORTUNITIES TO SERVE

Figure 7: Reach out

In a nutshell

You have reached in and identified your through line. You have learned how to reset that line when new information presents itself. Now, it is time to reach out to serve.

A duty to care

When I started in finance, I kept hearing the words, 'We have a duty *of* care'. I always wondered why we didn't say, 'We have a duty *to* care'. The nuance is small but important. As leaders, sweating the small stuff matters. We must collaborate. We must listen. We must improvise. Because leadership cannot be transactional. It must be relational. It must be respectful. The word respect comes from the Latin meaning to see again (re-spect). It is not I think therefore I am. It is I am seen therefore I am.

Two summers ago, my family and I travelled through Japan. It was a memorable trip in so many ways. As we boarded our flight home after an incredible three-week stay, I happened to glance out of the window. As the plane pulled away from the parking stand, the entire ground staff was assembled at the gate, bowing and waving at us. It was a deep sign of respect, one that needed no translation.

We can offer everyone respect if we care. The dignity of each person we encounter means everything to them. And reaching out is one of the easiest ways both to demonstrate respect and build relationships. Relationships, like our through lines, afford us stability in the face of chronic uncertainty. Why? Because relationships remind us that we cannot do this alone. That we must step up to reach out when needed and step back to reach in and reset. Solid in our core. Committed to doing well together.

In my line of work, every problem I have ever solved has followed a standard path. It starts with frustration over a problem which leads me to ask: Why hasn't anyone done anything about this? It follows with if you don't, who will? I then gather those I think could take part in building a solution, in owning their parts and in contributing to the whole. We deconstruct the problem and inevitably its thorny layers. We dig and dig and dig to get to the bottom of the proverbial bin. We usually take copious notes. We follow up. We escalate when we need to. Every single time, this tends to get us closer to a solution if not to the solution itself. I connect those who can help. I aim to reorient and facilitate throughout. To me that is the joy in leadership – gathering the right folks and iterating to find the best possible solutions given the information we have available. Put another way, leadership requires care.

Yet care feels sorely lacking in the workplace. In this hyperconnected era, where social media platforms boast billions of users and technology bridges the gaps between continents, we find ourselves paradoxically disconnected. We are inundated with likes, clicks and notifications, yet genuine connection eludes us. While the digital age enables effortless communication, it also unwittingly fills our space. Constant notifications clutter our attention. Online interactions prioritize quantity over quality. Virtual communication decreases face-to-face interactions. Curated platforms exacerbate comparison. We have mastered the art of appearing connected while silently battling the profound disconnection within. The very tools designed to bring us closer have, in many ways, driven us further apart.

BetterUp's Insights Report found that more than 40% of UK employees felt disconnected from coworkers. Almost a quarter do not have even a single friend at work. Many connect less frequently, have smaller networks, and spend less time and effort on relationship building.[137] The consequences of this disconnection are profound. Disconnection costs UK companies an estimated £340 billion a year[138] in measurable things such as absenteeism and employee turnover. Loneliness and mental health struggles are on the rise. Our ability to empathize and understand one another is declining. We yearn for genuine connections, for a sense of belonging, yet find ourselves adrift in an ocean of superficial interactions.

Technology has not contributed to this state alone. The breakneck pace and relentless demands of our lives leave us feeling like cogs in a vast machine. We are so caught up in the pursuit of success, wealth and goals that we inadvertently sacrifice what matters most: meaningful connections. We are built to connect. Since our earliest days, connection helped keep us safe, fed and able to handle life's challenges. It enabled cultural transmission and evolution. It powered our thinking, creativity, collaboration and innovation.

Connection has two parts: the size of our networks and the feelings we experience within them. It is both an art and a science. Connection engenders belonging and nurtures purpose. And it arises from a solution that is available to us all. A beautifully simple solution that can allow us to see differently. We must reach out. That is when collective brilliance is unlocked, showcasing how the whole is greater than the sum of the parts. That is when care comes into its own. Reaching out makes us feel fulfilled. And it often pays dividends. When you least expect it.

In the mid-1800s, the Choctaw people of the USA gathered $140 to send to the Irish people who were suffering and dying during the great famine. The Choctaw sent the money with a note that said, 'We know what it is to be starving, to have no land and to not be able to return to your land. We hear of your hunger and death; it is our wish that this money will help to ease some of your suffering'. Fast forward to the last couple of years during the height of COVID. The Choctaw people received funds from Ireland for $1.7 million with a note that said: 'We Have Not Forgotten! We read of the death of Indigenous Elders, the lack of health care, clean water, and nutritional food. We give you this money with the hope that it will provide some support to you and ease your suffering.'[139]

Company means connection

The word company comes from the Latin word *companis*. *Com* meaning with and *panis* meaning bread. Roman merchants would gather, break bread, and connect. The art of connecting is integrated into the meaning of the companies we work for. Shouldn't we consider it essential to what we do and how we do it?

Technological advancements have optimized the friction out of our lives. In so doing, have we optimized ourselves out of building connection too? Have we stopped gathering? In *The Art of Gathering*, Priya Parker offers constructive ways to gather with intention. Workplaces are no different. As leaders, we must make time to gather with intention, asking ourselves what, how, when and why we gather. 'The data show that rebuilding social capital and culture isn't just nice to have – it's a business imperative.'[140] The pandemic gave us a once in a lifetime opportunity to transform how we work.

By creating new rituals of connection, we create a more human workplace, no matter where we are located.

So what does all of that have to do with reaching out? Well, at its core, when you reach out, you connect. When you connect, you feel seen, you feel heard. You matter.[141] You find meaning.

Every Sunday morning, my father gets on a call with some of his oldest friends. There are sometimes four of them, at others more, but the call is something he rarely misses. They have known each other for several decades, witnessed highs and lows in each other's lives. And boy do they have stories to tell. They dial in from around the world, the US, Australia, India and the UK. They come together without fail. I have noticed how much he looks forward to that hour every week. It fills him up.

The power of connection is that it energizes us. Conversely, when we are disconnected, we experience loneliness. The US Surgeon General recently declared a new public health epidemic in America: loneliness. Even before the COVID-19 pandemic, some estimates suggest that over half of US adults reported experiencing measurable levels of loneliness. According to the National Institute on Ageing, prolonged social isolation equates to smoking 15 cigarettes a day. Some studies have even estimated that loneliness could shorten a person's life span by as many as 15 years.[142]

The antidote to loneliness is connection. Connection is a fundamental human need. It empowers us, motivates us, and allows us to flourish. If as leaders we care about those in our charge, we must connect with them. Then our teams feel valued and visible in the workplace. We cultivate connection.

Think about this for a moment. Who do you call when thing go well? Who do you call when things go wrong? The answers to both those questions matter. Because they inform what connection means to you. Cultivating that connection matters in life. It matters at work. Those connections will help you see what you cannot. They help you learn what you do not know.

Following the pandemic, the Great Resignation, an idea proposed by Professor Anthony Klotz, predicted that a large number of folks would resign as they were no longer willing to tolerate jobs that left them feeling stressed and fatigued. A notable power shift occurred. Workers demanded more from their leaders, and leadership teams fought to adapt their internal value propositions to retain talent. As we have seen repeatedly, leadership does not exist in a vacuum. Everyone's wellbeing matters. But this is not all. A gap exists between leaders' perceptions and their teams' feelings.

Accounting firm Deloitte partnered with independent research firm Workplace Intelligence to survey 2,100 employees and leaders across four countries.[143] The research pointed to an interesting theme: every one of us, whether we lead teams or not, is a human first. Leaders acknowledged their struggles with wellbeing. However, they seemed unaware of the extent to which their employees were struggling. Fewer than two out of three employees rated their health as good or excellent. Leaders, on the other hand, consistently overestimated the wellbeing of their teams across various measures (physical, mental, social and financial). This care gap matters. We must close it.

Our through lines can bridge this gap. Because when we return to our core, we understand that we are subject to the same emotions that drive us all. That certain things motivate us while others don't. That we are multi-faceted human beings and that our lives comprise both ups and downs. Once we understand that we are just one of many, we can then reach out to those around us (in this case our teams) to better understand their circumstances. We can reach out with authenticity.

Businesses appear so focused on delivering wellbeing to their employees that we sometimes forget that wellbeing takes work by employees too. But to appreciate that nuance, we must empathize with each other, whether we are leaders or not. Then we do not rescue,[144] we simply witness. We care.

What happens if we don't? We fit right into the stereotypes that abound about leadership – that we don't care; that we exist only to increase the bottom line; that we do so at the expense of our people; that we treat people like capital; and the list goes on. Scroll through your LinkedIn feed and you will be spoiled for choice when it comes to individualistic, angry and cynical posts about why leaders are in it to win it.

An outside job

Self-awareness has two parts: internal and external. We explored the importance of internal self-awareness as we started reaching in. External self-awareness completes the picture. As a leader you must work on both types of self-awareness to be fully tooled up. Understanding how others view us allows us to exhibit genuine care. And as Professor

Tasha Eurich and her team of researchers demonstrated after scouring over 50 years' of research on self-awareness: 'For leaders who see themselves as their employees do, their employees tend to have a better relationship with them, feel more satisfied with them and see them as more effective in general.'[145]

The double-edged sword of experience and power means that as we move through our careers, we may be at risk of building a false sense of certainty about our performance, our skills and our attributes. This can often be down to less time or even less information. However, external self-awareness counteracts that. Being willing to listen to frequent critical feedback from those around you is the key.

I have boundless enthusiasm. I love the upside. I believe that the glass is half full. As I have wandered through a variety of leadership paradoxes, many have told me to temper my enthusiasm. They have guided me to understand that emotional consistency is critical. That my emotions must be understood and managed before I can lead with impact. I have been listening.

I used to believe that critical feedback, from those I did not align with, did not matter. But I have changed my perspective. I believe that even if we don't agree with everything, there are truths lying in wait. Those themes warrant care.

My struggle has been that when I heard the words, 'you're too emotional', I heard, 'change yourself'. When I attempted to do that (which was completely inauthentic) it never lasted for long. Instead, the feedback highlighted a need for emotional agility. A need to understand my emotions, assess why they arose, and then do something about them. My through line helped me understand those moments. Now, in moments when I hear words which bring forth anger, sadness, resentment or even joy, my through line reminds me to embrace the paradox. I pause. I figure there are only two options – continue carrying the emotions or set them down. The choice is mine. And only when I have given myself some time, do I respond. That is what care looks like. The ability to use the information to create space for everyone to respond in their own time and in their own way.

I have understood that caring does not come in one size. It does not mean being nice, soft or permissive. We can be both caring and demanding. We can be both empathetic and exacting. Care can show up in diverse ways, for different people. And so emotional agility continues to be a skill I am striving to develop. I am just as enthusiastic as ever, but I temper my enthusiasm until I am sure that it is worth sharing.

As leaders, we must cultivate external self-awareness to embrace care. The impact on our external world is significant when we do. Whether we realize it or not, those in our care notice it too. We don't care in order to receive rewards, appreciation or even recognition. We care because we can. It is free to access and free to give. Yet it has immeasurable impact.

Deep care

> People don't care how much you know – until they know how much you care.[146]

In the 1950s, the Asch Conformity Experiment[147] studied how individuals yielded to or defied a majority group. The experiments found that people were willing to ignore facts to adopt the norms, beliefs and behaviours of fellow group members (or what is sometimes described as the in-group). Yet, our businesses are stronger when we challenge and explore. We have seen how adapting to change and uncertainty requires us to stay open, to ideate and to innovate. So how do we encourage diversity of thought? We must care.

Richard Branson says it beautifully, 'Employees come first. If you take care of your employees, they will take care of your clients.'[148] In the highest performing companies, it is a norm that colleagues must support one another's efforts to do the best work that they can. It is true in my business. I believe that leaders can do few things more important than encouraging a culture of care within their business. Let me be clear. I don't mean performative care like duvet days or organizing happy hours. I mean the deep care associated with connecting, coaching and guiding.

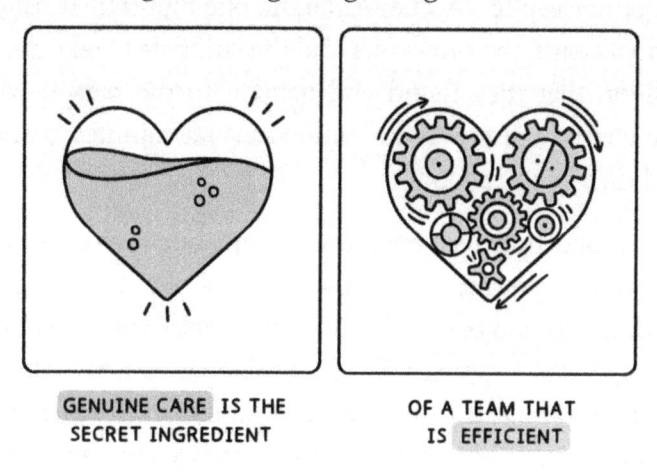

GENUINE CARE IS THE SECRET INGREDIENT

OF A TEAM THAT IS EFFICIENT

Figure 8: Deep care

This is true for several reasons. Caring allows efficiency to take on a whole new meaning. We know that we don't assign tasks optimally, that projects always take unexpected turns and that various parts of different projects go at different speeds. When we want people to work in tandem with us, they will not care how much we know until they know that we genuinely care about them. Then everyone embraces the goals. Everyone becomes an active contributor. Everyone engages.

Care will not occur organically without some element of nurturing. Individuals may be driven to compete, may feel uncomfortable asking for help or feel distrustful of those offering it. And incentive structures may inadvertently discourage care. A great example of care circulated on social media a few years ago.[149]

They brought balloons to a school. One was given to every student, who had to inflate it, sign their name on it and throw it in the hallway. The professors then mixed all the balloons. The students were given five minutes to find their own balloon. Despite a hectic search, no one found their balloon. At that point, the professors told the students to take the first balloon that they found and hand it to the person whose name was written on it. Within several minutes everyone had their own balloon.

Care is like those balloons. You can care, but finding care takes everyone. Care encourages the diversity of thought required to find solutions to thorny problems. This encourages courage. This creates safe spaces that prize nonconformity. To fight our need to belong. This discomfort can engender creativity. We need all types of perspectives to participate in the creation of solutions. Rather than working to win, working with care encourages collaboration, a dynamic interaction with differences of opinion, across multiple points and multiple networks. Small shifts can lead to larger paradigm shifts. Indigenous scholar Tyson Yunkaporta studies complex systems and noted, 'Solutions to complex problems take many dissimilar minds and points of view to design, so we have to do this together, linking up with as many other us-toos as we can to form networks of dynamic interaction.'[150] And surely that is at the heart of empowered leadership?

As I thought about why care matters, I considered four interdependent components of caring that facilitate common ground, safety and trust. I call it the CARE cycle (see Figure 9).

1. **Connection**: a biological need that is increasingly scarce in today's online world.
2. **Attention**: a highly prized commodity required to build adaptable systems.
3. **Refraction**: the power to use language to impact the speed and direction of problem-solving and to build trust.
4. **Expansion**: the network effect to build collective impact.

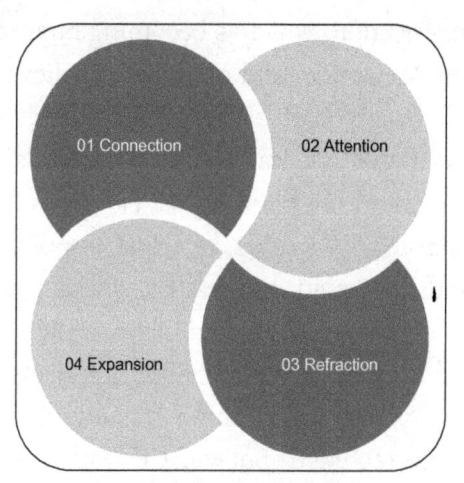

Figure 9: The CARE cycle

As we saw with the example of Stockholm's Enskilda Bank, jazz offers a beautiful portal into care. Jazz ensembles rely on each other to lead, collaborate and improvise. Underpinning it all is a care that honours each contribution. Musicians naturally connect, pay attention, refract and expand each other. This care could be shorthand for a love. A love of the craft. A love of the path. A love of mastery. As James Baldwin said, 'Love takes off the masks we fear we cannot live without and know we cannot live within.'[151]

As leaders, we don't need to know more than anyone else, but we must care. Showing care is not an admission of weakness. Modelling care is a source of strength. Let's look at the CARE cycle in more detail.

1. **Connection:** Gianpiero Petriglieri, Associate Professor of Organizational Behaviour at INSEAD stated, 'As a leader, you are always relating to a tradition that you are trying to preserve, expand, or change.'[152] When we take on leadership roles, we become responsible for goals, people and decisions, which can sometimes feel isolating. This isolation contrasts with our basic need for connection, which is becoming rarer in our digital world. What if we did not have to believe that leaders must always lead alone? Shared leadership allows others to take the lead too, fostering collaboration. Liz Wiseman, in her book *Impact Players*, talks about this beautifully. 'As leaders, our first response is to jump in and fill a void, but leaders who act as multipliers know to hold back and allow others the chance to fill it first.'[153] Think about projects where one person controls everything – many of us have done this, me included. But what if leaders aimed to step

back and create space for others to lead? This is true collaboration. John Patitucci, a renowned American bass player, describes leadership as using pauses to let others shine.[154] Silence then becomes a canvas for collaboration and creativity. The best teams are the ones that unearth the best thinking from everyone. Connection is the glue that holds teams together.

2. **Attention**: High performance requires attention. Great leaders know that this requires being willing to listen and hear others. To create adaptable businesses, we must pay attention to what others are saying (or not saying). In a jazz ensemble, players must listen to all those playing with them, at once. The skill of active listening is an art form and a discipline. When Taylor Swift goes on stage, she has a metronome in her ear, ensuring she keeps in time with the music. Think of the metronome as the leader's reminder to listen. The leader's job is to ensure that the best ideas are generated, the richest information is being exchanged and the most interpersonally risky moves are being taken – safely. Without that metronome on stage, things get off beat and off pitch quickly. We revert to whomever sings first, loudest and most. We must not mistake confidence for competence.

3. **Refraction**: In science, refraction occurs when the direction or speed of light or sound is changed through interference. In leadership, refraction occurs when leaders use language to change the direction or speed of a conversation. The rigour of how we use our words is something that we have the means to claim. Our language has the power to lift. It has the power to

unify. But it also has the power to malign, to separate and divide. It is likely that this has always been true. Linguists demonstrate the power of language to shape our thoughts – for better or worse. The world is mostly undefined. 'Walking through an empty office. Moving out of a childhood home. Struggling to write something original. Experiences like these often lack the perfect word. John Koenig spent more than a decade writing his own dictionary.'[155] Austrian linguist and philosopher Ludwig Wittgenstein famously said that '[t]he limits of my language represent the limits of my world'.[156] Every single word is invented. So inventing your own is not a limitation – rather it is a path to unlocking new possibilities. To push through into the unknown with panache. 'We allow our words to define us, but I think the natural order of things is that we define words. We imbue them with meaning. We pour ourselves into them. That is how it should be. We are the ones that mean something. All words are made up.'[157] As leaders, it is our duty to shape our language. Just as conductors have batons, artists have brushes or surgeons have scalpels, we have language. Refraction requires humility. The humility to give others the opportunity to contribute. To build on others' ideas. To let others shine. This, of course, can lead to conflict when there are differing visions of what is to be created. In jazz, these conflicts are resolved in real time, using the guiding principle 'serve the music'. What if in leadership the guiding principle could be 'serve the through line'? Then we might refrain from advancing our personal agenda to create something improved.

4. **Expansion**: In jazz, improvisation means a song will never be played the same way twice. Contrast that with well-intended but sometimes counterproductive leadership practices that try to ensure conformity (we want to do the same thing, in the same way, every time). There is wisdom in balance. While jazz artists understand structure and form, they also innovate within them. The same should be true for all of us. Fear of the unknown, fear of failing, fear of looking foolish may drive us to stay safe. But as Miles Davis once said, 'Do not fear mistakes. There are none'.[158] In jazz, a note is neither right nor wrong. It is the note that follows that will make the difference. For leaders, this should reinforce the power of creating a culture that encourages both experimentation and continuous learning. Then our actions can expand and make the difference.

The empty chair

Right now, in conference rooms around the world, leaders are having countless conversations about how to improve employee engagement. I know I did. It was a unique metric of how everyone was feeling, and I was determined to make sure every single member of the team felt enriched by their work. But engagement and commitment are very different things. And commitment requires care.

You may know about the concept of the empty chair. Employed in counselling settings as a form of Gestalt Therapy, the idea of putting yourself in someone else's shoes is fundamental to the practice. This empty chair technique, first used at Sears, has since been adopted by many, including Amazon. When Amazon holds important meetings, people at the company keep one chair empty.

> It's there to remind those assembled who's really the most important person in the room: the customer. Seeing it, encourages meeting attendees to take the perspective of that invisible but essential person. What is going through her mind? What are her desires and concerns? What would she think of the ideas we are putting forward?[159]

The empty chairs serve to remind leaders of the non-obvious stakeholders. Whether that is clients, environmental impact, or purpose. Those chairs are essential as they force us to take on different perspectives and encourage us to step out of the status quo.

The ability to motivate and inspire your teams depends on understanding your teammates' perspectives, getting inside their heads, and seeing the world through their eyes. That empty chair serves as a reminder of the importance of another's perspective. Care is built, one chair at a time.

Leading with care fosters an environment where individuals can develop self-determination by meeting fundamental psychological needs and by creating a supportive workplace culture. First, we need autonomy, competency and connection. When leaders demonstrate care, they help fulfil those needs. This in turn promotes intrinsic motivation. This autonomy-supportive leadership mindset closes the care gap because leaders understand employees' perspectives, offer meaningful choices and encourage self-initiation. Employees feel supported and able to thrive. Leaders feel supported with a workforce that supports the company's objectives. It is a win-win.

The Deloitte University Leadership Centre for Inclusion report, 'Uncovering Talent', reveals that 61% of all employees 'cover' their identities in some way – not necessarily hiding something, but downplaying it for fear of drawing unwanted attention or making others uncomfortable.[160] High performing companies recognize that diverse perspectives can strengthen their performance, and that homogeneity can cause blind spots. (I love the example of the right-handed YouTube engineers who realized 10% of videos were being uploaded upside down because they had not considered how left-handed users would manoeuvre their phones.) But to unlock the benefits of diversity, we must make it safe for everyone in our teams to uncover their identities.

Caring leadership also contributes to a sense of psychological safety[161] allowing everyone to uncover those identities. Amy C. Edmonson PhD, professor of leadership and management at Harvard Business School, has done extensive work on the value of psychological safety. When each member of a team feels safe enough to take risks, express their thoughts and make decisions without fear of negative consequences, we see innovation, performance and wellbeing thriving. We create an environment where dissent is valued. Employees take initiative and develop a sense of ownership over their work. Google is famous for prizing a culture of psychological safety, allowing employees to spend 20% of their time on projects of their choice.

Through care, we empower our team members by trusting them with responsibilities and providing them with opportunities for growth. Empowerment involves delegating authority, sharing information and providing resources which helps everyone feel capable. Fundamentally, research illustrates that caring leadership leads to higher job satisfaction, increased engagement and better performance.[162]

Caring innovation

Founded in 1916 by brothers John and Walter Wegman, Wegmans Food Markets are a family-owned, regional supermarket chain in the US. Unlike many brands, when this one arrives in neighbourhoods, it is greeted with enthusiasm and even joy. Why is that?

Walter E. Wegman founded his grocery empire from a pushcart. With his brother John, the two would peddle fresh produce to Rochester homemakers in 1915. Their parents were in the grocery business and provided the produce. A year later, the brothers opened their first food market – the Rochester Fruit & Vegetable Company. Throughout the booming 1920s, the brothers scaled up their business to include retail groceries and baked goods. During the Great Depression, Wegman's essential service and innovations ensured their continued success. Before it was fashionable to do so, they took the essential step in the 1930s of opening a 20,000-foot retail store that included a cafeteria that was large enough to seat 200 people. They introduced refrigerated display windows, vaporized water sprays on produce to keep things fresh, frozen foods, circular checkout counters and sophisticated in-house processing and production systems.

In 1953, Wegmans introduced progressive employee benefits to its 350+ full-time staff. In the 1970s they began donating to food banks and became the first supermarket chain in New York to offer 24-hour services in some of the stores. In 1984, they began handing out lucrative scholarships to workers. They provided academic assistance and part-time gigs to 14- and 15-year-old city school kids who needed an extra push to finish high school.

The company has become a beloved part of many families, known for their commitment to quality, service and community. Wegmans consistently appears on Fortune's 100 Best Companies to Work For list. They are widely recognized for their strong commitment to creating a positive work culture through training and development, scholarships and educational support and active involvement in the communities in which they operate.

Today the stores offer nutrition and cooking classes, recycling programmes, frequent shopper discounts and natural food health centres. They sell seafood, and they even have an organic farm and a cheese cave with its own room for Brie. They maintain their hometown culture and have stayed out of the limelight. With a through line that seems to emerge organically – everyone must eat – they exemplify a culture of care both within their corporate structure and beyond.

Wegmans feels like a fitting example of CARE. They are connected to their people and their community. They pay attention to the needs of their staff and customers. They refract the joy of others in the language they use and the way they serve. And they expand their network, their reach and their service model as things change. Do they always get everything right? No. But they remain grounded in their through line to reach in, reset and reach out.

Design thinking

What makes your workplace tick?

Design thinking[163] is a methodology that adopts the user-centric approach. It focuses on understanding 'the needs of the person you're designing for such that you can create something that's valuable to them'.[164] This applies equally when considering employee commitment. Perspective-taking is at the heart of the conversation. How can we make sense of what is going on? Do we examine it from multiple perspectives? Can we reach out of our experience and consider the emotions, values and beliefs of our users?

Global design and innovation consultancy, IDEO, is renowned for its human-centred approach to design and its unique workplace culture that emphasizes care and collaboration. Its core philosophy is centred around the idea that design should prioritize and understand the needs, behaviours and experiences of people. This approach extends into the business where empathy and care are paramount. IDEO fosters a highly collaborative environment where multidisciplinary teams work together to solve complex problems. This collaboration is rooted in mutual respect, open communication and a genuine interest in other people's perspectives. Team members are encouraged to share ideas freely and build on each other's contributions. Employees are encouraged to take ownership of their projects and make decisions. This empowerment is further supported by a culture which values creativity, experimentation and learning from failure. Employees feel trusted and respected, which enhances their sense of responsibility and commitment. Fundamentally, psychological safety underpins everything that they do. Innovation is fostered and all voices are heard.

The firm is high performing. It has received accolades for innovations in business, government, healthcare and is regularly invited to advise others on how to increase innovation. And it has done so while prioritizing people. It is a beautiful example of the through line – understanding what makes you tick so you can empower others to do the same. IDEO reaches out with ease.

While IDEO is in the field of innovation or design, they have much in common with each one of our companies. Why? Because, just like all of us, they tackle complex problems. They seek to provide an attractive work environment. They want to draw the best talent into their firm, and they want to retain those employees.

IDEO solves thorny problems with care. They connect. They pay attention. They refract by shaping ideas through collaboration. And they constantly expand their reach. How do they do it? Cultural norms are crystallized into the way they work. These norms drive how they reach out. They shape comprehension, behaviours and value. They expand a unique way of being and leading. The ground rules are clear.

1. Care is modelled at all levels of the organization. Interactions are encouraged across job function – consistently. Status is no barrier for being asked to care.

2. Care is two-sided, without a need for pay back, only to pay it forward.

3. Those asking for help (as a proxy for care) choose who they approach for it. Those approached are often those who are trusted, accessible and competent.[165]

4. By building flexibility into schedules, they can engage in unplanned ways. Slack exists to facilitate care.

5. Care is a metric – during interviews and promotions – and is modelled by all. Intrinsic incentives reinforce it. In IDEO's employee surveys, caring correlates with job satisfaction.

The pillars of CARE are exemplified in the business. First, they connect. They believe that regardless of role, each member of the team plays a vital role in ensuring the business creates impact: 'We are creative people at IDEO. All of us. Some practice design, some do not. Whether you work in operations, finance, marketing, design, or IT, you have a vital role to play in keeping us great and helping achieve our purpose of creating impact.'[166]

Notice the lack of comparison within the statement. They could have said greater or best and they chose not to. They collaborate. They even restate it; in case we missed it the first time. 'The most powerful asset we have in our arsenal is the word "we".'[167]

Next, attention is placed on the most fundamental values. Every member of staff receives 'The Little Book of IDEO' which codifies the seven principles they believe in. This normalizes expectations and makes care central to the work they do.[168]

Third, the clarity of expectations encourages a refraction of ideas. This creates space for innovation to happen. They embrace ambiguity and get comfortable with discomfort. They learn from failures consistently. Everyone takes ownership as they prize collective responsibility.

And finally, they expand their reach by remembering to 'talk less, do more'. As they explain: 'Nothing is a bigger buzzkill than over-intellectualizing. Design is about rolling up your sleeves and making things.' They get to it. They make others successful by going out of their way to help others succeed. IDEO make their secret sauce, free to share and free to understand. They understand that care drives impact.

Complicate the narrative: not every caring encounter is a resounding success

I have been part of interactions where care sometimes misses the mark. In other words, not every encounter with care will work. Timing matters. Receptivity matters. But perhaps most of all, trust matters. Providing care at a time, place or on a subject when time, receptivity or trust are not present will sometimes exacerbate the problems.

Let us think of an example. You are working, head down. Your to-do list is overflowing and you have several upcoming deadlines to meet. A colleague walks past your desk and offers to help. You silently weigh up the options. You could stop what you are doing, explain your priorities, and spend some time bringing your colleague up to speed. This will mean that you spend at least an hour stepping outside of the work you must complete. You weigh up your options and decide to turn them down gently.

I often hear about this type of conundrum. Frequently, it comes with the statement, 'I would just be faster doing it myself'. I totally get it. I have been there. But we might want to ask ourselves whether this is a long-term solution or a short-term problem. Because over the long term we want to encourage our teams to be able to both receive and offer care. And in so doing, not only do we build more resilient teams, but we also build expertise across our teams. Importantly, our company cultures then combine care with individual responsibility and productivity. These are not mutually exclusive at all. But sometimes, when viewed simplistically, they can be seen as such.

Leadership is reaching out

Nicholas Epley is the John Templeton Keller Distinguished Service Professor of Behavioral Science and Neubauer Family Faculty Fellow at the University of Chicago's Booth School of Business. He studies social cognition – how thinking people think about other people. He aims to understand why smart people routinely misunderstand each other. He studies the power of reaching out. In fact, he has evaluated how reaching out can make us feel better. Our perception of what others think drives an unwillingness to reach out. We may wonder: What if I say the wrong thing? What if I don't say enough? What if they think I'm strange? We systematically underestimate how much our outreach means to others.

We've talked a great deal about agency and choice in the last few chapters. We have choices to make when we consider the power of reaching out. Do we speak to others? Do we compliment others? Do we open ourselves up to difficult or meaningful conversations? Social choices will involve a tension between connection and worry, approach and avoidance. And generally, our inner compass will tend to tilt us towards avoidance more frequently than it should.

So what should we do? We must practice. Once you start, you will notice things you hadn't noticed before. You will start seeing things. This is essential in leadership. I remember a former CEO of mine who every time they walked down the hall would intentionally look down at the floor so that folks didn't engage with them. The result. No connections. Limited trust. On the other hand, in my current business, senior team members make a point of walking the floor. Speaking to everyone. Engaging folks in questions. Noticing the small stuff. The result. High levels of trust.

When you take an interest in others, they share things with you that you wouldn't otherwise learn. I believe this is foundational for leadership. If you know your team, if you understand their motivations, you can better coach, guide and mentor them. You can better harness collective capabilities with more information and insight. This is leadership amplified. This is caring personified.

Nick tells a wonderful story of a time he went to speak at a hedge fund conference. The room was full of folks who, as Nick described, wore suits that he would never be able to afford. They were stiff. Reserved. And not connecting. So on the spur of the moment, he decided to shake things up. He put three questions up onto the screen: If I was going to be friends with you what is the one thing that you want me to know about you? If a crystal ball dropped down from the heavens above what is the one thing you would want to know? Tell me about the last time you cried in front of another person.[169]

The room visibly cringed. Nick wasn't sure how it was going to go. He stayed with the feelings of discomfort and broke the group into teams of two. And then he left them to it. After a few moments, the room roared to life. Conversations started happening. It became loud, almost raucous. The move from dread to delight was palpable. Folks started laughing. They started crying. They ended up hugging. Connections were built in the moment. The day progressed differently from that point on.

Your turn

If you want to build a culture of care within your team, unit or business, there are some critical ways in which you can do this. Remember the CARE cycle and use it to build up a set of behaviours that encourage others to do the same. Then reach out and make these explicit.

If you want your team to keep improving on what they do, the ways they serve and the ways they execute, then you need them to care. They should be encouraged not only to balance one another's workloads but also to build the trust to examine, challenge, build and refine one another's ideas. You can do this by illustrating how caring produces better outcomes than competition on its own. We call it restlessness in my team. The restlessness to keep caring – to seek to examine, challenge, build and refine each other's ideas. And to remember that this is always in service of each other, our clients and our business. It is never personal, but it always matters.

Next, try to ensure that expectations are clear. As we learned, at IDEO they offer every employee a little book which spells out their most cherished values. In our business we offer every employee our purpose on a page. Chief among this is our dream – to be the place that goes above and beyond; to put heart and understanding into financial investing. New joiners understand the importance of those norms. We believe that care is a productive activity. We are armed to celebrate the moments when we see caring's positive impact.

We work hard to foster elevated levels of trust. We discourage political battles and encourage everyone to admit to and learn from mistakes. We eradicate blame and create interdisciplinary opportunities for connection both formally and informally. We use meetings and training sessions to teach each other how to seek, find, give and receive help effectively.

We try to avoid 'too many cooks' by finding the right cooks for the right jobs in every circumstance. We tend to come together in interdisciplinary groups to solve thorny problems, dissolving those groups when the work is done. We try not to overload people and remember that slack is essential.

Here are four examples of specific tools you can use at any time within the framework of the CARE cycle.

1. **Question to connect**: To build connection, model it, create space for it, and build opportunities for everyone to do it. Ask questions. Learn about each other. Edgar Schein, business theorist, psychologist and foundational researcher in organization behaviour said: 'Questions are taken for granted rather than given

a starring role in the human drama. Yet all my teaching and consulting experience has taught me that what builds a relationship, what solves problems, what moves things forward is asking the right questions.'[170] In my company, we offer every staff member the opportunities to gather to connect. Whether that's eating their lunch in a communal area when they're in the office, organizing social events that are combined with learning a new skill (e.g. cooking, dancing, cocktail making) or something as small as asking people to turn on their videos on virtual calls, each interaction is valued. We are explicit with our expectations. None of this is the sole remit of leadership. Anyone can do it. But if you don't model it, no one can see it.

2. **Brainwrite to pay attention**: To build attention, you might try brainwriting instead of brainstorming. Research shows that brainstorming can sometimes subdue the quieter voices in a room. As the humourist Dave Barry quipped, 'If you had to identify, in one word, the reason why the human race has not achieved, and never will achieve, its full potential, that word would be: "meetings".'[171] So instead, encourage brainwriting. Carnegie Mellon Professor of Organizational Behaviour, Anita Woolley, and her colleagues explain that collective intelligence is unlocked when you have balanced participation.[172] Brainwriting is one way to unlock this. Ask everyone to generate ideas individually. Then the team can gather to select the promising ideas. The facilitator's job is to coordinate, communicate and encourage debate on the various ideas. This not only opens the

floor to everyone but ensures all voices count. There may be no more immediately effective expression of care than giving someone your full attention. Being genuinely interested in what that person has to say or how they are feeling is possible once all ideas are collected.

3. **Loop to refract**: To refract ideas, you might use a technique such as looping to ensure that you are both opening the floor and understanding the messages being communicated. That you are unearthing both what is being said and what remains unsaid. I first learned about this technique from Amanda Ripley and Hélène Biandudi Hofer, introduced earlier. The idea is that when someone is speaking, you stop considering how you want to respond. Instead, you simply listen. You aim to summarize what you are hearing (and not hearing). You give the other person a chance to respond, clarify, amend their comments. And you keep going until you are sure the person feels heard (often the words, 'That's exactly what I mean' will be your signal that you have got it all). Then (and only then) do you invite other comments or engagement. You might even consider a third side.[173] Often in conversations, we immediately anchor to only two sides of an argument. But by encouraging the discovery of a third (who else is affected by this problem?) you explore new ways of approaching the discussion. This ensures that ideas are upheld for a period, and that they are built on as you move forward. Some questions you can ask might be: what is oversimplified about this issue? What is the other

side of the argument? What is the question nobody is asking? When you ask powerful questions, you will experience three counterintuitive signals. You may be wrong. You may feel uncomfortable. You may become quiet. That is OK.

4. **Appreciate to expand**: Finally, expansion occurs when you value all of the above. When you as a leader can demonstrate that these behaviours are worthwhile and that they work. A few years ago, we decided to encourage every member of the team to write a note to one other, randomly selected member of staff. The note had to have one reason they appreciated the person. At the end of the year, every member of the team received a card with three notes from members of the team. The impact was profound. Not only was it deeply satisfying for the person writing the notes, but the receiver felt seen and valued. This simple act of appreciation expanded impact which translated into higher commitment in the workplace.

6

A line to inspire: if you don't, who will?

The ability to inspire is one of the single most important leadership skills that separates great leaders from average ones.[174]

In a nutshell

Leadership isn't just about managing tasks – it's about inspiring others. True leadership is about creating meaning and fostering mastery, not chasing short-term success. The through line is a portal to inspiration. Reaching in identifies it. Resetting adapts it. Reaching out shares it. The beauty of this line is that, if integrated well, it can help you inspire. This is for two reasons. First, because it offers the world a user's guide to you. Your native genius shines through so those around you can find what they need more easily. Second, it centres you. So you can draw on your greatest attributes depending on the context in which you find yourself. The combination inspires. And in the context of leadership, inspiration engenders performance, retention, innovation and mastery. Ultimately, if you don't step up to inspire, who will?

What is inspiration?

Let's start with a simple truth: leaders inspire. It's not just about managing tasks or people. It's about making meaning. It's about igniting something in the hearts of those around you. Because if you don't, who will?

The word inspiration comes from the Latin word, *inspirare*, meaning to breathe or blow into. Inspiration results from the interplay of two parts of our brains: the default mode network, the region of our brains that is responsible for mind wandering and daydreaming, and the executive network, the area that governs higher order functions. In other words, inspiration encourages us to both pay attention and dream.

When I learned about the science behind inspiration, I was reminded of the ancient texts I had explored as a child. *Chitta* is a Sanskrit word meaning heart-mind. It is your mental landscape. The sum of your focus, emotional agility, clarity and awareness. Inspiration requires *chitta*. It serves as a reminder that our heart and our mind are deeply interconnected. Neuroscience and spiritual traditions agree. When both are activated, we are inspired.

Science shows that inspiration stems from three things: self-awareness, self-discipline and self-esteem. The work you have done in uncovering your through line can support all three. By reaching in, you build self-awareness, clarifying your self-concept. You understand your intrinsic motivators. Correspondingly, you build self-discipline, the ability to do what needs to be done. You don't rest on your laurels. By resetting, you constantly evaluate new information. You seek feedback from those around to continuously recalibrate yourself and your through lines. And so from this work stems your ability to reach out authentically with self-esteem. You understand who you are, and you know how you wish to lead.

Reach in, reset, reach out. Do those three things and you will inspire those around you.

If you don't inspire, who will?

> Inspiring leaders are those who use their unique combination of strengths to motivate individuals and teams to take on bold missions—and hold them accountable for results.[175]

Inspiring leaders are not born, they are made. The key to great leadership? It's not in what you do but in understanding who you are. When you tap into your through line, you figure out what drives you, what makes you tick. And when you're in touch with that, you're able to reach out and inspire others. It's like handing the world your user's manual. You give people the chance to see you clearly and know exactly what they can rely on you for.

Inspiration is critical in today's business landscape. Leadership is anything but generic. Context, strategy, business model and culture all matter. Leadership is not about managing people, processes or tasks. Instead, it is about igniting meaning within our teams (and inside ourselves). Inspiration emerges when we create a shared vision that appeals to values, emotions and aspirations. Inspiration originates from having done the work on your through line. Understanding your through line allows you to maximize the capabilities that support your leadership. By first understanding your values, your emotions and your aspirations, you can then align these (intentionally) with those of your teams. We reach in, we reset, we reach out. When we understand our way of being, we can change our way of leading to align with what we aspire to achieve. This ensures that our teams are then part of something that is propulsive and evolving. They become part of something larger than themselves. They understand what you, as a leader, are aiming to achieve. They find meaning. This inspires.

In 2015, Bain Consulting conducted a large-scale research effort with the Economist Intelligence Unit to deconstruct and teach inspiration. They wanted to define inspirational leaders and quantify the skills required to become one. The research identified 33 traits. If we enhance our CARE cycle of leadership based on this information, we might notice that inspiration is the output. The graphic in Horwitch and Callahan's article illustrates some of the most notable traits grouped into our four components: connecting with others (connection), developing inner resources (attention), setting the tone (refraction), and leading the team (expansion). For full details on the work and the attributes, I would encourage you to explore Bain's work.[176]

The research identified one mandatory attribute. Centredness, sat at the nexus of the 32 other elements and was core to inspiration. No one combination of attributes was more powerful than any other. Having just four attributes shifted the ability to inspire. Having one nearly doubled the chance of being inspiring. But centredness was a prerequisite.

> Centeredness is a state of greater mindfulness, achieved by engaging all parts of the mind to be

fully present. It improves one's ability to stay level-headed, cope with stress, empathise with others and listen more deeply. Centeredness is the nexus of the other 32 elements and a mandatory skill. [It] is a precondition to using one's leadership strengths effectively.[177]

Our through lines lead to centredness because they tap into our core. That core balances us. When we are balanced, we can understand our intrinsic attributes with calm. Importantly, we can reach out with CARE.

01 Connection
Vitality, humility, empathy, development, listening, expressiveness, commonality

02 Attention
Self-awareness, flexibility, independence, expression, self-esteem, optimism

Inspiration
Centredness

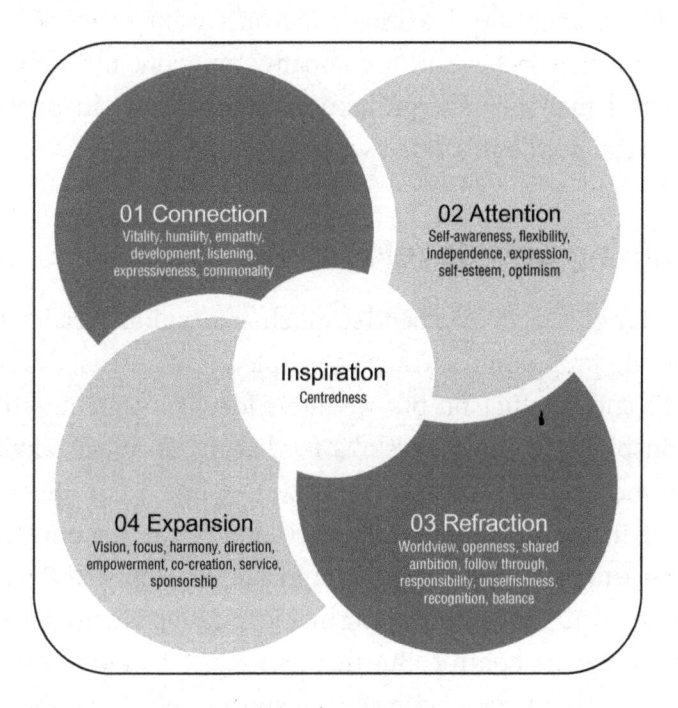

04 Expansion
Vision, focus, harmony, direction, empowerment, co-creation, service, sponsorship

03 Refraction
Worldview, openness, shared ambition, follow through, responsibility, unselfishness, recognition, balance

Figure 10: CARE for inspiration

A growing body of research shows that bolstering strengths is more effective than fixing weaknesses. In fact, the data show that it is more effective to develop a distinguishing strength rather than simply neutralizing weaknesses. According to Gallup research, the odds of increased engagement with a strengths-based approach outweighs one which focuses on neutralizing weaknesses.[178]

Get the balance right, and the results speak for themselves. Inspiration allows us to harness the collective capabilities within any team. When you inspire, people perform, innovate and stick around. Leadership isn't about the daily grind; it's about unlocking potential. 'Individual inspiration is the gateway to employee discretionary energy.'[179] In an increasingly fluid world, our teams want to work hard because they believe in a company's mission, not only for external metrics (pay, promotions, incentives). Inspiration shifts the needle in all that we do.

Training and development

It's strange, isn't it? We spend so much time building leadership training programmes, training people to hit targets, develop skills and be efficient, but we rarely focus on teaching them to inspire. Performance skills tend to be specific, tangible and measurable. The results are well-defined. On the other hand, inspirational skills tend to be difficult to describe, hard to measure and challenging to cultivate. It's almost as if we've resigned ourselves to thinking that inspiration is a mysterious force we can't control. But that's wrong. Inspiration can be trained. And it starts with self-awareness, self-discipline and self-esteem. Inspire your teams and they will find meaning.

We are meaning-making machines. And when we cannot find it, we fall away disinterested or continue to achieve without a sense of agency or excitement. Inspiration provides an antidote to a lack of meaning and discontent. Discovering and cultivating our attributes is one way. Our through lines offer a portal to implementation. Then we can reach every employee. Through the systematic teaching of this framework, we can foster authenticity, prize learning and honour the complexity of relationships. Collective understanding enables unique contributions.

Mastery over success

Inspiration supports a mindset of mastery. Mastery reminds us that leadership is neither enduring nor permanent. We may be given respect, opportunities or time. But mastery reminds us that none of these is for us. We are just holding them in safekeeping. They result from a role. And that role requires humility and grace. Mastery reinforces that we are each but another human on the path. And being a leader is never given, it is earned.

Author, professor and art curator Sarah Lewis, explores how mastery underpins creativity. She defines mastery as the 'ever onwards, almost'.[180] It is not an endpoint or a tick box, instead it is a quest orienting us towards the long term. In business, steering away from success (a short-term achievement) and towards mastery (a long-term pursuit) reorients us towards our core and our purpose. As leaders, this shift is crucial. When we focus on mastery, we're not just looking for wins, we're striving for deeper, more lasting impact.

Staying curious, asking questions and embracing discomfort is the path to mastery. In the workplace, it's about creating space for continuous learning and encouraging the kind of dissent that breeds creativity. As children, we ask questions as we learn new skills, without fear of failing or judgement. It is not about external validation, rather it is an internal quest. Our cultures prize consensus, knowledge and certainty. Sometimes at all costs. Yet, embracing a mindset of mastery may be exactly what we need. The fear of standing out or being different would then dissipate. Psychological safety would underpin our workplaces. We would thrive on continuous learning. James Baldwin once said, 'It is true that the more one learns, the less one knows'.[181] We should embrace not knowing. We could then lean into generative questioning and discomfort. Openness to feedback would make us stronger. Dissent would be encouraged. Creativity would become foundational.

What if we could be the doubter? What if we belonged not because we were just like everyone else but because we were different? What if the ideas we don't want to hear, are the ones we most need to pay attention to? What if the thing that makes you uncomfortable is the thing you need most?

The Queasy Eagle

It began like any other team meeting. Members of the Mayo Medical Ventures team gathered for what would become a milestone moment. Executive director of Mayo Medical Ventures, Rick Colvin, and medical director, Richard Brubaker, gathered the group to celebrate near-wins. They highlighted the projects that had started out well but ultimately failed to come to fruition. They then presented the teams with what was dubbed the Queasy Eagle Award.

'I've never been to a meeting where people felt so uplifted and truly recognised the power of trying new things.'[182] They had succeeded in institutionalizing safe ways to discuss both wins and failures. They had inspired their team.

From through line to inspiration

Commencement speeches seek to engender inspiration in their audiences. The speeches often have the power to give us goosebumps, to move us to act, and to admire what we hear. They distil down life's lessons into digestible chunks. Often, they work best when their through lines are profound yet light, simple yet nuanced, funny yet gut wrenching.

I went on a little quest. To listen to as many speeches as possible. To read those that were available in print. To distil down what made them work. I wanted to bucket these speeches into the three factors that interconnect to deliver inspiration: self-awareness, self-esteem and self-discipline. Because proving the point would have then been simple. If A equals B and B equals C then A equals C. No such luck!

However, as I was working through tens of commencement speeches, I noticed something fascinating. Every single speaker chose to draw on their lived experience. They chose to tell stories about what worked for them and why. They exhibited moral courage. They aimed to connect with their audience by paying attention to their experience, noticing the minute details that made them who they were, expanding these lessons into something new – inspiration. Those that worked, often had components of the three pillars of inspiration woven into them. Was it correlation or causation

– I don't know. Can I prove that inspiration is the root of all great speeches? No. But I know how I respond when I hear something inspiring, and I'm sure you do too.

The speeches are clear. Simple to digest. Yet nuanced too. Every single one of them offers a unifying thread – a through line that resounds within the words. There are those that talk about doing great work. Those that reinforce the importance of play. Others that talk about starting small and sweating the small stuff. 'Making your bed will also reinforce the fact that little things in life matter. If you can't do the little things right, you will never do the big things right.'[183] (Note: As ever, there are always multiple stories you can tell. I recently heard Trevor Noah talk about his new children's book, *Into the Uncut Grass,* and he writes a whole story about the perils of being bound to making your bed!) Those that point out that life (and leadership) is a team sport. That while you might stand alone as you lead, collective mastery depends on your team, your mentors, and even your competitors. These influences make us who we are. We learn about learning how to think. How hard work and discomfort can be the best teachers. How failure can offer a portal into clarity, conviction and originality. How change is the only constant. 'This is your time, and it feels normal to you, but really there is no normal. There is only change, and resistance to it and then more change.'[184] And each speech highlights our ability and the responsibility to listen, build and contribute. That this comes by understanding and becoming ourselves.

> You have, which is a rare thing, that ability and the responsibility to listen to the dissent in yourself, to at least give it the floor, because it is the key—not only

to consciousness—but to real growth. To accept duality is to earn identity. And identity is something that you are constantly earning. It is not just who you are. It is a process that you must be active in. It is not just parroting your parents or the thoughts of your learned teachers. It is now more than ever about understanding yourself so you can become yourself.[185]

Our through lines are a portal to inspiration. They showcase how we are each on a quest to find the best ways to tell our stories. They illustrate the power of the human spirit. They underscore that we can empower others if we empower ourselves. And perhaps most importantly, that when we reflect on our lessons, we have the power to change the world.

Inspiration to change the world

Peter Drucker once said, 'A healthy business can't exist in a sick society'.[186] The health of any business depends fundamentally on the health of society, or that piece of it which the business serves.

Established in 1973, rock climber and nature lover Yvon Chouinard had a bold idea. He wanted to inspire environmental change. And through unwavering courage and a conviction in a simple mission, he has done so through his company, Patagonia.

Patagonia's mission combines exploration with preservation. The brand's vision is to 'build the best product, cause no unnecessary harm, and use business to inspire and implement solutions to the environmental crisis'. It seems that the more they grow, the better they do. Customers repeatedly cite the positive action that the brand supports in them. And in 2022 the company revised its mission. They made the bold declaration that, 'We're in business to save our home planet'.[187] This larger-than-life mission made them one of the most discussed pieces of advertising of 2022.

Since 1985, Patagonia has used sustainable and recycled materials in their products that are built for durability and aim to minimize waste. You may remember their 'Don't Buy This Jacket' campaign. The paradox of a retailer encouraging less consumption was striking. Customers were encouraged to repair or reuse gear to extend its lifespan. Counterintuitive from a profitability standpoint but valuable at its core. The ethical decision which was good for the planet turned out to be good for business too. This impact-driven decision built enduring customer loyalty and trust.

Storytelling features front and centre in all that the company does. By launching a storytelling hub featuring interviews with activists, scientists and customers, they draw us in and help us understand their brand's value and purpose. Through email marketing and social media, customers can get involved. The company shared stories of regular folks advancing the change we need to see. They champion their customers' passions. They never push their products. And that is not all. The company puts its money where its mouth is. They donate 1% of sales to grassroots environmental organizations. Their employees volunteer over 4,000 hours each year for environmental causes. In 2016, their 'Black Friday Pledge' donated 100% of sales to environmental organizations chosen by customers. Everything they do is aligned with their through line – to save our home planet. They are unafraid to take a stand on social issues that matter to their purpose. It inspires smaller businesses to speak up.

Patagonia don't just make products. They want to change the world. Their mission isn't about selling jackets. It's about saving the planet. They espouse what they believe in. They affect policy and practice by showing their conviction to lead. They are an inspiration. Their through line serves to build brands that matter. Simply put, their brand shapes culture. They remind us that visionary brands can inspire change.

Your turn

Time is a finite resource. Energy is renewable. Defined in physics as the capacity to work, energy stems from four parts of us: our bodies, our minds, our emotions and our spirit. Inspiration requires that we manage our energy.

When Alessandro Volta invented the voltaic pile, he produced a simple and reliable source of energy. By alternating discs of zinc and silver (or copper and pewter) separated by paper or cloth soaked either in salt water or sodium hydroxide, he built a steady source of electricity. As leaders we must find ways to renew and sustain our energy to inspire. We must build a leadership voltaic pile using our through lines to provide a reliable source of energy for inspiration.

Here are some questions to uncover your attributes and consider how you manage your energy. Gather a list of the questions you find helpful and add them here.

- What are four of your core attributes that you'd like to continue to work on? If you are unsure what your strengths are, I find the VIA Character Strengths survey quite useful (www.viacharacter.org/survey). There are many other ways of uncovering your attributes. Chief among these is asking those around you to provide you with feedback, and cross-referencing these against the work conducted by Bain. Happy digging.

- What have you learned this year and how are you applying it?

- What skills or knowledge do you need to acquire to continue to grow?

- How are you managing your energy to maximize your contributions?

- When was the last time you switched off and reset?[188]

7

A line to go further: what is next?

Tell me what you plan to do with your one wild, precious life.[189]

Figure 11: Rewilding

Rewilding

Since the 1930s, the UK has lost 97% of its wildflower meadows.[190] Rewilding has achieved newfound focus in recent years. The reasons are plentiful. Wildflowers sustain biodiversity. They support other wildlife. They provide food year-round. Their complex root systems hold on to rainwater and stop nutrients from washing away. They help us fight disease and climate change.

Leadership books, courses and externalities tell us that there is one way to lead. That we must clip and prune our teams into perfect shapes. Instead, what if we accepted that each of us are wildflowers? We don't need shaping. We only require nourishment. We need to care so those around us can care for others. Be willing to receive care. The focus, the function and the development, these are individual choices. Our job is only to provide the fertile ground to allow everyone to become their glorious selves.[191]

The work is 'delicious, confounding, frustrating, necessary'.[192] We cannot (and must not) curate every opportunity. When we centre our self-worth on the success of those in our charge, not only do we put pressure on them, but we limit their potential. In fact, when we constantly rescue and attend to others, we take away their ability to build agency. That agency is essential to growth.

Instead, we must embrace complexity and nuance. We should let those around us find their way. As we understand who we are, how we lead becomes lighter. We get better at listening. We appreciate the nuance of relationships. We let the wildflowers grow, free of constraints and in their own time and way.

What is next?

I appreciate art. But my best efforts at drawing always ended with a picture of a house. Somehow, the structural comfort of drawing something concrete helped me overcome a deep-seated fear of the unknown. In 2001, a friend and I decided to take a portraiture class. The teacher encouraged us to bring in a photograph of someone we wished to draw. In the first class, she explained that, as budding artists, we sometimes get stuck when we look at something we recognize, limited by the lines that we see (or don't see) in a picture. So she asked us to turn the picture upside down. Why? Because the picture then morphs into something quite different: shades of colour, distinct shapes, many blurred lines. The recognizability shifts. Our perception shifts. And instead of anchoring on the reality of an image or in what we see, we can deconstruct a whole into separate parts.

I tell that story because our through lines are just like that upside-down picture. They are a representation of many distinct experiences that we have been a part of during our lives. When each is looked at discretely they don't necessarily show us a path forward. But when we step back, when we evaluate our lives like an upturned picture, we glimpse themes, shapes, colours, textures that we did not even realize were there. In reaching in, we uncover what is true about who we are. In resetting, we adapt that image to the external information we are provided with daily. And in reaching out, we put that information to use as we aim to serve those around us. All the while, our through lines are almost imperceptible. Yet they are there. They keep us grounded. They connect us. Those threads link our values to our behaviours. They shape our character and our leadership style. And they empower us when we need it most.

Thank you for spending some time with me. I hope apertures have opened to allow you to explore your through lines and what you hope for in leadership. Continue to challenge yourself. Steer into discomfort. Embrace new ideas. Expand them. But most of all, please share them. I leave you with words I penned while thinking about leadership. It was a sort of manifesto, unfiltered and raw. I encourage you to craft your own.

> Follow your heart but take your brain with you.
> Remember your purpose.
> Maintain an eagerness to learn.
> Do what is right not what is easy.
> Be comfortable with messy: test and learn.
> Breathe (before you speak, act, or respond).
> Treat failure and success equally.
> Speak up when things go well; speak up when things go poorly.
> Serve those around you: giving is a lifestyle.
> Have faith (in yourself and each other): build up those around you.
> Contribute to a culture of openness and compassion.
> Allocate resources to the things that matter.
> Reach in and find your through line.
> Reset, every day, to adapt.
> Reach out. That is what you are built for.

There is no such thing as an ending. Just a place where you leave the story. And it is your story now. I spent 40 years scrubbing floors, and the last months of my life as co-manager of a hotel halfway across the world. You have no idea now what you will become. Do not try and control it. Let go. That is when the fun starts. Because as I once heard someone say, there is no present like this time.[193]

Notes

[1] C. S. Lewis, quoted in Sherman, J. R. (1982). *Rejection.* Pathway Books.

[2] Palmer, P. (2015). *Let Your Life Speak: Listening for the voice of vocation.* Jossey Bass.

[3] Jones, L. (2024, September 20). *LinkedIn.* Linkedin.com. www.linkedin.com/posts/luvvie_the-intersection-of-our-personal-lives-and-activity-7236472893990125568-Annt/

[4] Shankar, M. (Host). (2024, July 1). What comes after gold, with Olympian Missy Franklin. [Audio podcast episode]. In *A Slight Change of Plans.* Pushkin Industries. www.pushkin.fm/podcasts/a-slight-change-of-plans/what-comes-after-gold-with-olympian-missy-franklin

[5] No discussion on leadership would be complete without a reference to imposter syndrome. Originally coined by psychologists Pauline Rose Clance and Suzanne Ines in 1978, the research focused on high-achieving women. You can read more about the myths, misconceptions and impacts here. Tulshyan, R. and Burey, J. A. (2022, August 4). *Stop Telling Women They Have Imposter Syndrome.* https://hbr.org/2021/02/stop-telling-women-they-have-imposter-syndrome

[6] Brown, B. (2024, June 26). *A Dare to Lead + BetterUp Partnership.* Brené Brown. https://brenebrown.com/articles/2024/06/26/a-dare-to-lead-better up-partnership/

[7] Brown, B. (Host). (2024, April 24). What's coming (and what's here). [Audio podcast episode]. In *Dare to Lead.* https://brenebrown.com/podcast/whats-coming-and-whats-here/#listen

[8] Corrigan, K. (Host). (2024, April 1). Being well in the modern world. (No. 1) [Video podcast episode]. In *Tell Me More.* www.pbs.org/video/the-state-of-well-being-in-america-8elqnq/

[9] www2.deloitte.com/us/en/pages/about-deloitte/articles/burnout-survey.html

[10] www.deloitte.com/uk/en/about/press-room/poor-mental-health-costs-uk-employers-51-billion-a-year-for-employees.html

[11] Gibbs, N. (2023, May 31). 'At Harvard, Tom Hanks offered an increasingly rare moment of grace'. *Washington Post*. www.washingtonpost.com/opinions/2023/05/31/tom-hanks-commencement-harvard/

[12] Hanks, T. (2023, May 26). Tom Hanks delivers the Commencement Address | Harvard Commencement 2023. YouTube. https://youtu.be/dkPo5nfEk1w

[13] Petula Clark is a legendary British singer and actress, best known for her hit song *Downtown*, which became an anthem in the 1960s. With a career that spans over seven decades, she's one of the most enduring pop icons, blending classic pop with a touch of elegance. Beyond *Downtown*, she's had numerous hits, including 'I Know a Place' and 'Don't Sleep in the Subway'. Petula was also a star in films and on stage, and her influence on modern pop music is still felt today. She's like the British answer to icons like Dionne Warwick or Barbra Streisand, a true pioneer who brought a sophisticated sound to the swinging 60s.

[14] Coined by American sociologist Ruth Useem in the 1950s, the term third-culture kid was conceived for expatriate children who spent their formative years overseas, shaped by the multicultural, peripatetic spheres of their parents.

[15] Keys, A. (2020). *More Myself*. Flatiron.

[16] Ward, T. B., Patterson, M. J. and Sifonis, C. M. (2004). Conceptual combination and the creation of new ideas: constraint-based and pre-inventive processes in creative cognition. *Journal of Experimental Psychology: Learning, Memory, and Cognition*, 30(5), 1023–1032. https://doi.org/10.1037/0278-7393.30.5.1023. Mehta, R. and Zhu, M. (2016). Creating when you have less: the impact of resource scarcity on product use creativity. *Journal of Consumer Research*, 42(5), 767–782. https://doi.org/10.1093/jcr/ucv051. Moreau, C. P. and Dahl, D. W. (2005). Designing the solution: the impact of constraints on consumers' creativity. *Journal of Consumer Research*, 32(1), 13–22. https://doi.org/10.1086/429597. Liberman, N. and Förster, J. (2009). The effect of psychological distance on perceptual focus. *Journal of Experimental Social Psychology*, 45(2), 485–489. https://doi.org/10.1016/j.jesp.2008.12.002

[17] We could think about impact as our desire to be good ancestors (instead of leaving a legacy).

[18] From the Latin word for 'patchwork garment', a cento is a literary work collaged entirely from other authors' verses or passages. In their earliest forms, centos were often composed as tributes to other authors.

[19] See: Kellerman, B. (2012). *The End of Leadership*. Harper Business.

[20] Lamott, A. (2003, May 8). *UC Berkeley Commencement* [Keynote].

[21] Lamott, A. (1994). *Bird by Bird: Instructions on writing and life.* (p. 119). Canongate Books Ltd.

[22] Boyce, S. and Robay, D. (Hosts). (2024, March 25). Writing your own story. (No. 1) [Audio podcast episode]. In *The Bright Side*. Hello Sunshine. https://omny.fm/shows/the-bright-side/reese-witherspoon-on-writing-your-own-story

[23] Confucius. (2006). *The Essential Analects: Selected passages with traditional commentary*. Hackett Publishing.

[24] Karsh, Y. (n.d.). *Character, like a photograph, develops in darkness* [Quote]. BrainyQuote. www.brainyquote.com/quotes/yousuf_karsh_163621. Yousuf Karsh is an Armenian-Canadian photographer.

[25] Grant, S. (2024, July 10). Video: Thasunda Brown Duckett, President & CEO, TIAA – 'I Rent My Title, I Own My Character'. www.sherylgrant.com/post/video-thasunda-brown-duckett-president-ceo-tiaa-i-rent-my-title-i-own-my-character#:~:text=Thasunda%20explained%20that%20titles%20are%20rented%20and%20temporary.,can%20claim%20it%20and%20proclaim%20it.%20It%E2%80%99s%20yours.%22

[26] Sarah Lewis beautifully defines mastery as a near win, an every onwards almost. I hold that definition close because I think we should all prize the path rather than the goal. Lewis, S. (Guest) and Raz, G. (Host). (2022, July 3). The importance of a near miss. [Audio podcast episode]. In *Wisdom from the Top*. iHeart. www.iheart.com/podcast/139-wisdom-from-the-top-30131202/episode/the-importance-of-a-near-miss-sarah-99361945/

[27] Godin, S. (2023). *The Song of Significance*. Random House.

[28] Maxwell, J. C. (1997). *Becoming a Person of Influence: How to positively impact the lives of others*. Thomas Nelson. John C. Maxwell is an author, pastor and speaker who has written extensively on leadership.

[29] McKinsey. (2022, August 17). *What Is Leadership? A definition and way forward*. www.mckinsey.com/featured-insights/mckinsey-explainers/what-is-leadership

[30] Senge, P. M. (1990). *The Fifth Discipline: The art and practice of the learning organization*. Doubleday/Currency.

[31] Le Gentil, H. (2021, October 25). *Leaders, Stop Trying to Be Heroes*. https://hbr.org/2021/10/leaders-stop-trying-to-be-heroes

[32] Winfrey, O. (2024, August 21). *Oprah Winfrey's speech at the Democratic National Convention* [Transcript]. Democratic National Convention. www.rev.com/blogs/transcripts/oprah-winfrey-democratic-national-convention-2024

[33] Walsch, N. D. (n.d.). Life begins at the edge of your comfort zone [Quote]. In *Conversations with God*.

[34] David, S. (2017, February). *The gift and power of emotional courage* [Video]. TED. www.ted.com/talks/susan_david_the_gift_and_power_of_emotional_courage?subtitle=en. See also: David, S. (2016). *Emotional Agility: Get unstuck, embrace change and thrive in work and life*. Avery Publishing Group.

[35] Neal, J. (2006). *Edgewalkers: People and organizations that take risks, build bridges, and break new ground*. Praeger.

[36] Kyte, L. (2018, August 14). Why Is Rebecca Solnit Hopeful? Lion's Roar. www.lionsroar.com/the-truth-teller/

[37] Elkin, L. (2017, July 11). The Collector: Rebecca Solnit on Textual Pleasure, Punk, and More. *The Daily Beast*. www.thedailybeast.com/the-collector-rebecca-solnit-on-textual-pleasure-punk-and-more

[38] Solnit, R. (2013). *The Faraway Nearby*. Granta Books.

[39] Grant, A. (Host). (2019, December 3). The internet doesn't need your opinion on everything with Rebecca Solnit. (No. 381) [Audio podcast episode]. In *WorkLife*. TED Audio Collective. https://podcasts.apple.com/ca/podcast/the-internet-doesnt-need-your-opinion-on-everything/id1346314086?i=1000657705504

[40] Weir, K. (2017, March 2). *The Philosopher Queen: Rebecca Solnit*. Elle. www.elle.com/culture/books/a42862/the-philosopher-queen-rebecca-solnit/

[41] Pandya, H. (2023, March 29). *The best joke in Mae Martin's Netflix comedy special 'SAP.'* Vulture. www.vulture.com/article/mae-martin-sap-comedy-special-snow-globes.html

[42] Collins, J. and Porras, J. I. (1996). Building your company's vision. *Harvard Business Review*, 74(5), 65–77.

[43] Baldwin, J. A. (1962). 'The Fire Next Time'. In *The New Yorker*. Also, quoted in *History Workshop Journal*, 83(1), Spring 2017, 230–240. https://doi.org/10.1093/hwj/dbx006

[44] Arthur Brooks defines moral courage as defending those we disagree with in the presence of those you agree with. Brooks, A. C. (2024, September 19). The right way to say the unsayable: how to speak truth without fear – but avoid alienating everyone you know. *The Atlantic*. www.theatlantic.com/ideas/archive/2024/09/speaking-truth-without-fear/679901/

[45] Knowles, B. (2023, November 6). *CFDA Fashion Awards* [Keynote].

[46] Biography.com (2021, May 21). *Constantin Stanislavski – Method, Quotes & Facts*. Biography. www.biography.com/actors/constantin-stanislavski

[47] www.ey.com/en_us/insights/consulting/is-gen-z-the-spark-we-need-to-see-the-light-report/gen-z-finding-meaning

[48] Borgschulte, M., Guenzel, M., Liu, C. and Malmendier, U. (2020). CEO Stress, Aging, and Death. *NBER*, 28550. https://doi.org/10.3386/w28550

[49] Adkins, B. A. (2024, April 9). Only one in 10 people possess the talent to manage. *Gallup.com*. www.gallup.com/workplace/236579/one-people-possess-talent-manage.aspx

[50] Grant, A. (Host). (2019, December 3). The internet doesn't need your opinion on everything with Rebecca Solnit. (No. 381) [Audio podcast episode]. In *WorkLife*. TED Audio Collective. https://podcasts.apple.com/ca/podcast/the-internet-doesnt-need-your-opinion-on-everything/id1346314086?i=1000657705504

[51] Ma, Y. (n.d.). *A composition is always more than the sum of its parts*. Retrieved from www.allgreatquotes.com/quote-468143/

[52] Aristotle. (n.d.). *Knowing yourself is the beginning of all wisdom*. Goodreads. www.goodreads.com/author/quotes/2192.Aristotle

53 Eurich, T. (2023, April 6). What self-awareness really is (and how to cultivate it). *Harvard Business Review*. https://hbr.org/2018/01/what-self-awareness-really-is-and-how-to-cultivate-it

54 Tasha Eurich and colleagues found that there are two types of self-awareness: Internal self-awareness (how clearly, we see our own values, passions, aspirations, fit with our environment, reactions, and impact on others) and external self-awareness (understanding how other people view us). Here we are addressing internal self-awareness.

55 Self-concept clarity is a metacognitive view (our awareness of our thinking) of our certainty about the shape of our identity.

56 Hogan, R. and Warrenfeltz, R. (2003). Educating the modern manager. *Academy of Management Learning & Education*, 2(1), 74–84.

57 I will note here that to garner trust you need three things: authenticity, logic and empathy.

58 Leary, K. and Wilkinson, R. (2020). Leading with intentionality: the 4P framework for strategic leadership (RWP20-029). *Harvard Kennedy School Faculty Research Working Paper Series*. https://dash.harvard.edu/handle/1/37371395?show=full

59 Ben Okri, Nobel Prize for Literature. Okri, B. (1996). *Birds of Heaven*. Phoenix House.

60 Peppernell, C. (2018). *Pillow Thoughts II: Healing the heart*. Andrews McMeel Publishing.

61 Sparks, N. (Writer) and Katz, R. (Director). (2016). *The Choice* [Film script]. Lionsgate.

62 Wrzesniewski, A. (2022, July 26). *To be happier at work, think flexibly about your job—and yourself*. Yale Insights. https://insights.som.yale.edu/insights/to-be-happier-at-work-think-flexibly-about-your-job-and-yourself

63 According to recent research, meaning is made up of three parts: comprehension, mattering and purpose. Comprehension refers to having clarity about one's life events. Mattering refers to having a sense that one's life is significant. Purpose refers to pursuing goals that are in line with one's values.

64 Creativity is thinking up new things. Innovation is doing new things.

65 Spain, S. and Kim, J. (2018). Leadership, work careers, and self-concept clarity. In J. Lodi-Smith and K. DeMarree (eds), *Self-Concept*

Clarity: Perspectives on assessment, research, and applications (pp. 165–176). Springer.

[66] Ancona, D. L., Malone, T. W., Orlikowski, W. J. and Senge, P. M. (2007). In praise of the incomplete leader. *Harvard Business Review*, 85(2), 92–100. https://hbr.org/2007/02/in-praise-of-the-incomplete-leader

[67] Grant, A. (2023). *Hidden Potential: The science of achieving greater things.* WH Allen.

[68] Ingram, P. and Choi, Y. (2022, November 1). What does your company really stand for? *Harvard Business Review*. https://hbr.org/2022/11/what-does-your-company-really-stand-for

[69] Ripley, A. (2018, June 27). Complicating the narratives. *Solutions Journalism*. https://thewholestory.solutionsjournalism.org/complicating-the-narratives-b91ea06ddf63

[70] Wadhwa, V. (2009, July 8). The anatomy of an entrepreneur. Kauffman Foundation. Duke University.

[71] www.sixwordmemoirs.com/

[72] Tagishcharley – Sixwordmemoirs.com

[73] cummings, e. e. (1958). A poet's advice to students. In G. J. Firmage (ed.), *e.e. cummings: A miscellany* (p. 13). Harvard University Press.

[74] Ripley, A. (2021). *High Conflict: Why we get trapped and how we get out.* Simon and Schuster.

[75] Chödrön, P. (2001). *The Places that Scare You: A guide to fearlessness in difficult times.* Shambhala Publications.

[76] Gilbert, E. (2015). *Big Magic: Creative living beyond fear.* Riverhead Books.

[77] Kahneman, D. (n.d.). Quote by Daniel Kahneman: 'Nothing in life is as important as you think it is, while you are thinking about it'. BrainyQuote. www.brainyquote.com/quotes/daniel_kahneman_567029

[78] Porcelli, A. J. and Delgado, M. R. (2009). Acute stress modulates risk taking in financial decision making. *Psychological Science*, 20(3), 278–283.

[79] Arnsten, A. F. T. (2009). Stress signaling pathways that impair prefrontal cortex structure and function. *Nature Reviews Neuroscience*, 10(6), 410–422.

[80] Sinha, R. (2008). Chronic stress, drug use, and vulnerability to addiction. *Annals of the New York Academy of Sciences*, 1141(1), 105–130.

[81] Charles Handy, author and philosopher specializing in organizational behaviour.

[82] Qin, S., Hermans, E. J., van Marle, H. J., Luo, J. and Fernández, G. (2009). Acute psychological stress reduces working memory-related activity in the dorsolateral prefrontal cortex. *Biological Psychiatry*, 66(1), 25–32.

[83] Schwabe, L. and Wolf, O. T. (2009). Stress prompts habit behavior in humans. *Journal of Neuroscience*, 29(22), 7191–7198.

[84] Unknown.

[85] Guillen, L. and Florent-Treacy, E. (2011). Emotional intelligence and leadership effectiveness: the mediating influence of collaborative behaviors. *INSEAD Working Paper No. 2011/23/IGLC. SSRN.* https://ssrn.com/abstract=1759991 or http://dx.doi.org/10.2139/ssrn.1759991

[86] Emotional labour was a term originally coined by sociologist Arlie Hochschild, in the 1983 book *The Managed Heart: Commercialization of human feeling* (University of California Press). It highlights a complexity of leading – that we sometimes must manage our emotions in the workplace, and this can cause fatigue. Be aware of it.

[87] Ovans, A. (2015, April 15). How emotional intelligence became a key leadership skill. *Harvard Business Review*. https://hbr.org/2015/04/how-emotional-intelligence-became-a-key-leadership-skill

[88] Goleman, D. (1998). *Working with Emotional Intelligence*. Bantam Books.

[89] Weinstein, N., Brown, K. W. and Ryan, R. M. (2009). A multi-method examination of the effects of mindfulness on stress attribution, coping, and emotional well-being. *Journal of Research in Personality*, 43(3), 374–385.

[90] Ashley, G. and Reiter-Palmon, R. (2012). Self-awareness and the evolution of leaders: the need for a better measure of self-awareness. *Journal of Behavioral and Applied Management*, 14, 2–17. 10.1037/t29152-000

[91] Silvia, P. J. and O'Brien, M. E. (2004). Self-awareness and constructive functioning: revisiting 'the human dilemma'. *Journal of Personality*, 72(1), 29–52.

[92] Sutton, A., Williams, H. M. and Allinson, C. W. (2015). A longitudinal, mixed method evaluation of self-awareness training in the workplace. *European Journal of Training and Development*, 39(7), 610–627.

[93] Gardner, W. L., Avolio, B. J., Luthans, F., May, D. R. and Walumbwa, F. (2005). 'Can you see the real me?' A self-based model of authentic leader and follower development. *The Leadership Quarterly*, 16(3), 343–372.

[94] Gilbert, E. (2013, November 6). The 'Stubborn Gladness' of Elizabeth Gilbert's favorite poet. *The Atlantic*. www.theatlantic.com/entertainment/archive/2013/11/the-stubborn-gladness-of-elizabeth-gilberts-favorite-poet/281158/

[95] Pennebaker, J. W. (1997). *Opening Up: The healing power of expressing emotions*. Guilford Press. Pennebaker, J. W. (2011). *The Secret Life of Pronouns: What our words say about us*. Bloomsbury Press. Pennebaker, J. W. and Beall, S. K. (1986). Confronting a traumatic event: toward an understanding of inhibition and disease. *Journal of Abnormal Psychology*, 95(3), 274–281. Pennebaker, J. W., Kiecolt-Glaser, J. K. and Glaser, R. (1988). Disclosure of traumas and immune function: Health implications for psychotherapy. *Journal of Consulting and Clinical Psychology*, 56(2), 239–245.

[96] I note that there could have been many other explanations for what he saw, but please bear with me on this one.

[97] Lipa, D. (Host). (2023, November 17). Tim Cook: What it takes to run Apple. (No. 41) [Audio podcast episode]. In *Dua Lipa at Your Service*. BBC Sounds. www.bbc.co.uk/programmes/p0cgz10v/episodes/downloads

[98] Kleiner, K. (2011, September). Lunchtime leniency: Judges' rulings are harsher when they are hungrier. *Scientific American*. www.scientificamerican.com/article/lunchtime-leniency/#:~:text=Researchers%20at%20Ben%20Gurion%20University%20in%20Israel%20and

[99] Ryff, C. D. and Singer, B. (1998). The contours of positive human health. *Psychological Inquiry*, 9(1), 1–28.

[100] Rafaeli-Mor, E., Gotlib, I. H. and Revelle, W. (1999). The meaning and measurement of self-complexity. *Personality and Individual Differences*, 27(2), 341–356.

[101] Collins, J. C. and Porras, J. I. (1996). Building your company's vision. *Harvard Business Review*, 74(5), 65–77.

[102] Wadhwa, H. (2020, April 7). *Three shifts in leadership mastery*. Columbia Business School. https://business.columbia.edu/leadership/ideas-work/three-shifts-leadership-mastery

[103] Chiu, M. and Salerno, H. (2019). *Changing change management*. Gartner. www.gartner.com/en/human-resources/trends/changing-change-management

[104] Gervais, M. (Host). (2019, December 3). Inner master, outer impact: The essence of a great leader. (No. 441) [Audio podcast episode]. In *Finding Mastery*. https://findingmastery.com/podcasts/hitendra-wadhwa/

[105] www.hopperslondon.com

[106] Wadhwa, H. (Finding Mastery). (2024, April 3). *Inner Mastery, Outer Impact: The Essence of a Great Leader* [Audio podcast episode]. Finding Mastery with Dr. Michael Gervais. https://audio.listennotes.com/e/p/d22180fdc8564b66945334099985f878/.

[107] Amaechi, J. (2021). *The Promises of Giants*. Nicholas Brealey.

[108] *Dare to Lead List of Values*. (2023, November 14). Brené Brown. https://brenebrown.com/resources/dare-to-lead-list-of-values/#

[109] Amaechi, J. (2021). *The Promises of Giants*. Nicholas Brealey.

[110] Gilbert, E. (2015). *Big Magic: Creative living beyond fear*. Riverhead Books.

[111] Shankar, M. (Host). (2024, August 19). Olympian Gabby Thomas on choosing happiness. (No. 124) [Audio podcast episode]. In *A Slight Change of Plans*. Pushkin Industries. https://omny.fm/shows/a-slight-change-of-plans/olympian-gabby-thomas-on-choosing-happiness

[112] Eurich, T. (2023, April 6). What self-awareness really is (and how to cultivate it). *Harvard Business Review*. https://hbr.org/2018/01/what-self-awareness-really-is-and-how-to-cultivate-it

[113] Lewis, S. E. (2014, March 1). Embrace a near win [Conference presentation]. TED. www.ted.com/talks/sarah_lewis_embrace_the_near_win?subtitle=en

[114] Gartner.com (n. d.). Organizational change management. www.gartner.com/en/human-resources/insights/organizational-change-management#:~:text=Change%20is%20the%20new%20constant,34%25%20are%20a%20clear%20success

[115] Adams, G. S., Converse, B. A., Hales, A. H. and Klotz, L. E. (2021). People systematically overlook subtractive changes. *Nature*, 592, 258–261.

[116] Pradhan, K. (2019, April 2). In the dense mangrove forests straddling the India-Bangladesh border, tigers and a mythical goddess unite Hindus and Muslims. BBC. www.bbc.com/travel/article/20190329-the-people-who-live-with-tigers#:~:text=Royal%20Bengal%20tigers%20are%20known%20for%20their%20intelligence,a%20mask%20on%20the%20back%20of%20their%20head

[117] Eger, E. E. (2017). *The Choice: Embrace the possible*. Scribner Book Company.

[118] Noah, T. (2016). *Born a Crime: Stories from a South African childhood*. Doubleday Canada.

[119] Deci, E. L., Koestner, R. and Ryan, R. M. (1999). A meta-analytic review of experiments examining the effects of extrinsic rewards on intrinsic motivation. *Psychological Bulletin*, 125(6), 627–668.

[120] Mullainathan, S. and Shafir, E. (2013). *Scarcity: Why having too little means so much*. Times Books.

[121] American Psychological Association. (2017). *Stress in America: Coping with Change*. APA.

[122] Ryan, R. M. and Deci, E. L. (2000). Self-determination theory and the facilitation of intrinsic motivation, social development, and well-being. *American Psychologist*, 55(1), 68–78.

[123] Wrzesniewski, A., McCauley, C., Rozin, P. and Schwartz, B. (1997). Jobs, careers, and callings: people's relations to their work. *Journal of Research in Personality*, 31(1), 21–33.

[124] Deci, E. L. and Ryan, R. M. (2008). Self-Determination Theory: A macro theory of human motivation, development, and health. *Canadian Psychology*, 49(3), 182–185.

[125] David, S. (2016). *Emotional Agility: Get unstuck, embrace change, and thrive in work and life*. Avery Publishing Group.

[126] Shankar, M. (Host). (2024, July 8). Surrender is not in my DNA. [Audio podcast episode]. In *A Slight Change of Plans*. Pushkin Industries. www.youtube.com/watch?v=T-fAjTlijIM

[127] Olympics.com (2021, August 30). Brad Snyder talks historic first triathlon gold for USA and that moment in Afghanistan. https://olympics.

com/en/news/brad-snyder-talks-historic-first-triathlon-gold-for-usa-and-that-moment-in-afgha

[128] Buckingham, M. and Goodall, A. (2019, May 14). The power of hidden teams. *Harvard Business Review*. https://hbr.org/2019/05/the-power-of-hidden-teams

[129] Edmondson, A. C. and Corsi, E. Leading culture change at SEB. Harvard Business School Case 621-074, February 2021.

[130] Grant, A. (Host). (2024, June 25). How novelist Gabrielle Zevin learned to enjoy failure. [Audio podcast episode]. In *Worklife*. TED Audio Collective. https://podcasts.apple.com/us/podcast/worklife-with-adam-grant/id1346314086

[131] Stevenson, B. (2014). *Just Mercy: A story of justice and redemption*. Spiegel & Grau.

[132] Curiosity is seen as a motive to explore within definite and accepted frames whereas wonder engenders exploration because there is doubt about the frames.

[133] Johnson, C. (1955). *Harold and the Purple Crayon*. HarperCollins Children's Books.

[134] Ellenhorn, R. (2022). *Purple Crayons: The art of drawing a life*. HarperCollins.

[135] Keys, A. and Jay-Z. (2009). 'Empire State of Mind'. On *The Blueprint 3*. Roc Nation.

[136] Keys, D. (1982). *Earth at Omega: Passage to planetization* (p. 79). Brenden Press.

[137] Yang, L., Holtz, D., Jaffe, S., et al. (2022). The effects of remote work on collaboration among information workers. *Nature Human Behaviour*, 6, 43–54. https://doi.org/10.1038/s41562-021-01196-4

[138] Cholteeva, Y. (2022, August 23). Three in five workers are disengaged and costing UK economy billions, study finds. www.peoplemanagement.co.uk/article/1796442/three-five-workers-disengaged-costing-uk-economy-billions-study-finds

[139] https://www.choctawnation.com/about/history/irish-connection/#:~:text=Their%20relationship%20began%20in%201847%2C%20when%20the%20Choctaws%2C,to%20support%20the%20Irish%20during%20the%20Potato%20Famine

[140] Microsoft (2022, September 22). Hybrid work is just work: are we doing it wrong? Worktrend Index. www.microsoft.com/en-us/worklab/work-trend-index/hybrid-work-is-just-work

[141] Remember the research that showed that meaning comes from three things: comprehension, mattering and purpose.

[142] Kroll, M. M. (2022, May 2). Prolonged social isolation and loneliness are equivalent to smoking 15 cigarettes a day. Extension. https://extension.unh.edu/blog/2022/05/prolonged-social-isolation-loneliness-are-equivalent-smoking-15-cigarettes-day#:~:text=Loneliness%20is%20the%20feeling%20of%20being%20alone%2C%20regardless

[143] Fisher, J. and Silverglate, P. H. (2022, June 22). The C-suite's role in well-being. Deloitte Insights. www2.deloitte.com/us/en/insights/topics/leadership/employee-wellness-in-the-corporate-workplace.html

[144] Help is the sunny side of control. When we relinquish our need to control, we can witness because we care.

[145] Eurich, T. (2023, April 6). What self-awareness really is (and how to cultivate it). *Harvard Business Review*. https://hbr.org/2018/01/what-self-awareness-really-is-and-how-to-cultivate-it

[146] Roosevelt, T. (1905, October 25). *People don't care how much you know until they know how much you care.* Speech delivered in Memphis, Tennessee. www.goodnewsnetwork.org

[147] Larsen, K. (1974). Conformity in the Asch experiment. *Journal of Social Psychology*, 94(2), 303–304.

[148] Richard Branson. Your Thought Partner. (2019, October 23). *10 inspiring quotes from successful CEOs to help you win at employee engagement.* Your Thought Partner. www.yourthoughtpartner.com/blog/10-inspiring-quotes-from-successful-ceos-to-help-you-win-at-employee-engagement

[149] Snopes. (2020, November 3). *Teacher fills hallway with balloons for heartwarming student activity – fact or fiction?* www.snopes.com/fact-check/teacher-fills-hallway-balloons/

[150] Yunkaporta, T. (2019). *Sand talk: How Indigenous thinking can save the world.* HarperOne.

[151] Baldwin, J. A. (1963). *The Fire Next Time.* Vintage Books.

[152] Gianpiero Petriglieri.

[153] Wiseman, L. (2021). *Impact Players: How to take the lead, play bigger, and multiply your impact.* Harper Business.

[154] Enright, E. (2021, March 27). John Patitucci's sustained intensity. *DownBeat Magazine.* https://downbeat.com/news/detail/john-patituccis-sustained-intensity

[155] Narisetti, R. (Host). (2022, January 26). *Author Talks: The made-up words that make our world* [Interview with John Koenig]. McKinsey & Company. www.mckinsey.com/featured-insights/mckinsey-on-books/author-talks-the-made-up-words-that-make-our-world

[156] Ludwig Josef Johann Wittgenstein was an Austrian philosopher who worked primarily in logic, the philosophy of mathematics, the philosophy of mind and the philosophy of language.

[157] Narisetti, R. (Host). (2022, January 26). *Author Talks: The made-up words that make our world* [Interview with John Koenig]. McKinsey & Company. www.mckinsey.com/featured-insights/mckinsey-on-books/author-talks-the-made-up-words-that-make-our-world

[158] Davis, M. (1990, December). Do not fear mistakes. There are none. *SPIN*, 30.

[159] Pink, D. H. (2014). *To Sell is Human: The surprising truth about moving others.* Canongate Books, Ltd.

[160] Bourke, J., Dillon, B. and Deloitte. (2018). The diversity and inclusion revolution. *Deloitte Review*, 22, 82–85. www2.deloitte.com/content/dam/insights/us/articles/4209_Diversity-and-inclusion-revolution/DI_Diversity-and-inclusion-revolution.pdf

[161] Edmondson, A. C. (1999). Psychological safety and learning behavior in work teams. *Administrative Science Quarterly*, 44(2), 350–383.

[162] Seibert, S. E., Wang, G. and Courtright, S. H. (2011). Antecedents and consequences of psychological and team empowerment in organizations: a meta-analytic review. *Journal of Applied Psychology*, 96(5), 981–1003.

[163] Design thinking was coined in 2003 by IDEO co-founder David Kelley.

[164] Mortensen, D. (2020, July 10). *Stage 1 in the design thinking process: empathise with your users.* Interaction Design Foundation – IxDF. www.interaction-design.org/literature/article/stage-1-in-the-design-thinking-process-empathise-with-your-users

[165] Amabile, T. M., Fisher, C. M. and Pillemer, J. (2014, January 1). IDEO's culture of helping. *Harvard Business Review.* https://hbr.org/2014/01/ideos-culture-of-helping

[166] IDEO (n.d.). The Little Book of IDEO. Ideo.com. https://lboi.ideo.com/

[167] IDEO (n.d.). The Little Book of IDEO. Ideo.com. https://lboi.ideo.com/

[168] IDEO (n.d.). The Little Book of IDEO. Ideo.com. https://lboi.ideo.com/

[169] Vedantam, S. (Host). (2024, August 19). The gift of other people. [Audio podcast episode]. In *The Hidden Brain*. Hidden Brain Media. https://hiddenbrain.org/podcast/you-2-0-the-gift-of-other-people/

[170] Schein, E. A. (2021). *Humble Inquiry: The gentle art of asking instead of telling*. Berrett-Koehler Publishers.

[171] Adam, G. (2023, October 24). Why brainstorming doesn't work. Time.com. https://time.com/6327515/brainstorming-doesnt-work-essay/

[172] Woolley, A. W., Aggarwal, I. and Malone, T. W. (2015). Collective intelligence and group performance. *Current Directions in Psychological Science*, 24(6), 420–424.

[173] Fisher, R. and Ury, W. (2012). *Getting to Yes: Negotiating an agreement without giving in*. Random House Business.

[174] Kurter, H. L. (2020, February 29). 7 powerful characteristics of a truly inspirational leader. Forbes. www.forbes.com/sites/heidilynnekurter/2020/02/29/7-powerful-characteristics-of-a-truly-inspirational-leader

[175] Garton, E. (2017, April 25). How to be an inspiring leader. *Harvard Business Review*. www.bain.com/insights/how-to-be-an-inspiring-leader-hbr/

[176] Horwitch, M. and Callahan, M. W. (2016, June 9). How leaders inspire: cracking the code. Bain.com. www.bain.com/insights/how-leaders-inspire-cracking-the-code/

[177] Horwitch, M. and Callahan, M. W. (2016, June 9). How leaders inspire: cracking the code. Bain.com. www.bain.com/insights/how-leaders-inspire-cracking-the-code/

[178] Sorenson, B. S. (2020, January 30). How employees' strengths make your company stronger. Gallup.com. www.gallup.com/workplace/231605/employees-strengths-company-stronger.aspx

[179] Horwitch, M. and Callahan, M. W. (2016, June 9). *How leaders inspire: cracking the code*. Bain.com. www.bain.com/insights/how-leaders-inspire-cracking-the-code/

[180] Raz, G. (Host). (2024, July 3). The importance of a near miss: Sarah Lewis (Harvard). Apple Podcasts. https://podcasts.apple.com/us/podcast/the-importance-of-a-near-miss-sarah-lewis-harvard/id1460154838?i=1000660990455

[181] Plimpton, G. and Elgrably, J. (Interviewers). (1984). James Baldwin: An interview. *The Paris Review*, 89, 71–106.

[182] Suzanne Leaf-Brock, quoted in Harty, E. (2014, March 13). Celebrating failed attempts to fly. *In the Loop*. Mayo Clinic. https://intheloop.mayoclinic.org/2014/03/13/celebrating-failed-attempts-to-fly/

[183] McRaven, W. R., Admiral (2014, May 16). Find courage to change the world [Commencement speech, University of Texas at Austin].

[184] Streep, M. (2010, May 18). The success fairy [Commencement speech, Barnard College].

[185] Whedon, J. (2013, May 26). Contradictions and tensions [Commencement speech, Wesleyan College].

[186] Drucker, P. F. (1973). *Management: Tasks, responsibilities, practices*. Harper & Row.

[187] https://eu.patagonia.com

[188] Ransom, H. (2024, June 16). Mid-year check-in: 5 questions for leaders to reflect and re-energise. Love Mondays. www.linkedin.com/pulse/mid-year-check-in-5-questions-leaders-reflect-holly-ransom-5lioc/ Holly Ransom is a social entrepreneur who founded Emergent to bring leadership insights to live. You can find out more about Holly here: hollyransom.com.

[189] Oliver, M. (2013). *New and Selected Poems, volume one* (p. 133). Beacon Press.

[190] HuffPost UK. (2020, August 10). *The UK has lost over 97% of natural wildflower meadows – and they're crucial to biodiversity*. HuffPost UK. www.huffingtonpost.co.uk/entry/wildflower-meadows-uk-wildflowers-biodiversity_uk_5f3683bec5b65bbd8c8bfdab

[191] Duffy, C. (Host). (2024, August 19). How to be an adult – and how to raise one. [Audio podcast episode]. In *How to Be a Better Human*. TED Audio Collective. https://play.prx.org/listen?ge=prx_357_7e5540e8-2813-4c70-b08f-250de5e4bb1a&uf=https%3A%2F%2Ffeeds.feedburner.com%2FHowToBeABetterHuman

[192] Duffy, C. (Host). (2024, August 19). How to be an adult – and how to raise one. [Audio podcast episode]. In *How to Be a Better Human*. TED Audio Collective. https://play.prx.org/listen?ge=prx_357_7e5540e8-2813-4c70-b08f-250de5e4bb1a&uf=https%3A%2F%2Ffeeds.feedburner.com%2FHowToBeABetterHuman

[193] Madden, J. (Director). (2015). *The Second-Best Exotic Marigold Hotel* [Film]. Fox Searchlight Pictures.

Bibliography

Adams, G. S., Converse, B. A., Hales, A. H., & Klotz, L. E. (2021). People systematically overlook subtractive changes. *Nature*, 592(7853), 258–261.

Adkins, B. A. (2024, April 9). *Only One in 10 People Possess the Talent to Manage*. Gallup.com. www.gallup.com/workplace/236579/one-people-possess-talent-manage.aspx

Amabile, T. M. Fisher, C. M., & Pillemer, J. (2024, April 9). IDEO's Culture of Helping. *Harvard Business Review*. https://hbr.org/2014/01/ideos-culture-of-helping

Amaechi, J. (2021). *The Promises of Giants*. Nicholas Brealey.

American Psychological Association. (2017). *Stress in America: Coping with Change*. APA

Ancona, D. L., Malone, T. W., Orlikowski, W. J., & Senge, P. M. (2007). In praise of the incomplete leader. *Harvard Business Review*, 85(2), 92–100. https://hbr.org/2007/02/in-praise-of-the-incomplete-leader

Arnsten, A. F. T. (2009). Stress signalling pathways that impair prefrontal cortex structure and function. *Nature Reviews. Neuroscience*, 10(6), 410–422.

Ashley, G., & Reiter-Palmon, R. (2012). Self-awareness and the evolution of leaders: The need for a better measure of self-awareness. *Journal of Behavioral and Applied Management*, 14, 2–17. 10.1037/t29152-000.

Baldwin, J. A. (1962). *The Fire Next Time*. The New Yorker.

Baldwin, J. A. (1963). *The Fire Next Time*. Vintage Books.

Borgschulte, M., Guenzel, M., Liu, C., & Malmendier, U. (2021). *CEO Stress, Aging, and Death*. NBER Working Paper Series. https://doi.org/10.3386/w28550

Bourke, J., Dillon, B., & Deloitte. (2018). The diversity and inclusion revolution: eight powerful truths. *Deloitte Review*, 22, 82–85. www2.

deloitte.com/content/dam/insights/us/articles/4209_Diversity-and-inclusion-revolution/DI_Diversity-and-inclusion-revolution.pdf

Boyce, S., & Robay, D. (Hosts). (2024, March 25). Writing your own story. (No. 1) [Audio podcast episode]. In *The Bright Side*. Hello Sunshine. https://omny.fm/shows/the-bright-side/reese-witherspoon-on-writing-your-own-story

Brooks, A. C. (2024, September 19). Speaking truth without fear. *The Atlantic*. www.theatlantic.com/ideas/archive/2024/09/speaking-truth-without-fear/679901/

Brown, B. (2024, June 26). *A Dare to Lead + BetterUp Partnership*. https://brenebrown.com/articles/2024/06/26/a-dare-to-lead-betterup-partnership/

Brown, B. *Dare to Lead List of Values* (2023, November 14). https://brenebrown.com/resources/dare-to-lead-list-of-values/#

Brown, B. (Host). (2024, April 24). What's coming (and what's here). [Audio podcast episode]. In *Dare to Lead*. https://brenebrown.com/podcast/whats-coming-and-whats-here/#listen

Buckingham, M., & Goodall, A. (2019, May 14). The power of hidden teams. *Harvard Business Review*. https://hbr.org/2019/05/the-power-of-hidden-teams

Chiu, M., & Salerno, H. (2019). *Changing change management*. Gartner. www.gartner.com/en/human-resources/trends/changing-change-management

Chödrön, P. (2001). *The places that scare you: A guide to fearlessness in difficult times*. Shambhala Publications.

Cholteeva, Y. (2022, August 23). *Three in five workers are disengaged and costing UK economy billions, study finds*. www.peoplemanagement.co.uk/article/1796442/three-five-workers-disengaged-costing-uk-economy-billions-study-finds

Collins, J. C., & Porras, J. I. (1996). Building your company's vision. *Harvard Business Review*, 74(5), 65–77. https://hbr.org/1996/09/building-your-companys-vision

Confucius. (2006). *The Essential Analects: Selected passages with traditional commentary*. Hackett Publishing.

Corrigan, K. (Host). (2024, April 1). Being Well in the Modern World. In *Tell Me More with Kelly Corrigan*, Season 7, Episode 1. PBS.org. www.pbs.org/video/the-state-of-well-being-in-america-8elqnq/

Cummings, E. E. (1958). *A poet's advice to students*. In G. J. Firmage (ed.), E.E. Cummings: A Miscellany. Harvard University Press.

David, S. (2016). *Emotional agility: Get unstuck, embrace change, and thrive in work and life*. Avery Publishing Group.

David, S. (2017, February). *The gift and power of emotional courage* [Video]. TED. www.ted.com/talks/susan_david_the_gift_and_power_of_emotional_courage?subtitle=en

Deci, E. L., Koestner, R., & Ryan, R. M. (1999). A meta-analytic review of experiments examining the effects of extrinsic rewards on intrinsic motivation. *Psychological Bulletin*, 125(6), 627–668.

Deci, E. L., & Ryan, R. M. (2008). Self-determination theory: A macro theory of human motivation, development, and health. *Canadian Psychology*, 49(3), 182–185.

Drucker, P. F. (1973). *Management: Tasks, responsibilities, practices*. Harper & Row.

Duckworth, C., & Alexander, M. (2016). *How leaders inspire: Cracking the code*. Bain & Company. https://media.bain.com/Images/BAIN_BRIEF_Inspirational_Leadership.pdf

Duffy, C. (Host). (2024, August 19). How to be an adult – and how to raise one. [Audio podcast episode]. In *How to Be a Better Human*. TED Audio Collective. https://play.prx.org/listen?ge=prx_357_7e5540e8-2813-4c70-b08f-250de5e4bb1a&uf=https%3A%2F%2Ffeeds.feedburner.com%2FHowToBeABetterHuman

Edmondson, A. C. (1999). Psychological safety and learning behavior in work teams. *Administrative Science Quarterly*, 44(2), 350–383.

Edmondson, A. C., & Corsi, E. (2021). *Leading culture change at SEB*. Harvard Business School Case 621-074.

Eger, E. E. (2017). *The Choice: Embrace the possible*. Scribner Book Company.

Elkin, L. (2017, July 11). The Collector: Rebecca Solnit on Textual Pleasure, Punk, and More. *The Daily Beast*. www.thedailybeast.com/the-collector-rebecca-solnit-on-textual-pleasure-punk-and-more

Ellenhorn, R. (2022). *Purple Crayons: The art of drawing a life.* HarperCollins.

Ellerman, B. (2012). *The end of leadership.* Harper Business.

Enright, E. (2021, March 27). John Patitucci's sustained intensity. *DownBeat Magazine.* https://downbeat.com/news/detail/john-patituccis-sustained-intensity

Eurich, T. (2023, April 6). What self-awareness really is (and how to cultivate it). *Harvard Business Review.* https://hbr.org/2018/01/what-self-awareness-really-is-and-how-to-cultivate-it

Fisher, J., & Silverglate, P. H. (2022, June 22). The C-suite's role in well-being. *Deloitte Insights.* www2.deloitte.com/us/en/insights/topics/leadership/employee-wellness-in-the-corporate-workplace.html

Fisher, R., & Ury, W. (2012). *Getting to Yes: Negotiating an agreement without giving in.* Random House Business.

Gardner, W. L., Avolio, B. J., Luthans, F., May, D. R., & Walumbwa, F. (2005). 'Can you see the real me?' A self-based model of authentic leader and follower development. *The Leadership Quarterly,* 16(3), 343–372.

Gartner.com (n. d.). *Organizational change management.* www.gartner.com/en/human-resources/insights/organizational-change-management#:~:text=Change%20is%20the%20new%20constant,34%25%20are%20a%20clear%20success

Garton, E. (2017, April 25). How to be an inspiring leader. *Harvard Business Review.* www.bain.com/insights/how-to-be-an-inspiring-leader-hbr/

Gervais, M. (Host). (2019, December 3). Inner mastery, outer impact: The essence of a great leader. (No. 441) [Audio podcast episode]. In *Finding Mastery.* https://findingmastery.com/podcasts/hitendra-wadhwa/

Gibbs, N. (2023, May 31). 'At Harvard, Tom Hanks offered an increasingly rare moment of grace'. *Washington Post.* www.washingtonpost.com/opinions/2023/05/31/tom-hanks-commencement-harvard/

Gilbert, E. (2013, November 6). The 'Stubborn Gladness' of Elizabeth Gilbert's favourite poet. *The Atlantic.* www.theatlantic.com/entertainment/archive/2013/11/the-stubborn-gladness-of-elizabeth-gilberts-favorite-poet/281158/

Gilbert, E. (2015). *Big magic: Creative living beyond fear.* Riverhead Books.

Godin, S. (2023). *The Song of Significance*. Random House.

Goleman, D. (1998). *Working with Emotional Intelligence*. Bantam Books.

Goleman, D. (2015, April 15). How emotional intelligence became a key leadership skill. *Harvard Business Review*. https://hbr.org/2015/04/how-emotional-intelligence-became-a-key-leadership-skill

Grant, A. (2023, October 24). Why Brainstorming Doesn't Work. *Time*. https://time.com/6327515/brainstorming-doesnt-work-essay/

Grant, A. (2023). *Hidden Potential: The science of achieving greater things*. WH Allen.

Grant, A. (Host). (2019, December 3). The internet doesn't need your opinion on everything with Rebecca Solnit. (No. 381) [Audio podcast episode]. In *WorkLife*. TED Audio Collective. https://podcasts.apple.com/ca/podcast/the-internet-doesnt-need-your-opinion-on-everything/id1346314086?i=1000657705504

Grant, A. (Host). (2024, June 25). How novelist Gabrielle Zevin learned to enjoy failure. [Audio podcast episode]. In *Worklife*. TED Audio Collective. https://podcasts.apple.com/us/podcast/worklife-with-adam-grant/id1346314086

Grant, S. (2024, July 10). Video: Thasunda Brown Duckett, President & CEO, TIAA – 'I Rent My Title, I Own My Character'. *FIT for Life*. www.sherylgrant.com/post/video-thasunda-brown-duckett-president-ceo-tiaa-i-rent-my-title-i-own-my-character#:~:text=Thasunda%20explained%20that%20titles%20are%20rented%20and%20temporary.,can%20claim%20it%20and%20proclaim%20it.%20It%E2%80%99s%20yours.%22

Guillen, L., & Florent-Treacy, E., Emotional Intelligence and Leadership Effectiveness: The Mediating Influence of Collaborative Behaviors (February 11, 2011). *INSEAD* Working Paper No. 2011/23/IGLC. http://dx.doi.org/10.2139/ssrn.1759991

Hanks, T. (2023, May 26). Tom Hanks delivers the Commencement Address. *Harvard Commencement*. YouTube. https://youtu.be/dkPo5nfEk1w

Harty, E. (2014, March 13). *Celebrating failed attempts to fly*. In the Loop. Mayo Clinic. https://intheloop.mayoclinic.org/2014/03/13/celebrating-failed-attempts-to-fly/

Hochschild, A. R. (1983). *The managed heart: Commercialization of human feeling*. University of California Press.

Hogan, R., & Warrenfeltz, R. (2003). Educating the modern manager. *Academy of Management Learning & Education*, 2(1), 74–84.

Horwitch, M. and Callahan, M. W. (2016, June 9). *How Leaders Inspire: Cracking the code*. Bain.com. www.bain.com/insights/how-leaders-inspire-cracking-the-code/

HuffPost UK. (2020, August 10). The UK has lost over 97% of natural wildflower meadows – and they're crucial to biodiversity. *HuffPost UK*. www.huffingtonpost.co.uk/entry/wildflower-meadows-uk-wildflowers-biodiversity_uk_5f3683bec5b65bbd8c8bfdab

Ingram, P. and Choi, Y. (2022, November 1). What does your company really stand for? *Harvard Business Review*. https://hbr.org/2022/11/what-does-your-company-really-stand-for

Johnson, C. (1955). *Harold and the Purple Crayon*. HarperCollins Children's Books.

Jones, L. (2024, September 20). LinkedIn. Linkedin.com. www.linkedin.com/posts/luvvie_the-intersection-of-our-personal-lives-and-activity-7236472893990125568-Annt/

Kahneman, D. (n.d.). Quote by Daniel Kahneman: 'Nothing in life is as important as you think it is, while you are thinking about it.' *BrainyQuote*. Retrieved October 20, 2024, from www.brainyquote.com/quotes/daniel_kahneman_567029

Karsh, Y. (n.d.). Character, like a photograph, develops in darkness [Quote]. *BrainyQuote*. www.brainyquote.com/quotes/yousuf_karsh_163621

Keys, A. (2020). *More Myself*. Flatiron Books.

Keys, A., & Jay-Z. (2009). *Empire State of Mind*. On The Blueprint 3. Roc Nation.

Kleiner, K. (2011, September). Lunchtime leniency: Judges' rulings are harsher when they are hungrier. *Scientific American*. www.scientificamerican.com/article/lunchtime-leniency/#:~:text=Researchers%20at%20Ben%20Gurion%20University%20in%20Israel%20and

Knowles, B. (2023, November 6). CFDA Fashion Awards [Keynote].

Kroll, M. M. (2022, May 2). Prolonged social isolation and loneliness are equivalent to smoking 15 cigarettes a day. *Extension*. https://extension.

unh.edu/blog/2022/05/prolonged-social-isolation-loneliness-are-equivalent-smoking-15-cigarettes-day#:~:text=Loneliness%20is%20the%20feeling%20of%20being%20alone%2C%20regardless

Kurter, H. L. (2020, February 29). 7 powerful characteristics of a truly inspirational leader. *Forbes*. www.forbes.com/sites/heidilynnekurter/2020/02/29/7-powerful-characteristics-of-a-truly-inspirational-leader

Kyte, L. (2018, August 14). Why Is Rebecca Solnit Hopeful? *Lion's Roar*. www.lionsroar.com/the-truth-teller/

Lamott, A. (1994). *Bird by Bird: Instructions on writing and life*. Canongate Books Ltd.

Lamott, A. (2003, May 8). UC Berkeley Commencement [Keynote].

Larsen, K. (1974). Conformity in the Asch experiment. *Journal of Social Psychology*, 94(2), 303–304.

le Gentil, H. (2021, October 25). *Leaders, Stop Trying to Be Heroes*. https://hbr.org/2021/10/leaders-stop-trying-to-be-heroes

Leary, K., & Wilkinson, R. (2020). *Leading with intentionality: The 4P framework for strategic leadership* (RWP20-029). Harvard Kennedy School Faculty Research Working Paper Series. https://dash.harvard.edu/handle/1/37371395?show=full

Lewis, S. E. (2014, March 1). Embrace a near win [Conference presentation]. *TED*. www.ted.com/talks/sarah_lewis_embrace_the_near_win?subtitle=en

Lewis, S. E. (Guest), & Raz, G. (Host). (2022, July 3). The Importance of a Near Miss. [Audio podcast episode]. In *Wisdom from the Top*. iHeart. www.iheart.com/podcast/139-wisdom-from-the-top-30131202/episode/the-importance-of-a-near-miss-sarah-99361945/

Liberman, N., & Förster, J. (2009). The effect of psychological distance on perceptual focus. *Journal of Experimental Social Psychology*, 45(2), 485–489. https://doi.org/10.1016/j.jesp.2008.12.002

Lipa, D. (Host). (2023, November 17). Tim Cook: What it takes to run Apple. (No. 41) [Audio podcast episode]. In *Dua Lipa at Your Service*. BBC Sounds. www.bbc.co.uk/programmes/p0cgz10v/episodes/downloads

Ma, Y. (n.d.). *A composition is always more than the sum of its parts*. Retrieved from www.allgreatquotes.com/quote-468143/

Madden, J. (Director). (2015). *The Second-Best Exotic Marigold Hotel* [Film]. Fox Searchlight Pictures.

Maxwell, J. C. (1997). *Becoming a person of influence: How to positively impact the lives of others*. Thomas Nelson.

McKinsey (2022, August 17). *What Is Leadership? A definition and way forward*. www.mckinsey.com/featured-insights/mckinsey-explainers/what-is-leadership

McRaven, W. R., Admiral (2014, May 16). *Find courage to change the world* [Commencement speech, University of Texas at Austin].

Mead, M. (n.d.). *Never doubt that a small group of thoughtful, committed citizens can change the world; indeed, it's the only thing that ever has*. Retrieved from www.quoteinvestigator.com

Mehta, R., & Zhu, M. (2016). Creating when you have less: The impact of resource scarcity on product use creativity. *Journal of Consumer Research*, 42(5), 767–782. https://doi.org/10.1093/jcr/ucv051

Microsoft (2022, September 22). Hybrid work is just work: Are we doing it wrong? *Worktrend* Index. www.microsoft.com/en-us/worklab/work-trend-index/hybrid-work-is-just-work

Moreau, C. P., & Dahl, D. W. (2005). Designing the solution: The impact of constraints on consumers' creativity. *Journal of Consumer Research*, 32(1), 13–22. https://doi.org/10.1086/429597

Mortensen, D. (2020, July 10). Stage 1 in the Design Thinking Process: Empathise with Your Users. Interaction Design Foundation – IxDF. www.interaction-design.org/literature/article/stage-1-in-the-design-thinking-process-empathise-with-your-users

Mullainathan, S., & Shafir, E. (2013). *Scarcity: Why having too little means so much*. Times Books.

Narisetti, R. (Host). (2022, January 26). Author Talks: The made-up words that make our world [Interview with John Koenig]. McKinsey & Company. www.mckinsey.com/featured-insights/mckinsey-on-books/author-talks-the-made-up-words-that-make-our-world

Neal, J. (2006). *Edgewalkers: People and organizations that take risks, build bridges, and break new ground*. Praeger.

Noah, T. (2016). *Born a Crime: Stories from a South African childhood*. Doubleday Canada.

Okri, B. (1996). *Birds of Heaven*. Phoenix House.

Oliver, M. (2013). *New and selected poems*, Volume One. Beacon Press.

Olympics.com (2021, August 30). Brad Snyder talks historic first triathlon gold for USA and that moment in Afghanistan. https://olympics.com/en/news/brad-snyder-talks-historic-first-triathlon-gold-for-usa-and-that-moment-in-afgha

Palmer, P. (2015). *Let Your Life Speak: Listening for the voice of vocation*. Jossey Bass.

Pandya, H. (2023, March 29). The best joke in Mae Martin's Netflix comedy special 'SAP.' Vulture. www.vulture.com/article/mae-martin-sap-comedy-special-snow-globes.html

Parker, P. (2018). *The art of gathering: How we meet and why it matters*. Riverhead Books.

Pennebaker, J. W. (1997). *Opening Up: The healing power of expressing emotions*. Guilford Press.

Pennebaker, J. W. (2011). *The Secret Life of Pronouns: What our words say about us*. Bloomsbury Press.

Pennebaker, J. W., & Beall, S. K. (1986). Confronting a traumatic event: Toward an understanding of inhibition and disease. *Journal of Abnormal Psychology*, 95(3), 274–281.

Pennebaker, J. W., Kiecolt-Glaser, J. K., & Glaser, R. (1988). Disclosure of traumas and immune function: Health implications for psychotherapy. *Journal of Consulting and Clinical Psychology*, 56(2), 239–245.

Peppernell, C. (2018). *Pillow Thoughts II: Healing the heart*. Andrews McMeel Publishing.

Peppernell, C. (n.d.). You can't skip chapters; that's not how life works. *Goodreads*. Retrieved October 20, 2024, from www.goodreads.com/quotes/11641432-you-can-t-skip-chapters-that-s-not-how-life-works-you

Petriglieri, G. (2023, April 24). Driving organizational change without abandoning tradition. *Harvard Business Review*. https://hbr.org/2023/04/driving-organizational-change-without-abandoning-tradition

Pink, D. H. (2014). *To Sell is Human: The surprising truth about moving others*. Canongate Books, Ltd.

Plimpton, G., & Elgrably, J. (Interviewers). (1984). James Baldwin: An interview. *The Paris Review*, 89, 71–106.

Porcelli, A. J., & Delgado, M. R. (2009). Acute stress modulates risk taking in financial decision making. *Psychological Science*, 20(3), 278–283.

Pradhan, K. (2019, April 2). In the dense mangrove forests straddling the India-Bangladesh border, tigers and a mythical goddess unite Hindus and Muslims. *BBC*. www.bbc.com/travel/article/20190329-the-people-who-live-with-tigers#:~:text=Royal%20Bengal%20tigers%20are%20known%20for%20their%20intelligence,a%20mask%20on%20the%20-0back%20of%20their%20head

Qin, S., Hermans, E. J., van Marle, H. J., Luo, J., & Fernández, G. (2009). Acute psychological stress reduces working memory-related activity in the dorsolateral prefrontal cortex. *Biological Psychiatry*, 66(1), 25–32.

Rafaeli-Mor, E., Gotlib, I. H., & Revelle, W. (1999). The meaning and measurement of self-complexity. *Personality and Individual Differences*, 27(2), 341–356.

Ransom, H. (2024, June 16). Mid-year check-in: 5 questions for leaders to reflect and re-energise. *Love Mondays*. www.linkedin.com/pulse/mid-year-check-in-5-questions-leaders-reflect-holly-ransom-5lioc/

Ripley, A. (2018, June 27). Complicating the narratives. *Solutions Journalism*. https://thewholestory.solutionsjournalism.org/complicating-the-narratives-b91ea06ddf63

Ripley, A. (2021). *High Conflict: Why we get trapped and how we get out.* Simon and Schuster.

Roosevelt, T. (1905, October 25). *People don't care how much you know until they know how much you care.* Speech delivered in Memphis, Tennessee. Retrieved from Good News Network.

Ryan, R. M., & Deci, E. L. (2000). Self-determination theory and the facilitation of intrinsic motivation, social development, and well-being. *American Psychologist*, 55(1), 68–78.

Ryff, C. D., & Singer, B. (1998). The contours of positive human health. *Psychological Inquiry*, 9(1), 1–28.

Schein, E. A. (2021). *Humble Inquiry: The gentle art of asking instead of telling.* Berrett-Koehler Publishers.

Schwabe, L., & Wolf, O. T. (2009). Stress prompts habit behavior in humans. *Journal of Neuroscience*, 29(22), 7191–7198.

Seibert, S. E., Wang, G., & Courtright, S. H. (2011). Antecedents and consequences of psychological and team empowerment in organizations: a meta-analytic review. *Journal of Applied Psychology*, 96(5), 981–1003.

Senge, P. M. (1990). *The Fifth Discipline: The art and practice of the learning organization*. Doubleday/Currency.

Shankar, M. (Host). (2024, August 19). Olympian Gabby Thomas on choosing happiness. (No. 124) [Audio podcast episode]. In *A Slight Change of Plans*. Pushkin. https://omny.fm/shows/a-slight-change-of-plans/olympian-gabby-thomas-on-choosing-happiness

Shankar, M. (Host). (2024, July 1). *What Comes After Gold* with Olympian Missy Franklin. (No. 75) [Audio podcast episode]. In *A Slight Change of Plans*. Pushkin. www.pushkin.fm/podcasts/a-slight-change-of-plans/what-comes-after-gold-with-olympian-missy-franklin

Shankar, M. (Host). (2024, July 8). Surrender is not in my DNA. [Audio podcast episode]. In *A Slight Change of Plans*. Pushkin. www.youtube.com/watch?v=T-fAjTlijIM

Sherman, J. R. (1982). *Rejection*. Pathway Books.

Silvia, P. J., & O'Brien, M. E. (2004). Self-awareness and constructive functioning: Revisiting 'the human dilemma'. *Journal of Personality*, 72(1), 29–52.

Sinha, R. (2008). Chronic stress, drug use, and vulnerability to addiction. *Annals of the New York Academy of Sciences*, 1141(1), 105–130.

Snopes. (2020, November 3). Teacher fills hallway with balloons for heartwarming student activity – Fact or Fiction? *Snopes*. www.snopes.com/fact-check/teacher-fills-hallway-balloons/

Solnit, R. (2013). *The Faraway Nearby*. Granta Books.

Sorenson, B. S. (2020, January 30). How employees' strengths make your company stronger. Gallup.com. www.gallup.com/workplace/231605/employees-strengths-company-stronger.aspx

Spain, S.M., & Kim, J. (2017). Leadership, work careers, and self-concept clarity. In J. Lodi-Smith & K. DeMarree (eds), *Self-Concept Clarity*. Springer. https://doi.org/10.1007/978-3-319-71547-6_9

Sparks, N. (Writer), & Katz, R. (Director). (2016). *The Choice* [Film script]. Lionsgate.

SPIN Magazine. (1990, December). Do not fear mistakes. There are none. *SPIN*, 30.

Stanislavski, C. (2021). *Method, Quotes & Facts. Biography*. www.biography.com/actors/constantin-stanislavski

Stevenson, B. (2014). *Just Mercy: A story of justice and redemption*. Spiegel & Grau.

Streep, M. (2010, May 18). *The success fairy* [Commencement speech, Barnard College].

Sutton, A., Williams, H. M., & Allinson, C. W. (2015). A longitudinal, mixed method evaluation of self-awareness training in the workplace. *European Journal of Training and Development*, 39(7), 610–627.

Tulshyan, R., & Burey, J. A. (2022, August 4). *Stop Telling Women They Have Imposter Syndrome*. https://hbr.org/2021/02/stop-telling-women-they-have-imposter-syndrome

Vedantam, S. (Host). (2024, August 19). The gift of other people. [Audio podcast episode]. In *The Hidden Brain*. Hidden Brain Media. https://hiddenbrain.org/podcast/you-2-0-the-gift-of-other-people/

Wadhwa, H. (2020, April 7). *Three shifts in leadership mastery*. Columbia Business School. https://business.columbia.edu/leadership/ideas-work/three-shifts-leadership-mastery

Wadhwa, V. (2009, July 8). *The anatomy of an entrepreneur*. Kauffman Foundation. Duke University.

Walsch, N. D. (n.d.). *Life begins at the edge of your comfort zone* [Quote]. In Conversations with God.

Ward, T. B., Patterson, M. J., & Sifonis, C. M. (2004). Conceptual combination and the creation of new ideas: Constraint-based and pre-inventive processes in creative cognition. *Journal of Experimental Psychology: Learning, Memory, and Cognition*, 30(5), 1023–1032. https://doi.org/10.1037/0278-7393.30.5.1023

Weinstein, N., Brown, K. W., & Ryan, R. M. (2009). A multi-method examination of the effects of mindfulness on stress attribution, coping, and emotional well-being. *Journal of Research in Personality*, 43(3), 374–385.

Weir, K. (2017, March 2). The Philosopher Queen: Rebecca Solnit. *Elle*. www.elle.com/culture/books/a42862/the-philosopher-queen-rebecca-solnit/

Whedon, J. (2013, May 26). *Contradictions and tensions* [Commencement speech, Wesleyan College].

Winfrey, O. (2024, August 21). Oprah Winfrey's speech at the Democratic National Convention [Transcript]. *Democratic National Convention*. www.rev.com/blogs/transcripts/oprah-winfrey-democratic-national-convention-2024

Wiseman, L. (2021). *Impact Players: How to take the lead, play bigger, and multiply your impact*. Harper Business.

Woolley, A. W., Aggarwal, I., & Malone, T. W. (2015). Collective intelligence and group performance. *Current Directions in Psychological Science*, 24(6), 420–424.

Wrzesniewski, A. (2022, July 26). To be happier at work, think flexibly about your job – and yourself. *Yale Insights*. https://insights.som.yale.edu/insights/to-be-happier-at-work-think-flexibly-about-your-job-and-yourself

Wrzesniewski, A., McCauley, C., Rozin, P., & Schwartz, B. (1997). Jobs, careers, and callings: People's relations to their work. *Journal of Research in Personality*, 31(1), 21–33.

Yang, L., Holtz, D., Jaffe, S., et al. (2022). The effects of remote work on collaboration among information workers. *Nature Human Behaviour*, 6, 43–54. https://doi.org/10.1038/s41562-021-01196-4.

Your Thought Partner. (2019, October 23). 10 inspiring quotes from successful CEOs to help you win at employee engagement. *Your Thought Partner*. www.yourthoughtpartner.com/blog/10-inspiring-quotes-from-successful-ceos-to-help-you-win-at-employee-engagement

Yunkaporta, T. (2019). *Sand talk: How Indigenous thinking can save the world*. HarperOne.

Acknowledgements

Writing this book truly took a village, and what a wonderful, vibrant village it is.

To Alison Jones and Practical Inspiration Publishing: Thank you for believing in me when my ideas were just chaotic clouds. To Kelly Winter and Rachel Carter: Thank you for the care you took in copy editing, proofreading and generating my final manuscript. To Mary McCormick: Thank you for creating a beautiful cover for the book. To Ash Lamb: Your visuals brought clarity to my thoughts and pushed me to simplify (which is no easy feat). To Stephanie Belton: Thank you for managing to take incredible pictures despite my awkwardness.

To my teachers, professors, and coaches: You saw potential in me before I did and gave me space to learn at my own (sometimes glacial) pace. To Patti: Thank you for showing me the power of a 'through line' in action. To Sarah, Robin, and Remi: Your presence and drive inspire favourite versions of us all. To Kevin: Thank you for reminding us that everything starts with a purpose.

To my students: Thank you for trusting a fledgling teacher, sharing your dreams, and diving headfirst into learning. You taught me more than I could have imagined.

To my teammates: Thanks for tolerating my wild experiments, and smiling through it all. You've been champions of authenticity and growth. Daniela: You've pushed and supported me through self-doubt. Lucie: Your grounded perspective kept me real. Mike: You were the first to show me what leadership could look like. Ed L.: See, I wrote it down! Ed M.: You showed me how much we can learn from a climb – discomfort really is the price of growth. Ross: You are optimism incarnate. Mark: Chaos is normal; you're right, again. Caroline: You took a chance on me years ago, and I'm forever grateful.

To my friends, who bring love, laughter, and food to the table – literally and metaphorically – you light up the world. Special shout-outs to Jess, my oldest friend, and Reynald, Sylvie, Laurent, Kiki, and Christophe – you're priceless. Musi: Your wisdom helps me navigate leadership. Emily: You gave me your time which is priceless. Ruth: Your example makes us all better. Ajay and Anne: You embody connection at its best. Cris and Kyle: Thanks for stepping in when needed. Maiki: Your courage knows no bounds. Reemster and Fabs: Still divine, two decades later. Arun and Poojha:

You proved the power of community. Rofo: Our teaching-turned-learning journey is a gift I treasure. Geraud and Flo: Thank you for being my constants.

To my family: Annick and Alain, Clement and Severine, Ilan, Melvil, Ruben: thank you for inspiring me and cheering me on. Juju: You remind me of the power of storytelling. Anand: Your ability to find humour in everything makes you one of a kind. To the next generation – you know who you are – keep blazing new trails.

To Dad: You've showed me how to hope even when it was hard to find. To DM: I pick rabbit. Thank you for being willing to read, re-read, edit and discuss what must have felt like endless drafts. Ella, my amazing daughter: Thanks for putting up with my quirks. Don't ever hide your light. And last but never least, to Arnaud, my "best favourite": Thirty years in, and you still help me stretch, laugh, and live life to the fullest. Here's to our evolving 'through line.'

This book is a reflection of all of you. Thank you for being my village.

Index

A
acceptance 31–35
adaptability 68–69
Amaechi, John 81
Amazon 128
American haiku 57
Aristotle 46
Asch Conformity Experiment 121
attention (CARE cycle) 123, 125, 134, 140–141, 146
authenticity 39, 40–41, 46
autonomy 52, 100
awareness 17
  see also self-awareness

B
Bain Consulting 146
balanced participation 140
Baldwin, James 33, 149
Barry, Dave 140
beginner's mind 55, 56, 105–107
BetterUp's Insights Report 113–114
boldness, in leadership 98–99
brains, limited capacity of 73–74
Brooks, Arthur 165 n43
Brown, Brené 80
Brubaker, Richard 150
burnout 8

C
caffè sospeso 23
Callahan, M. 146
care, a line to
  caring innovation 130–132
  company means connection 115–118
  deep care 120–127, *121*
  design thinking 132–135
  a duty to care 112–115
  the empty chair 127–130
  leadership is reaching out 136–138
  not every caring encounter is a success 135–136
  in a nutshell 111
  outside job 118–120
  your turn 138–142
CARE cycle 123–127, *123*, 138, 139–142, 146, 147, *147*
caring
  deep care 120–127, *121*
  a duty 112–115
  ground rules for (IDEO) 133–134
  innovation 130–132
  not every encounter is a success 135–136
  to notice 23–27
cento 15, 162 n17
centredness, and inspiration 146–147
change 18, 73
  generative conversations 103–105
  a pain 78–79

and personal experience 93
and practice 93
change, a line to
  blank sheet of paper 105–107, 108, 109
  change leadership 90–95
  courage to keep revising 100–103
  ease or discomfort 96–100
  free solo 95–96
  in a nutshell 85–86
  sick and tired 86–88
  surrender and reset 88–90
  your turn 107–109
character 21–22
chitta 144
Choctaw people, and Irish people 114–115
Chödrön, Pema 63
Chouinard, Yvon 153
Clange, Pauline Rose 161 n4
clarification 74
Clark, Petula 10–11, 162 n12
Close, Chuck 20
Coca-Cola 106
cognitive clarity 68–69
collaboration, not comparison 134
Collins, Jim 31
colour 29–31
Colvin, Rick 150
comfort zone 26
commencement speeches 151–152
company, and connection 115–118
compassion practice 63–64
competence 52, 100
comprehension 51–52, 166 n62
Confucius 20–21
connection 52, 100, 113–115
  CARE cycle 123, 124–125, 134, 139–140, 146
  and company 115–118

consistency 47–48
  emotional 119–120
Cook, Tim 71
core values 55, 56
COVID-19 4, 64, 97, 105, 115–116
creativity 52–53, 56–59, 166 n63
crossing lines
  caring to notice 23–27
  hope in uncertainty 27–30
  in a nutshell 17
  see it to name it 19–20
  true colours 29–31
  unearthing a truth 31–35
  use it 21–23
  your turn 35
curiosity, use of term 172 n130

D

data
  emotions as 89–90
  information as 88
David, Susan 26
Davis, Miles 104, 127
Deci, Edward 52, 54–55
decision-making 64–67
deep care 120–127, *121*
Deloitte 117
Deloitte University Leadership Centre for Inclusion 129
design thinking 132–135
discomfort 13, 14, 21, 26–27, 34
  or ease 96–100
disconnection 113–115
Disneyland 106
disruption, navigating together 76
dissolution 101–103
dopamine 65
Drucker, Peter 153
Duckett, Thasunda 22
Dyson, Frank Watson 69

E

ease, or discomfort 96–100
Economist Intelligence Unit 146
Edmonson, Amy C. 129
emotional agility 68
emotional consistency 119–120
emotions, as data 89–90
empathy 97
empty chair 127–130
Epley, Nicholas 136, 137–139
Eurich, Tasha 46, 119
exercises (your turn)
  care, a line to 138–142
  change, a line to 107–109
  crossing lines 35
  inspire, a line to 155–156
  through line 58–59
  understand, a line to 79–84
expansion (CARE cycle) 123, 127, 135, 142, 146
expectations, clarity in 139
experience 51, 53–56, 159
external self-awareness 118–120
  see also self-awareness

F

fear, role of 99–100
feedback 119
flat packing 41–43
fMRI 74
food 77–79
Fortune 100: Best Companies to Work For 131
Frankl, Viktor 51–52, 166 n62
Franklin, Missy 4
free soloing 95–96
future: what's next? 158–159

G

Gallup 44, 147
Gartner survey 76
Gestalt Therapy 127
Gilbert, Elizabeth 69
Godin, Seth 23
Goethe 30
'golden thread' 31
Google 129
Great Resignation 117

H

hacking 41–43
Hanks, Tom 9–10
Harold and the Purple Crayon (Johnson) 106–107
Harvard Business Review 53
Harvard Business School 97, 129
Hemingway, Ernest 56
hidden in plain sight 18–19
history, as your story 18–19
Hofer, Hélène Biandudi 141
Honnold, Alex 95–96
hope, in uncertainty 27–30
Hoppers 78–79
Horwitch, M. 146
Hugander, Per 104

I

identity
  and clarification 74
  covering 129
IDEO 132–135, 139
  ground rules 133–134
  The Little Book of IDEO 134, 139
if you don't, who will? 9–10, 24, 50, 145–148
impostor syndrome 161 n4
Ines, Suzanne 161 n4
information, as data 88
Ingram, Paul 80
innovation 55, 166 n63
inspiration
  CARE cycle for 147
  and centredness 146–147

to change the world 153–155
through line to 151–153
what it is 144–145
words of 160
inspire, a line to
  if you don't, who will? 145–148
  inspiration to change the world 153–155
  mastery over success 149–150
  in a nutshell 143
  from through line to inspiration 151–153
  training and development 148–149
  what is inspiration? 144–145
  your turn 155–156
internal goal system 80
internal self-awareness 118
  see also self-awareness
intrapersonal skills 47
intrinsic motivation 54–55, 56
introspection 49–50, 67
Irish people, and Choctaw people 114–115

J
jazz ensembles 124–125, 126
job, reasons for doing 93

K
Kahneman, Daniel 65, 167 n76
Kauffman Foundation 56
Keys, Alicia 13, 108–109
Klotz, Anthony 117
Koenig, John 126

L
Lacks, Henriette 87
Lamott, Anne 19–20
leadership 37
  boldness and vulnerability in 98–99

change and 90–95
collaborative effort 25
disruptive 55
influencing 24
is reaching out 136–138
structures and categories 43–45
leadership impact 15, 162 n16
learning, made by many pieces 15
Lennon, John 109
Lewis, Sarah 149, 163 n25
life experiences 37
limitation 56–59
Lincoln, Abraham 79
lived experience 151
lockdown 8, 18, 62–63
  see also COVID-19
loneliness 116

M
Ma, Yo-Yo 45
majority groups 121
Martin, Mac 30
mastery
  inner 76–77
  journey towards 23, 163 n25
  over success 149–150
mattering 52, 166 n62
Maxwell, James Clerk 65
Maxwell, John C. 163 n27
Mayo, Elton 97
Mayo Medical Ventures 150
McDonald's 106
Mead, Margaret 111
meaning 51–52, 116, 166 n62, 172 n138
metabolic drag 8
mirror neurons 40
moral courage 34, 165 n43
motivation 52
  intrinsic 54–55, 56

N

Nadella, Satya 97
National Academy of Sciences 73–74
National Bureau of Economic Research 44
National Institute of Ageing 116
nature 71
Nelson, Admiral 30–31
neuroscience 40
  of stress 65–67
Noah, Trevor 93
nuance 54

O

Okri, Ben 50
outer impact, by inner mastery 77–79

P

pandemic *see* COVID-19
paradox 3, 10, 29, 31
Parker, Priya 115
past, the, accepting 31–35
Patagonia 153–155
Patitucci, John 124–124
Pennebaker, James 70–71, 72
Peppernell, Courtney 50
perfectionism 93
personal experience 93
perspective 71, 103–105
Porras, Jerry 31
possibility 20
potential 21
practice, and change 93
Prince 106
prioritizing, and clarification 74
psychological safety 129
purpose 56, 74, 139, 166 n62
  identifying 73
  on a page (Roberts) 82–84
  powering performance 97
purposing (Roberts) 82–84

Q

Queasy Eagle 150
questions
  quality of 21
  to uncover attributes 155–156
  understand, a line to 63
  'what' questions 35, 68
quick fixes 41–43
quilt metaphor 20–21

R

reach in 3, *61*
  see also understand, a line to
reach out 3, *111*
  see also care, a line to
red thread 30–31
refraction (CARE cycle) 123, 125–126, 134–135, 141–142, 146
Reith, John 69
relationships 112–113
replicability 72
reset 3, *85*
  prominent in parenthood 89
  and self-awareness 88
  surrender as 88–90
  see also change, a line to
resilience 47, 69, 73, 74, 75, 100
respect 112
restlessness 138
revising 100–103
rewards, intrinsic 99–100
rewilding 157–158
Ripley, Amanda 141
Roberts, Kevin 82–84
Rochester Fruit & Vegetable Company 130
Roethlisberger, Fritz 97
Roosevelt, Teddy 120
Ryan, Richard 52, 54–55

S

sandbars 51
scarcity, role of 99–100
Schein, Edgar 139–140
Sears 128
self-awareness 46–47, 118–120, 144, 165 n53
  and adaptability 68–69
  and cognitive clarity 68–69
  and emotional agility 68
  evacuate your lines 73–75
  and reset 88
  and uncertain environments 68
self-complexity 74
self-concept 46–47, 48, 166 n54
self-determination 128–129
self-discipline 144
self-esteem 144–145
Senge, Peter Michael 25
sensemaking 52
Sevestre, Heidi 96
sisu 98
six-word memoir 57–59
Smith, Larry 57–58
SMITH magazine 57
Snyder, Brad 101–103
social cognition 136
Solnit, Rebecca 27–29
soul, the 34–35, 81
Stanislavsky, Konstantin 38–40
Stanislavsky System 39–40
static, tuning out 69–73
Stockholm's Enskilda Bank (SEB) 103–105, 124
storytelling 154
  complicate the narrative 53–56
  integrate the stories 50–53
  with intent 48–50
  power of 5–6
strengths-based approach 147–148

stress 43–44, 65–67
surrender, as reset 88–90
Swift, Taylor 125

T

Taylor, Frederik 97
Theseus 30
third-culture kid 12, 162 n13
Thomas, Gabby 86
through line
  all the world's a stage 38–41
  avoid flat packing 41–43
  be consistent 47–48
  complicate the narrative 53–56
  finding 4–7
  formed over time 51
  integrate the stories 50–53
  know yourself 46–47
  leadership structures and categories 43–45
  leads to centredness 147
  in a nutshell 37–38
  one person, one story, six words 56–58
  a representation 159
  storytelling with intent 48–50
  understanding 145
  what it is 2
  your turn 58–59
  to lose your way is to learn the way 10–15
training and development 148–149
trust 47, 48, 135, 139, 166 n56
truth line 33–34
Tuskegee Syphilis Study 87

U

uncertainty
  in decision-making 64–67
  hope in 27–30
  and self-awareness 68
  in the system 7–8

understand, a line to
  daring to feel 62–64
  decision-making uncertainty 64–67
  evacuate your lines 73–75
  inner mastery 76–77
  an inside job 67–69
  in a nutshell 61–62
  outer impact 77–79
  questions to ask 63
  tune out static 69–73
  your turn 79–84
understanding, complexity for 54
Useem, Ruth 162 n13
user-centric approach 132–135

V
value cards (Ingram) 80
values 89–90
  and internal goal system 80
values-based living 55
VIA Character Strengths survey 155

Volta, Alessandro 155
vulnerability, in leadership 98–99

W
Wadwha, Hitendra 76–77, 78–79
Webb, Amy 7
Wegman, John 130
Wegman, Walter 130
Wegmans Food Markets 130–132
Weick, Karl 52
Wiseman, Liz 124
Wittgenstein, Ludwig 126, 173 n153
wonder, use of term 172 n130
Woolley, Anita 140
work, as a calling 100
Workplace Intelligence 117
writing, expressive 70–73
Wrzesniewski, Amy 51

Z
Zen Buddhism 55

A quick word from Practical Inspiration Publishing...

We hope you found this book both practical and inspiring – that's what we aim for with every book we publish.

We publish titles on topics ranging from leadership, entrepreneurship, HR and marketing to self-development and wellbeing.

Find details of all our books at: www.practicalinspiration.com

Did you know...

We can offer discounts on bulk sales of all our titles – ideal if you want to use them for training purposes, corporate giveaways or simply because you feel these ideas deserve to be shared with your network.

We can even produce bespoke versions of our books, for example with your organization's logo and/or a tailored foreword.

To discuss further, contact us on info@practicalinspiration.com.

Got an idea for a business book?

We may be able to help. Find out more about publishing in partnership with us at: bit.ly/PIpublishing.

Follow us on social media...

- @PIPTalking
- @pip_talking
- @practicalinspiration
- @piptalking
- Practical Inspiration Publishing

Gallery Books
Editor Peter Fallon

THE FIFTY MINUTE MERMAID

Nuala Ní Dhomhnaill
Paul Muldoon

THE
FIFTY MINUTE
MERMAID

Gallery Books

The Fifty Minute Mermaid
is first published
simultaneously in paperback
and in a clothbound edition
on 14 October 2007.

The Gallery Press
Loughcrew
Oldcastle
County Meath
Ireland

www.gallerypress.com

*All rights reserved. For permission
to reprint or broadcast these poems,
write to The Gallery Press.*

Poems in Irish © Nuala Ní Dhomhnaill 1998, 2007
Translations © Paul Muldoon 2007
This collection © The Gallery Press 2007

ISBN 978 1 85235 374 2 *paperback*
      978 1 85235 375 9 *clothbound*

A CIP catalogue record for this book
is available from the British Library.

Clár/Contents

PART ONE
Mo Mháistir Dorcha *leathanach* 12
  My Dark Master *page* 13
Dubh 16
  Black 17
An Obair 20
  The Task 21

PART TWO
Na Murúcha a Thriomaigh 26
  The Assimilated Merfolk 27
Cuimhne an Uisce 30
  A Recovered Memory of Water 31
An Mhurúch san Ospidéal 34
  The Mermaid in the Hospital 35
Na Murúcha agus an Litríocht 38
  The Merfolk and Literature 39
Na Murúcha agus an Bainne Cíche 40
  The Merfolk on Breastfeeding 41
Bunmhiotas na Murúch 44
  Founding Myth 45
Miotas Bunaidh Eile 48
  Another Founding Myth 49
Aurora Borealis 52
  Aurora Borealis 53
Easpa Comhbhróin 58
  Lack of Sympathy 59
Na Murúcha agus Galair Thógálacha 60
  The Merfolk and Infectious Diseases 61
Na Murúcha ag Ní a gCeann 64
  The Merfolk and Washing Hair 65
Na Murúcha i mBun Oibreacha Innealtóireachta 68
  Public Works 69
An Mhurúch agus Naomh Bréanainn 72
  The Merfolk and Saint Brendan 73

An Mhurúch agus Focail Áirithe 76
   The Mermaid and Certain Words 77
Glór an Uisce 80
   Water Voice 81
Poltergeist 82
   Poltergeist 83
Murúch Linbh gan Baisteadh 84
   An Unbaptised Merchild 85
Admháil Shuaithinseach 86
   A Remarkable Admission 87
Leide Beag 90
   A Tiny Clue 91
Leide Beag Eile 92
   Another Tiny Clue 93
Baisteadh na Murúch 96
   The Order of Baptism 97
Dúchas Arís 98
   Second Nature 99
Na Murúcha agus an Ceol 102
   The Merfolk and Music 103
An Mhurúch agus an Sagart Paróiste 108
   Mermaid with Parish Priest 109
Bás agus Aiséirí na Murúiche 114
   The Death and Rebirth of the Mermaid 115
Briseadh an Tí 118
   Wrecking the House 119
An Mhurúch ina hAthbhreith 120
   The Born-again Mermaid 121
An Mhurúch ag Coigilt na Tine 122
   The Mermaid Smooring the Fire 123
An Mhurúch is a Tigh 124
   The Mermaid and Her House 125
Teoranna 128
   Boundaries 129

An Mhurúch is a hInníon   132
   The Mermaid and Her Daughter   133
Melusine   136
   Melusine   137
Fáidhiúlacht na Murúiche   140
   The Mermaid's Gift of Prophecy   141
Filleadh na Murúiche ar an dTír-fó-Thoinn   142
   The Mermaid Returns to Land-Under-Wave   143
An Mhurúch i nDeireadh a Saoil Thiar   146
   The Mermaid Nears the End   147
An Mhurúch Seo 'gainne fó Thoinn Arís   148
   Our Mermaid Goes Under Again   149
Spléachanna Fánacha ar an dTír-fó-Thoinn   152
   Some Observations on Land-Under-Wave   153

Though in many of its aspects the visible world seems formed in love, the invisible spheres were formed in fright.
— Herman Melville, *Moby-Dick*

That is the secret delight of Hell — the fact that it is not denounceable, that it is secure from language, that it just is, but cannot be reported in the newspaper, cannot become public knowledge and cannot be brought by word within the realm of critical judgement.
— Thomas Mann, *Doctor Faustus*

PART ONE

Mo Mháistir Dorcha

Táimse in aimsir ag an mBás,
eadrainn tá coinníollacha tarraicthe.
Réitíomair le chéile ar feadh tréimhse is spás
aimsire, achar roinnt bliana is lae mar a cheapas-sa.

Bhuaileas leis ag margadh na saoire.
D'iarr sé orm an rabhas *hire*-áilte.
'Is maith mar a tharla; máistir ag lorg cailín
is cailín ag lorg máistir.'

Ní rabhas ach in aois a naoi déag
nuair a chuas leis ar dtúis faoi chonradh.
Do shíneas mo láimh leis an bpár
is bhí sé láithreach ina mhargadh.

Do chuir sé a chrúcaí im' lár
cé nar thug sé brútáil ná drochíde orm.
Ba chosúla le greas suirí nó grá
an caidreamh a bhí eadrainn.

Is tugaim a tháinte dubha chun abhann,
buaibh úd na n-adharca fada.
Luíonn siad síos i móinéir.
Bím á n-aoireacht ar chnoic san imigéin
atá glas agus féarach.

Seolaim ar imeall an uisce iad
is gaibheann siad scíth agus suaimhneas.
Treoraím lem' shlat is lem' bhachall iad
trí ghleannta an uaignis.

My Dark Master

I've gone and hired myself out. I've hired myself out to
   Death.
We drew up a contract and set the seal
on it by spitting in our palms. I would go with him to
   Lateeve
for a year and a day — at least, that was the deal

as I remember it. When I met him at the hiring-fair
he inquired if I'd yet
been taken: 'What a stroke of luck,' he declared,
'when a master who's set on a maid finds a maid who's set

on a master.' I was only nineteen years old
at the time the bargain was struck.
I made my mark on a bit of paper and was indentured
on the spot. What a stroke of luck,

I declare, what a stroke of luck that I fell
into his clutches. Not, I should emphasize again,
that he meddled with or molested me for, to tell
you the truth, our relationship was always much more akin

to walking out, or going steady. I lead his blue-black cows
with their fabulously long horns
to water. They lie down in pastures of clover and fescue
and lucerne. I follow them over hills faraway and green.

I lead them down beside Lough Duff
where they find rest and where they are restored.
I drive them with my rod and my staff
through the valleys of loneliness. Then I might herd

Is siúlaim leo suas ar an ard
mar a mbíonn sciollam na móna le blaiseadh acu
is tagann míobhán orm i mbarr an mháma
nuair a chím faid mo radhairc uaim ag leathadh

a thailte is méid a ríochta,
an domhan mór ba dhóigh leat faoina ghlaic aige
is cloisim sa mhodardhoircheacht bhróin
na hanamnacha ag éamh is ag sioscadh ann.

Is tá sé féin saibhir thar meon.
Tá trucailí óir agus seoda aige.
Ní bheadh i gcarn airgid Déamair
ach cac capaill suas leo.

Ó táimse in aimsir ag an mbás,
is baolach ná beidh mé saor riamh uaidh.
Ní heol dom mo thuarastal ná mo phá
nó an bhfaighidh mé pá plaic' nó cead aighnis uaidh.

them to a mountain-pass, to a summit
where they browse on bog-asphodel and where I, when I
look down, get somewhat
dizzy. His realm extends as far as the eye

can see and beyond, so much so
a body might be forgiven for thinking the whole
world's under his sway. Particularly after the sough-sighs
of suffering souls

from the darkness. He himself has riches that are untold,
coming down as he is with jewels and gems.
Even John Damer of Shronel, even his piles of gold
would be horse-shit compared to them.

I've hired myself out to death. And I'm afraid that I'll not
ever be let go. What I'll have at the end of the day
I've absolutely no idea, either in terms of three hots and a cot
or if I'll be allowed to say my say.

Dubh

Ar thitim Shrebrenica, 11ú Iúil 1995

Is lá dubh é seo.
Tá an spéir dubh.
Tá an fharraige dubh.

Tá na gairdíní dubh.
Tá na crainn dubh.
Tá na cnoic dubh.
Tá na busanna dubh.
Tá na carranna a thugann na páistí ar scoil ar maidin dubh.

Tá na siopaí dubh.
Tá a bhfuinneoga dubh.
Tá na sráideanna dubh (is ní le daoine é).
Tá na nuachtáin a dhíolann an cailín dubh go bhfuil an
    folt láidir dubh uirthi
dubh, dubh, dubh.

Tá an damh dubh.
Tá an gadhar dubh.
Tá capall úd Uíbh Ráthaigh dubh.
Tá gach corréan a scinneann amach as an ealta dubh.
An chaora dhubh a sheasann amach de ghnáth i lár an tréada,
ní heisceacht í níos mó mar tá na caoirigh ar fad dubh.

Tá na prátaí dubh.
Tá na turnapaí dubh.
Tá gach bileog cabáiste a chuirfeá síos i dtóin corcáin dubh.

Tá an sáspan dubh.
Tá an ciotal dubh.
Tá gach tóin corcáin as seo go Poll Tí Liabáin dubh.

Black

On the fall of Srebrenica, 11 July 1995

A black day, this.
The sky is black.
The sea is black.

The gardens are black.
The trees are black.
The hills are black.
The buses are black.
The cars bringing the kids to school are black.

The shops are black.
Their windows are black.
The streets are black (and I don't mean with people).
The newspapers sold by the dark girl with the great head of
    dark hair
are black, black, black.

The ox is black.
The hound is black.
The very horse from Iveragh is black.
The bird suddenly out of sync with the flock is black.
The black sheep that stood out from the ordinary run of sheep
      no longer stands out, for all the sheep are black.

The spuds are black.
The turnips are black.
Every last leaf of cabbage in the pot is black.

The saucepan is black.
The kettle is black.
The bottom of every pot from here to the crack of doom is
    black.

Tá na Caitlicigh dubh.
Tá na Protastúnaigh dubh.
Tá na Seirbigh is na Crótaigh dubh.
Tá gach uile chine a shiúlann ar dhromchla na cruinne
an mhaidin dhubh seo samhraidh, dubh.

Tá na polaiticeoirí ar sciobaidh
is iad ag baint na gcos is na n-eireaball dá chéile
ag iarraidh a chur ina luí orainn
nach fada go mbeidh gach dubh ina gheal.
Is an té a leomhadh a mhisneach dó
nó a chreidfeadh an méid a deireann siad
níor mhiste dó b'fhéidir an cheist a chur
ab ann ab amhlaidh a chiallaíonn sé seo anois
nach mbeidh ins gach dubhthréimhse ach seal?

Ach ní dhéanfadsa.
Mar táimse dubh.
Tá mo chroí dubh
is m'intinn dubh.
Tá m'amharc ar feadh raon mo radhairc dubh.
Tá an dubh istigh is amuigh agam chughainn.

Mar gach píosa guail nó sméar nó airne,
gach deamhan nó diabhal nó daradaol,
gach cleite fiaigh mhara nó íochtar bhonn bróige,
gach uaimh nó cabha nó poll tóna
gach duibheagán doimhin a shlogann ár ndóchas,
táim dubh dubh dubh.

Mar tá Srebrenica, cathair an airgid,
'Argentaria' na Laidne,
bán.

The Catholics are black.
The Protestants are black.
The Serbs and the Croatians are black.
Every tribe on the face of the earth this blackest of black
    mornings black.

The politicians are scuffling about
biting the legs and the tails off each other
trying to persuade us
to look on the bright side.
Anyone who might be inclined
to take them at their word
would do well, maybe, to ask
why they think it goes without saying
that every black cloud has a silver lining.

I myself won't be the one.
For I'm black.
My heart is black and my mind is black.
Everything that falls into my field of vision is black.
I'm full of black rage.
There's a black mark against all our names.

Like each and every lump of coal, every blackberry and sloe
and demon and devil and Devil's Coachman,
every grave and cave and arsehole,
every bottomless pit in which we lose all hope,
I'm black as black can be.

Now that Srebrenica, that silver city —
'Argentaria', as the Romans called it —
is blank.

An Obair

An móta is bábhún Normannach a chonac isteach thar chuirtín
 crann
is mé ag tiomáint thar bráid go tapaidh ar an mbóthar,
áit éigin faoin dtuath in aice le Cill Mhaighneann
i gContae na Mí, a thugann an ainm don áit. Sin í An Obair.

É sin is an cara mná is ansa liom ar domhan ag fáil bháis go mall
in Ospidéal an Adelaide: an grianghraf thíos im' phóca dínn
 beirt inár mná óga
a tógadh lá Márta, an chéad lá earraigh i nGairdín na mBláth in
 Ankara
na Tuirce, sinn ag gáirí is gan tuairim againn ar cad a bhí
 romhainn;

aghaidh na mná Moslamaí ón Ailgéir a chonac le déanaí sa
 nuachtán
nuair a hinsíodh di go rabhthas tar éis an scornach a ghearradh
ar ochtar leanbh óg dá clann; an file iomráiteach Seirbeach
a bhí ina cheannaire ar mhórchampa géibhinn; an staraí
 litríochta
a chaith a chuid ama saor lena chairde ag imirt caide le plaosc
 dhaonna;

m'fhear céile a chaith sé lá i gcóma is mé ag féachaint amach
 fuinneoga
an tseomra feithimh ar an solas ag dorchú amuigh ar an mbá
idir Dún Laoghaire is Binn Éadair, is ar theacht is imeacht na
 taoide;
trácht trom ar an mbóthar mar a raibh an saol Fódlach ag rith
 sall
is anall, ag plódú ar nós na nduilleog a bhí ag péacadh ar gach
 aon chrann;

The Task

It's from the massive Norman earthworks I glimpsed through
   a curtain of trees
as I drove quickly past,
somewhere near Kilmainham, County Meath,
that the place took its name. Nobber. From the Irish *an obair*,
   'the task'.

From that and my dearest friend slowly dying
in the Adelaide Hospital; the photograph deep in my pocket
   of us as young women,
taken on a March day, the first day of spring in the Botanic
   Gardens in Ankara,
laughing, with no sense of what was to come;

the face of the Muslim woman from Algeria I saw in a newspaper lately
after she was told lately that the throats
of eight of her children had been cut; the major Serbian poet
who was the commandant of a major camp; the literary
   historian
who enjoyed an off-moment with his friends, playing ball
   with a human skull;

my own husband who spent six days in a coma while I
   looked out the windows
of the waiting room at the light going down on the bay
between Dun Laoghaire and Howth, at the come and go of
   the tide;
heavy traffic on the road as the entire population of Ireland
   rushed here and there,
countless as bud-blasts from the trees;

é seo go léir a thabhairt faoi ndeara is áit a dhéanamh dó id'
   chroí gan pléascadh,
é seo uile is an móta Normannach a chonac is mé ag gabháil na slí,
áit éigin faoin dtuath in aice le Cill Mhaighneann i gContae na Mí,
An Obair. Sin í an obair. Sin í an obair nach éasca.

to take it all in, to make room in your heart without having
   your heart burst,
to take in not only this but that Norman motte and bailey
I passed near Kilmainham or thereabouts,
a place called Nobber. That's the task. *An obair*. A task that's
   far from easy.

PART TWO

Na Murúcha a Thriomaigh

Ar an gcarraig lom seo ar a gcuireann siad isteach
an t-am de ló is a ngainní á dtriomú acu
tagann galair cnis mar oighear is gríosach orthu
is codladh grifín ón mbríos gaoithe is fiú ón leoithne,
rud nár thaithíodar as a n-óige is nár chleachtadar riamh
ar na bánta íochtaracha, iad ag iomrascáil is ag déanamh
gleacaíochta leis na leanaí ríoga. Dar leo tá goin na ré
gach pioc chomh holc leis an ngréin á mbualadh;
gorm a bhíonn siad i ndiaidh goin na gealaí
is buí i ndiaidh an ghrian á leagadh.

Nuair a thagann an rua orthu is go méadaíonn an braon
ins na harasaipil níl luibh ná leigheas a thabharfadh
aon chabhair mura bpiocfá cúpla rúta de mheacan
an táthabha. Caitear é seo a bhaint i gcónaí
i dtaobh thall den abhainn is é a ullmhú
de dhroim uisce, chun ná geobhaidh an phiast bhaineann
a bholadh is ná neadóidh níos doimhne istigh
idir coirt is craiceann, idir feoil is leathar.
Deintear céirín ansan dó a thairricíonn an nimh.

Caitheann na mná muincí troma thart faoina muineál
is na fearaibh ceirteacha dearga
nó rud ar bith a chlúdódh rian na sceolbhach.
Deireann an dochtúir liom go bhfuil an sine siain
ar lár ina lán acu. Caitear an ribe tuathail
i mbarr a gceann a stoitheadh nó é a chuimilt go maith
le céir sara gcnagfaidh sí seo thar n-ais iontu.
'An gcualaís an cnag?' a fhiafraíonn sé díobh
nuair a tharlaíonn an leigheas. Tá dearmhad glan déanta acu
faoin am seo ar shuathadh mearathail na gcaisí doimhne
is ar chlaisceadal na míol mór sa duibheagán.

The Assimilated Merfolk

Barely have they put in on this bare rock
than their scales start drying out
and they suffer such skin complaints as windgall and blotching
and get pins-and-needles from the breezes, never mind the zephyrs,
unaccustomed as they were to either
on the underwater plains where they used to wrestle and besport
themselves with the princelings. As far as they're concerned,
   moonstroke
is every bit as serious as too much sun;
they turn blue after moonstroke
and yellow after the sun has laid them low.

If they happen to get shingles, or when a boil
comes to a head, there's no herb or native remedy that will offer
any respite except maybe a couple of roots of hellebore
from the opposite bank of the river, the hellebore itself prepared
somewhere over water, thereby ensuring that the she-grub won't
   get wind of it
and burrow deeper
between the outer and inner subcutaneous layers, between flesh
   and hide.
A poultice is made from this which draws out the poison.

The women wear heavy neck-ornaments
while the men favour red kerchiefs,
anything at all that hides the signs of their gills.
The doctor reports that the uvula
is displaced in the vast majority of them. The topmost hair
of their heads must either be torn out by the roots or thoroughly
   stiffened
with wax before the uvula snaps back.
'Did you hear the snap?' the doctor enquires of them
when the cure takes effect. By now they've clean forgotten
the dizzying churning of the deep currents
and, from the abyss, the whales' antiphonal singing.

Uair má seach airíonn siad fós é ag sioscadh
ar an ngaoith is tugann siad Port na bPúcaí air.
Cuireann siad fíor na croise idir iad agus é.

Sánn siad an fonn a ghabhann leis i gcúil an choicís
nó i bhfolach i bpoll sa chlaí i dteannta
lomadh na gruaige is bearradh na hingne,
an ionga úd a fuaireadar ón lia súl
is na spéaclaí nár chuireadar ariamh orthu.
Tá sé ag lobhadh ansan i gcónaí i dteannta
ceirteacha na gcneácha, an fhuil mhíosúil
is náireach leo, a meabhraíonn dóibh is a chuireann
in iúl an slabar is an glóthach tiubh
dár díobh iad. Ní fhreagraíonn siad d'éinne
a ghlaonn as a n-ainm is as a sloinne orthu
ó théann an ghrian ina luí. Tá sé suite meáite
is go daingean i gceann gach uile dhuine acu
gurb ionann freagairt do ghlaoch saolta
nó do ghlaoch síoraí.

Ní shínfeadh fear ná bean acu ar shúisín
ná ar leaba go mbeadh a gcosa sínte i dtreo na tine.
Dar leo gur cóiriú an duine mhairbh é sin.
Ní maith leo cloch a thabhairt isteach
'on tigh Dé Luain. Dá dtabharfadh leanbh
leis isteach i dteach í do chuirfí iachall air
í a chaitheamh amach arís. Tá cur ina coinne acu.
Fágann na rabhartaí earraigh a rianta fós
ar chlathacha cosanta a n-aigne; gach tonnchosc díobh
ina ghlib ag bruth farraige is ag brúscar raice —
focail a scuabtar isteach mar a bheadh carbháin charraige
ar líne bharra taoide nuair a bhuaileann an ré roithleacáin
aimsir ré an tSathairn, focail a thugann scáil
na seanré fós leo, focail ar nós
'más reamhar, com seang, meanmain uallaigh'.

From time to time they hear a snatch of it
on the wind and call it 'Port na bPúcaí'.
They make a sign of the cross between themselves and it.

They fling the air of the tune into the heap of leftovers
or hide it away in the same hole in the ditch where they dispose
of hair-clippings and nail-parings,
the ointment they got that time from the eye-doctor,
those eye-glasses they never wore.
The air of that tune is forever breaking down
along with the menstrual rags, the menstrual blood
they shy away from, reminiscent as it is
of the ooze and muck
from which they sprang. They never answer anyone
who calls them by their name or surname
once the sun's set. For they've determined,
and hold it now as an article of faith,
that to answer such a mortal call
is to answer an eternal one.

Not one of them, man or woman, would stretch out on a sofa
or a settle-bed if their legs were to be turned toward the fire.
They associate this with the laying out of the dead.
They don't like it if a stone is brought
inside the house on a Monday. If a child
were to bring one in he'd be compelled
to bring it out again. They really take against that.
The high spring tides leave their mark
on the sea-walls of their minds, the edge of every breaking wave
ragged with flotsam and jetsam and other wreckage,
words carried ashore like the shells of sea-urchins
and left at the high-water mark when they get the head-staggers
at the time of the Saturday moon, words that are still imbued
with the old order of things, phrases like
'wide-thighs, narrow-waist, hare-brain'.

Cuimhne an Uisce

Uaireanta nuair a bhíonn a hiníon
sa seomra folctha
ag glanadh a fiacla le slaod tiubh
is le sód bácála,
tuigtear di go líonann an seomra suas
le huisce.

Tosnaíonn sé ag a cosa is a rúitíní
is bíonn sé ag slibearáil suas is suas arís
thar a másaí is a cromáin is a básta.
Ní fada
go mbíonn sé suas go dtí na hioscaidí uirthi.
Cromann sí síos ann go minic ag piocadh suas
rudaí mar thuáillí láimhe nó ceirteacha
atá ar maos ann.
Tá cuma na feamnaí orthu —
na scothóga fada ceilpe úd a dtugaidís
'gruaig mhaighdean mhara' nó 'eireabaill mhadraí rua' orthu.
Ansan go hobann téann an t-uisce i ndísc
is ní fada
go mbíonn an seomra iomlán tirim arís.

Tá strus uafásach
ag roinnt leis na mothúcháin seo go léir.
Tar éis an tsaoil, níl rud ar bith aici
chun comparáid a dhéanamh leis.
Is níl na focail chearta ar eolas aici ar chor ar bith.
Ag a seisiún síciteiripeach seachtainiúil
bíonn a dóthain dua aici
ag iarraidh an scéal aisteach seo a mhíniú
is é a chur in iúl i gceart
don mheabhairdhochtúir.

Níl aon téarmaíocht aici,
ná téarmaí tagartha

A Recovered Memory of Water

Sometimes when the mermaid's daughter
is in the bathroom
cleaning her teeth with a thick brush
and baking soda
she has the sense the room is filling
with water.

It starts at her feet and ankles
and slides further and further up
over her thighs and hips and waist.
In no time
it's up to her oxters.
She bends down into it to pick up
handtowels and washcloths and all such things
as are sodden with it.
They all look like seaweed —
like those long strands of kelp that used to be called
'mermaid-hair' or 'foxtail'.
Just as suddenly the water recedes
and in no time
the room's completely dry again.

A terrible sense of stress
is part and parcel of these emotions.
At the end of the day she has nothing else
to compare it to.
She doesn't have the vocabulary for any of it.
At her weekly therapy session
she has more than enough to be going on with
just to describe this strange phenomenon
and to express it properly
to the psychiatrist.

She doesn't have the terminology
or any of the points of reference

ná focal ar bith a thabharfadh an tuairim is lú
do cad é 'uisce'.
'Lacht trédhearcach,' a deir sí, ag déanamh a cruinndíchill.
'Sea,' a deireann an teiripí, 'coinnibh ort!'
Bíonn sé á moladh is á gríosadh chun gnímh teangan.
Deineann sí iarracht eile.
'Slaod tanaí,' a thugann sí air,
í ag tóraíocht go cúramach i measc na bhfocal.
'Brat gléineach, ábhar silteach, rud fliuch.'

or any word at all that would give the slightest suggestion
as to what water might be.
'A transparent liquid,' she says, doing as best she can.
'Right,' says the therapist, 'keep going.'
He coaxes and cajoles her towards word-making.
She has another run at it.
'A thin flow,' she calls it,
casting about gingerly in the midst of words.
'A shiny film. Dripping stuff. Something wet.'

An Mhurúch san Ospidéal

Dhúisigh sí
agus ní raibh a heireaball éisc ann
níos mó
ach istigh sa leaba léi
bhí an dá rud fada fuar seo.
Ba dhóigh leat gur gaid mhara iad
nó slaimicí feola.

'Mar mhagadh atá siad
ní foláir,
Oíche na Coda Móire.
Tá leath na foirne as a meabhair
le deoch
is an leath eile acu
róthugtha do *joke*anna.
Mar sin féin is leor an méid seo,'
is do chaith sí an dá rud
amach as an seomra.

Ach seo í an chuid
ná tuigeann sí —
conas a thit sí féin ina ndiaidh
'cocs-um-bo-head'.
Cén bhaint a bhí
ag an dá rud léi
nó cén bhaint a bhí aici
leosan?

An bhanaltra a thug an nod di
is a chuir í i dtreo an eolais —
'Cos í seo atá ceangailte díot
agus ceann eile acu anseo thíos fút.
Cos, cos eile,
a haon, a dó.

The Mermaid in the Hospital

She awoke
to find her fishtail
clean gone
but in the bed with her
were two long, cold thingammies.
You'd have thought they were tangles of kelp
or collops of ham.

'They're no doubt
taking the piss,
it being New Year's Eve.
Half the staff legless
with drink
and the other half
playing pranks.
Still, this is taking it
a bit far.'
And with that she hurled
the two thingammies out of the room.

But here's the thing
she still doesn't get —
why she tumbled out after them
arse-over-tip . . .
How she was connected
to those two thingammies
and how they were connected
to her.

It was the sister who gave her the wink
and let her know what was what.
'You have one leg attached to you there
and another one underneath that.
One leg, two legs . . .
A-one and a-two . . .

Caithfidh tú foghlaim
conas siúl leo.'

Ins na míosa fada
a lean
n'fheadar ar thit a croí
de réir mar a thit
trácht na coise uirthi,
a háirsí?

Now you have to learn
what they can do.'

In the long months
that followed
I wonder if her heart fell
the way her arches fell,
her instep arches.

Na Murúcha agus an Litríocht

Cé go bhfuil léamh agus scríobh a dteanga féin acu
ó thángadar i dtír
is go raibh sí á foghlaim ag an aos óg
go dtí gur dúnadh scoil an oileáin síos
ag an Roinn um Oileáin Nuathriomaithe thiar ins na
    caogadaí
(baol ó mhaidhm nó sciorradh carraige an leathscéal)

níor thairricíodar chúchu a bpeannaibh
is níor luíodar riamh leis an litríocht.
Níor chumadar is níor cheapadar
is níor chuir gothaí na n-údar orthu féin.
Ba scorn leo gnásmhaireacht an dúigh
is níor dheineadar a mbuilín
ar an áit aoibhinn aisteach úd as a dtángadar.

An Chistin Fhomhuireach,
An tOileán a bhí Faoi Dhraíocht,
Seanscéalta ón dTír-fó-Thoinn,
nó *Maighdean Mhara ag Insint a Scéil Féin*
cuid de theidil na leabhar nár scríobhadar.

Tá aithreachas orthu gur fhágadar é
agus caitheamh i ndiaidh an tseanshaoil
ar mhórán; mar sin féin ní bhíd ag cáiseamh
mar is maith a thuigeann siad gur fíor
nach bhfuil aon dul siar.
Is cé nach mbeidh a leithéidí arís ann,
beag ná mór,
ní scríobhann siad dréachta filíochta ná caibidilí leabhar
ag maíomh as.

Fágann siad na cúraimí sin
faoi na Blascaodaigh.

The Merfolk and Literature

Although they could read and write their own language —
from the time they came out of the sea
it had been learned by the youngsters
until, of course, the island school was closed down
by the Department of Freshly Formed Islands
because of the constant danger of rockfalls and landslides —

they didn't take up their pens
to actually set down a literature.
They neither compiled nor composed
nor were afflicted by any of the affectations associated with
    authors.
They put no store in the customs and practices of the writing life
and never set out to cash in
on the lovely, strange world from which they'd sprung.

Submarine Cuisine,
The Enchanted Isle,
Legends from the Land under the Sea,
not to speak of *A Mermaid's Tail,*
are only some of the titles of books they didn't get round to
    writing.

It's not that they don't have regrets about leaving,
and many of them do indeed sigh
for the old ways, only that
they don't make a habit of bewailing their sad fate,
for they know right well
there's no going back.
And though their likes will never be seen again
in any shape or form,
they don't go writing screeds of poetry and prose,
making a huge deal of it.

They leave that kind of carry-on
to the crowd from the Blaskets.

Na Murúcha agus an Bainne Cíche

Diúltaíonn siad bainne cíche a thabhairt dá gclann
agus baineann siad de dheol iad i bhfad roimh am
(tar éis seachtaine uaireanta). Tá an nós seo ar bun
acu le deich nglún anuas nó ar a laghad dhá chéad bliain
ón am a thosnaíodar ag teacht aníos ar an míntír.

Leamhnacht is bainne saibhir a thugann siad dos na naíonáin
is iad siúd atá gustalach, tugann siad uachtar dóibh ar spúnóga
is gruth is im i dteannta iasc leathchoganta.
Ní mór leo dóibh na rudaí seo.

Bíonn leanbh ag an murúch bhaineann gach aon bhliain
ach toisc an ráta báis a bheith chomh hard acu
(suas le ceithre chéad in aghaidh gach míle)
tá an daonra ginearálta ag meath go tiubh.

Pianta boilg is trioblóidí díleáite is mó a mharaíonn na leanaí
agus cé gur léir don saol Fódlach gurb é an réimeas bídh
atá ag ídiú na leanbh orthu, ní shin é a chreideann siad féin.
Ní chloisfidh siad aon fhocal faoi. Níl aon bhaint eatarthu,
    dar leo.

Cuireann siad an milleán ar fad ar chomhachtaí seachtracha
nach bhfuil leigheas acu orthu, is nach bhfuil faoina smacht.
Séard atá ag marú na leanaí, a chloisféa iad a rá
ná an mí-ádh mór is an drochrath is cinniúintí eile
mar an moladh maol, an drochshúil, is cúrsaí ciorraithe tré
    chéile.

Tá sé deacair d'aon duine againne dul go bunrúta an scéil
gan trácht ar na luachanna siombalacha atá acu.

The Merfolk on Breastfeeding

They refuse point-blank to breastfeed their newborn
but wean them much too early,
sometimes after only a week. This has been their custom
for ten generations or, at the very least, the two hundred years
since they first ventured on to dry land.

What they do give the infants is sweet cow's milk and enriched
    cow's milk.
The wealthier among them spoonfeed them cream,
curds, butter, and pre-masticated fish.
They've come to think this is the infants' due.

The female merfolk have a child every year
but because of the high rate of infant mortality
(four hundred in every thousand)
the general population has declined.

Bellyaches and digestive woes are what usually do for the
    children
and, though it's obvious to everyone on the auld sod that it's
    their dietary regimen
that's eating away at their children, they give it no credence.
They won't hear of it. As far as they're concerned the two
    things are unconnected.

They lay the blame on outside influences
over which they've no control.
What's killing the children, you'll hear them say,
is the Great Ill Wind and General Misfortune and other kinds
    of bad cess
such as inappropriate praise or the evil eye or other kinds of
    witch-watchery.

It's difficult for a single person to get to the bottom of this
without taking into account their system of symbols.

Is fíor nach bhfuil íomhá ar bith acu de bhean ag deol
ná níl pictiúr na Maighdine Muire mar chuid dá samhlaíocht
   bheo.

Is faoin méid atá ar eolas againn faoina saol fó-thoinn
is léir go raibh réimeas leathan comhachta ag na murúcha
   baineanna
is go rabhadar, ar an mórgóir, saor ó smacht go mór
murab ionann is mar atá an cás acu anois ar an míntír.

Nuair a thángadar suas ar an dtalamh do luíodar le
   feirmeoireacht
is go háirithe le bólacht. Dhein dia beag acu
de tháirgí déiríochta. Dhein siombail onóra díobh.
Bhíodar mar bhunús mórtais is oinigh.

Do chloisfeá na filí acu ag cur síos de shíor
is ag caint ar 'fhoinse shíoraí bainne na mbó mbleacht,
a thugann sásamh cuí do leanaí agus is cúis onóra don
   mbantracht'.
Fiú sa chaint acu tugtar 'im mo chroí' nó 'an smearadh
   mullaigh'
ar an ní is mó is ansa leo riamh.

Is dóigh liom sa chás seo nach féidir a rá
gur treise dúchas ná oiliúnt. Séard a tharla ná
gur bhuaigh an t-uabhar is an mór-is-fiú
is an mórtas-cine-gan-cur-suas ar an loighic is an réasún
is ar eilimintí bunúsacha na daonnachta.

Mar is fíor sa deireadh, dá mhéid é a gcumas aithrise
is a mbua luí isteach leis an dtimpeallacht, dála na gcaimileon,
dúile uisce a bhí iontu sarar thriomaíodar, is ar an míntír
pé sórt dúile eile a dhein díobh, níor dhein daoine díobh.

It's the case that they have no statues of nursing mothers
and that images of the Madonna aren't part of their everyday
   imaginations.

From what we can determine about their underwater existence
it's obvious that the females had a wide range of powers
and that they were pretty much free of all oversight,
quite unlike their circumstances on dry land.

When they came ashore they would give themselves over to
   farming,
in particular dairy farming. They pretty much worshipped
dairy products. These would become symbols of honour.
A matter of kudos and self-congratulation.

Their poets, such as they are, hold forth interminably
on 'the inexhaustible bounty of the kine
which sustains the children and adds to the esteem of the
   women'.
Even in ordinary speech they call what they hold most dear
'the butter of my heart' and 'top of the milk'.

I suspect that in this instance it is not true to say
that nature is stronger than nurture. It looks very much as if
   raw pride and conceit
would get the better of them
and their newfound sense of their own importance
would overshadow all sense of reason and the basic elements
   of humanity.

For, let's face it, despite their adaptability
and their gift for fading into the woodwork, like chameleons,
they were water-dwellers before they came on land and,
   however we might describe
what they'd morph into, it certainly wasn't human beings.

Bunmhiotas na Murúch

A mórfhormhór
níl an luide is lú de chuimhne acu níos mó
ar cad sa diabhal a thug in airde ar an dtalamh iad
an chéad lá.

Bhíodar ag teitheadh ó rud éigin; sin an méid is léir dóibh.
Tá miotas acu ina thaobh fiú; ins an scéal
bhí taoiseach orthu a fuair ordú ó Dhia:
'Ardaigh do shlat is sín amach do láimh
os cionn na farraige is deighil ó chéile í,'
is ea a dúradh leis. Do dhein sé amhlaidh.
Do shéid an ghaoth as polláire sróine an dé
a dhein cnocáin des na huiscí is clathacha tiorma de thonnta.
Dheighil na huiscí óna chéile is chuaigh a mhuintir féin
ar chosán trí lár na farraige ar thalamh thirim
is na huiscí ina mballaí ar dheis is ar chlé acu.

Ansan do shín sé a láimh arís
is d'iaigh an fharraige.
An dream a bhí sa tóir orthu
do bádh gach éinne díobh, níor fhan fear inste scéil
nó anacail anama.
Dhein cíor thuathail ghlan díobh is chuadar go tóin poill
mar a dhéanfadh ualach cloch nó lasta luaidhe.
Shlog an fharraige iad scun scan
is deineadh ciota fogha díobh
i mbroinn na bóchna. Fiú cér dhíobh iad
nó cad ba shloinne dhóibh anois ní feasach d'éinne
nó cad ba chúis in aon chor leis an tóir.

Labhrann siad leis i dtaobh colúin thine is néil,
rud a chuireann ar scoláirí áirithe a chur i gcás
gur leis an gCríostaíocht a tháinig an scéal seo go léir
isteach, is gur bunaithe ar *Eaxodus* atá sé.

Founding Myth

Most of the merfolk
haven't the first idea
of what on earth brought them to dry land
in the first place.

They were in flight from something. That's as much as they remember.
They have a myth about being on the run
in which their leader was given an order by God:
'Raise on high your rod, and stretch forth your hand
over the waters and divide them one from the other,'
was what was said to him. He did the very same.
A wind blew from the nostrils of the god
that made hills out of the waters and dry banks of the waves.
The waters divided from each other and he and his people
walked on dry land through the sea
with walls of water to right and left.

The god stretched out his hand again
and the waters closed again.
The crowd that were in pursuit of them
were drowned to a man, not one of them living to tell the tale
or plead for his soul to be saved.
The sea swallowed them whole,
and they were dashed to bits
on the bosom of the ocean. The identity of the pursuers
is now completely lost
along with the reason for the pursuit.

They also speak of a pillar of fire and smoke which preceded them
which has led some scholars to posit
that this entire myth coincided with their conversion to Christianity
and that it's drawn mostly from *Exodus*.

Tá dream eile acu a deir a mhalairt —
gurb ann a bhí scéal dá shaghas, a bheag nó a mhór, i gcónaí
    ann
is nár dhein an Chríostaíocht ach craiceann breise
a chur air.

N'fheadar-sa féin cioca.
Ar leibhéal éigin,
ní chreidim ann, ach mar sin féin, ar chuma mhórán iontas
    eile
a bhaineas leo, ní bhréagnaím é.
Ní foláir ar deireadh nó tá bonn éigin leis
murab ionann is cuid des na scéalta eile a insíonn siad.

Others take the opposite view —
that founding myths pretty much the same as this have
    existed forever
and all that Christianity did
was to give it a veneer.

I don't give a hoot one way or the other.
At some level,
I don't believe it, though at the same time, like so many
    other miracles
having to do with the merfolk, I don't *not* believe it.
It seems there might be a factual basis for the story,
which is more than can be said of some of the other yarns
    they spin.

Miotas Bunaidh Eile

Tá scéal eile acu
mar gheall ar an áit as a dtagann siad
agus creideann siad go diongbhálta ann.

De réir dealraimh
nuair a bhí an cheannairc mhór
ar siúl ar Neamh
i gcoinne an Tiarna Dé Bhí
d'éiríodar seo amach ina reibiliúnaithe
faoi cheannas Shátain, Aingeal an Uabhair,
is dúirt gach uile dhuine acu i dteannta leis
'non serviam'.

Nuair a chuaigh an cath ina gcoinne
is go bhfuair fórsaí neimhe
faoi cheannas Mhíchíl Naofa Ard-Aingeal,
an lámh uachtair orthu,
do caitheadh amach as na Flaithis iad.

Do thit cuid acu san aer
is dhein an dream aerach díobh —
ní ár muintir féin, na mairbh
gur de chlann Éabha agus Ádhaimh iad —
ach na cinn dainséaracha, na deamhain aeir
a bhíonn de shíor is choíche fós
ag crá na ndaoine.

Na cinn a thit ar an dtalamh
dhein na púcaí díobh
is na cinn a thit san uisce
dhein díobh treabh na mara

atá riamh is choíche, ón lá sin fadó ó shoin
ag iarradh dreapadh leo thar n-ais

Another Founding Myth

They have yet another story
about their origins
which they all cling to like there's no tomorrow.

It seems that once upon a time
when there was that great insurrection
going on above in Heaven
and the angels rose up against The God of All
their forebears were among those
led by Satan, the angel of Luciferian pride,
and that they, too, took his vow
of 'non serviam'.

When the battle went against them
and the forces of Heaven,
under the command of Saint Michael, the Archangel,
    carried the day,
they were thrown out of Heaven.

Some of them fell into the air
and became the airy wee folk —
not our ancestors,
who sprang from Adam and Eve —
but the dangerous ones, the air demons
who still and always
bother ordinary people.

The ones that fell on the ground
became the pookas or land-fairies (in their underground
    mounds)
and those that fell into the sea became the sea-people,

who have been trying everything
since that day long ago

ar ais nó ar éigean
go dtí an áit as ar shíolraíodar.

Cuid acu, na cinn atá faoi chaibidil againn anseo,
dheineadar faoin am seo chomh fada leis an míntír é.

to climb back again
to the place from which they first fell.

Some of them, the ones who concern us here,
have so far made it only to dry land.

Aurora Borealis

Faoi mar a dhamhsann na *Borey Dancers* trasna na spéarthaibh,
ag coigilt na soilse ar a dtugann siad na Saighneáin —
chonacsa anuraidh iad im' sheasamh i bhFairbanks, Alaska,
is dhá oíche i ndiaidh a chéile níor thit orm oiread is aon néal
    amháin.
Ná creidim ód' bhéal gur róthaisteal eitleáin nó *jet-lag*
a bhain díom mo mheabhair, ag buaireamh mo chinn is mo
    chéille,
is munarb liú im' chluais é, a chuir go mór mé ar iomrall,
dar mo leabhar, do tuigeadh dom gur chuala monabhar bog caoin

na sféar. Muintir na háite, na treibheanna Atabascacha,
a mhaireann sa *taiga*, a thaithíonn na coillte tanaí
beithe, crainn chreathacha is giúise, nó sailearnach íseal,
do chreidfidís mé, is déarfadh gur féidir feadaíl
chun iad a tharrac i t'aice, go bhfreagraíonn siad don ghuth
    daonna,
is gur féidir iad a chaintiú, ach do ghuth a choimeád séimh is mín,
is má chaitheann tú seile orthu, rithfidh siad isteach ina chéile
is go dtabharfaidh siad fís duit, ach iad a láimhseáil ar an gcuma
    chuí.

Níos sia ó thuaidh, i measc lucht Inuit na réigiún im-mholach
deirtear gurb é atá ann ná na sprideanna ag lasadh trilseán
chun Bóthar na bhFlaitheas a réiteach d'anamnacha na nua-
    mharbh.
Bíd ag fleá is ag féasta, ag imirt chaide is ag iomrascáil
le cloigeann róin nó rosuailt — séard a chualas-sa, ní foláir, ná an
    siansán
a dheineann na *selamiut*, áitritheoirí na spéireach, le fonn
is iad ag rith i ndiaidh na caide ar pháirceanna imeartha an tsaoil
    eile
an sneachta ag geonaíl faoina gcosa is a mbuataisí ag déanamh
    gíoscáin.

Aurora Borealis

So it is that the Borey Dancers prance over the skies
raking over those embers they call the Northern Lights.
(I saw them last year when I was staying in Fairbanks, Alaska,
and for two nights in a row I didn't get a wink of sleep.)
I don't believe that it was simply too much flying about or jetlag
that put me out my senses, that caused me such a mental aberration,
for I swear on the Holy Book it seemed to me
I was hearing the sweet quiet murmuring

of the spheres. The locals, the Athabascan Indians
who live in the 'taiga', who frequent the sparse woods of birch,
quaking aspen trees and firs, or even just willow scrub,
they would have believed me, saying that if you whistled
you could pull them towards you, that they respond to the human
    voice
particularly if you sing to them soft and low
while, if you spit in their direction, their colours run into each other
    and fuse
and they can even give you inspiration, if you only know how to
    handle them right.

Further north, amongst the Inuit who inhabit the circumpolar
    regions
they say that these lights are the spirits lighting up torches
to guide the newly-arrived dead towards the Path of Heaven.
They spend their time in feasting and festivities, in feats of wrestling
and football played with seal- or walrus-skulls, so what I heard,
    it seems, was the sound
of the spirit-troop known as 'selamiut', the welkin-wanderers,
eagerly pursuing football in the great playing fields of the sky,
complete with the frost-hardened snow creaking and squeaking
    under their snowboots.

Deirtear sa Bhíobla, nuar a dhein an Rí Antiochus
ionradh ar an Éigipt, gur thaibhsigh an t-arm neamhaí
ag troid ins na Flaithis; ar feadh dathad lá agus oíche
go raibh marcaigh faoi éide in eagar, is lándíormaí
le sleánna agus claimhte ar tarraingt, gathanna á scaoileadh,
fothram toirní ag sciatha á dtógaint is sleánna ina gclipí,
glioscarnach as fallaingí óir is saighdiúirí ag imeacht cosa in airde.
Ní hionadh gur sceimhligh na daoine is gur thiteadar ar a
    nglúine ag guí.

Deireann lucht eolaíochta go bhfeidhmíonn an t-atmaisféar im-
    mholach
mar fheadán ga-chatóideach ollmhór, áit a soláthraíonn an maigh-
    néadaisféar
is gaoth shíoraí na gréine leictreoin faoi ardlastaí fuinnimh
a thiteann chun talaimh is a thálann solas infheicthe dá bharr.
Seo iad na Saighneáin, an *aurora borealis* nó *australis*
ag brath ar cén áit ina mbíonn tú, is iad lasta suas ina gcaor.
B'in iad a chonacsa, ar mo chuaird ceithre lá go hAlaska
iad ag scinneadh thar m'amharc ó phlasma saighneánta na spéire.

B'iad seo a thaibhsigh in aimsir an tSéasair Tiberias
in aice na Róimhe, nuair a las dath chomh craorac sa spéir
gur cheap díormaí an airm impiriúil go raibh cathair Ostia faoi
    léigear
is gur chuireadar chun bóthair láithreach bonn le cabhair faoina
    dhéin.
B'iad seo a thaibhsigh d'oilithrigh na meánaoiseanna
is a scanraigh chomh mór san iad gur thit na mílte i bfantaisí
is do phlódaíodar go Páras ina sluaite ag guí is ag paidreoireacht
ag impí na Maighdine, go gcoiscfeadh sí orthu fearg an Rí.

It is said in the Bible that when King Antiochus
led an attack into Egypt a heavenly host appeared
fighting in the skies; for forty days and forty nights
these horsemen charged about, in full uniform, whole battalions
   of them
wielding spears and swords, ballistic missiles being fired off,
the thunderous sounds of shields and spears in massed combat,
the flashes of gold raiment, soldiers galloping helter-skelter.
No wonder people were afraid and fell on their knees to pray.

According to scientists, what happens is that the whole circumpolar atmosphere
functions as an enormous discharge tube, where electrons
produced by the solar wind and the magnetosphere fall to earth,
these high-speed particles emitting visible light as they fall.
These are the Northern Lights — Northern or Southern,
   depending on where you are —
with their great balls of fire.
It was these I saw on my four-day trip to Fairbanks, Alaska,
as they shot out past my vision from the flaming plasma of the
   skies.

These are what appeared in the era of Tiberias Caesar,
not far from Rome, when the sky was lit up so blood-red
the Imperial legions thought the port city of Ostia was under
   siege
and rushed out to its relief.
It was the Aurora Borealis that appeared to mediaeval penitents
   and pilgrims
and frightened them so much that thousands of them fainted.
They shuffled along in hordes, praying vociferously to the
   Virgin Mary
in hopes that she might assuage the wrath of the King of Heaven.

Shoilsíodar síos ar na manaigh a leanaigh Naomh Bréanainn
go dtí na scairbhreacha crua ó thuaidh is na hoighearshruthaí.
Shoilsíodar síos, ní foláir, leis ar chosmhuintir Fhranklin
nuair a theip ar a n-iarrachtaí an Bealach Siar ó Thuaidh a aimsiú.
Do thit na mairnéalaigh as a seasamh, iad marbh le fuacht is le
  hocras
ón síormháirseáil tré fhásach feannaideach an Artaigh ó thuaidh.
Faid a shiúlaíodar ní foláir nó d'fhéachadar suas ins na flaithis
ar na soilse síoraí seo ag taitneamh gan taise, gan trua.

Tá's agam nach bhfuil sé ceart, cóir ná cothrom
rud beag chomh suarach lem' chroíse a chur i gcomparáid
le feiniméan síoraí, le rud atá chomh dosháraithe
le soilse na bhFlaitheas, le hiomrothlú na bpláinéad.
Ar a shon san, i gcead do chách is don saol i gcoiteann
cé gur mór an náire dhom bheith chomh lán d'áibhéal,
(níl aon leigheas agam air, mar ná feadar a mhalairt)
caithfidh mé a admháil, is a rá aon uair dheireanach amháin,

faoi mar a dhamhsann, ar an gcuma san go díreach, na *Borey
  Dancers*
thar réimsí fuara na spéireach mar ghuairneáin lasrach faoi
  éidreoir
ag soilsiú feadh na firmiminte in aon chaor amháin gléigeal
ag cogarnaíl is ag sioscadh, ag líonadh folús uafar an spáis lena
  nglór
is mar sin a scinneann mo dhántasa, faon agus tréithlag,
thar scáileán fluairiseach m'intinne is ansan síos ar phár
ag léimt idir catóid seo mo phearsan coinsiasaí, an chuid díom
  a aithním,
is an anóid, an chuid íogair anacrach úd, go seasann tú dó, a stór.

The Lights shone down on the monks who followed Saint Brendan
to the hard Northern reefs and glacier-fields.
They must have shone down on the hapless followers of Franklin
when they failed to find the North-West Passage.
The seamen fell, one by one, where they were standing, dead with
    cold and hunger
from the prolonged forced march through the dismal wastes of the
    Arctic North.
As they trudged on despairingly they must have looked up at the
    heavens
as these eternal lights shone down on them without pity or emotion.

Now I know it's not at all appropriate
to compare something as small and paltry as my heart
to an eternal phenomenon, something as impenetrable
as the lights of Heaven or the movement of the planets.
In spite of all that, and with apologies to one and all,
and though I'm ashamed to be so over the top
I just can't help it, for I know only that form of intellectual
    exchange,
I have to say, this one last time,

that just as the Borey Dancers prance in this particular way
over the cold expanses of the heavens, like great fire-gyres
lighting up the firmament in one bright band
whispering and hissing, filling with their voices the awesome
    emptiness above,
so my poems, poor and puny as they may be,
take off across the fluorescent screen of my mind and then down
    the page,
leaping between the cathode of my conscious personality, the
    part of me I recognize,
and the anode, that distressing part you seem to represent, my
    love.

Easpa Comhbhróin

Bhí cuid des na murúcha agus do thángadar i dtír
in oileáinín sceirdiúil, áit a raibh failltreacha diamhaire.
Bhí eagla a gcroí orthu go dtitfeadh a leanaí
leis an bhfaobhar. Rud a tharla leis minic go leor.
Is toisc gan na sceolbhaigh a bheith ag obair níos mó
bháití iad, nuair ná deintí mionrabh dóibh ar na clocha géara.

Is dála an mhéid a tharla do Pheig Sayers ar an Oileán
nuair a thit a mac féin le faill
d'fhan muintir na hinise amach go maith uathu
is níor thángadar ina slóite ar an dtórramh
nó fiú ag déanamh comhbhróin leothu.

Bhíodar lán de phiseoga,
á rá, má lean an méid sin den mí-ádh nó den drochrath iad
nach foláir nó bhí sé tuillte acu.
B'in a bhfuaireadar de láchas
ós na daoine gur chuadar ina measc.

Lack of Sympathy

There were some of the merfolk who came up on land
on one particularly blasted and bleak island, surrounded by
   precipitous cliffs.
They were always heart-afraid their youngsters
would fall over the edge. Something that happened often
   enough.
Since their gills had ceased to function
they drowned, when they weren't smashed to smithereens on
   the razor-rocks.

Such was the case with Peig Sayers on the Great Blasket
   Island
when her own son fell from a cliff
and the islanders gave them a very wide berth,
not showing up in their usual droves for the wake
or even dropping by to say they were sorry for their trouble.

They were so full of superstition
they said that anyone with so much bad luck and misfortune
   following them
must have done something to deserve it.
That's as much kindness as the merfolk ever saw
from the people among whom they'd fetched up.

Na Murúcha agus Galair Thógálacha

Bhí mórán acu
is níor éirigh leo an t-athrú saoil
a chur i gceart díobh.
Ní raibh sé de ghus nó de theacht aniar iontu
na cosa a thabhairt leo.
Bhuailtí taom trom orthu
is bhítí ag gabháil steallaidh dhóibh
le gach galar tógálach a ghaibheadh an treo.

An eitinn is mó a leag iad
ach bhain an t-íbhil reatha,
plucamas, an bhruitíneach, an calar agus an mhaláire
líon mór daonra is roinnt den laochas dóibh.
'Daonra maighdeanúil' a thugann lucht eipidéimeolaíochta
ar a leithéid na laethanta seo.
An uair úd dob é an léamh a deintí
ná gurb ann ab amhlaidh a sciob
na púcaí leo iad.

Bhí crosanna agus piseoga go forleathan
ina thaobh. Dá mbeadh triúr ban ag gabháilt aniar
sa bhaile céanna ag an am céanna
bhí sé ráite sa tairngreacht
go mbeadh duine acu sínte, siúráilte, faoin bhfód
bliain ón lá san.

Tharla a leithéid dom shin-sheanmháthair.
Uncail a céile, Tomás na bPúcaí,
bhíodh sé amuigh san oíche
ag imeacht i dteannta na bh*fairies*.
D'inis sé roimh ré
go mbeadh púr mhór ag imeacht ón áit
laistigh de ráithe — 'Do dheineas mo dhícheall
chun í a chimeád, ach ní fhéadfainn é.'

The Merfolk and Infectious Diseases

There were quite a lot of them
who never quite came to terms
with their great change of lifestyle.
They didn't have the inner resources or the recuperative
    power
to see them through.
They were particularly susceptible
to severe illnesses
and any infectious disease that was doing the rounds.

It was TB that made off with most of them
but the King's Evil,
mumps, measles, cholera and malaria
also put paid to quite a percentage of the population.
'A virgin population' is what they'd be called
by modern epidemiologists.
In those days, though, the way it was understood
was that the pookas
had swept them away with them.

Taboos and superstitions were rife
in this regard. If three women were found to be pregnant
in the same townland at the same time
it was widely prophesied
that one of them would definitely be dead and buried
within the year.

This is just what happened to my own great-grandmother.
Her husband's uncle, Thomas of the Pookas,
used to be out and about at night
with fairy folk.
He announced publicly beforehand
that a great calamity would strike the townland
within three months. 'I did my level best to stop them,'
says he, 'but I wasn't able to.'

Níor inis sé d'éinne
cioca den triúr a bheadh ina púr
go dtí gur cailleadh í.

D'imigh rud cosúil leis ar a hiníon chomh maith,
deirfiúr chríonna mo sheanmháthar.
Bhí sí ina hógbhean chomh hálainn, chomh breá
is d'fhéadfaí d'fháilt, í ina ceirtlín
dea-dhathach. Róbhreá a bhí sí.
Leagadh í gan choinne is í ag teacht ón sáipéal
is d'fheoigh is do mheathlaigh sí.
Naoi déag a bhí sí.
Ní áiteodh an sagart paróiste go dtí an deireadh
ar mo Neain
ná gurb iad na púcaí a d'fhuadaigh í.

He didn't tell anyone which of the three women would die
so tragically until his own niece was taken.

Something more or less the same happened to her daughter,
   as well,
my grandmother's eldest sister.
She was as fine and beautiful a young woman
as you would find anywhere, a well-made, fine-complexioned
   girl
with red hair. Too fine altogether she was.
She was struck down suddenly as she was coming from Mass
   one Sunday,
and she faded away and went into a decline.
She was only nineteen when she died.
To the very end of her days the parish priest himself
couldn't persuade my grandmother
that it wasn't the fairies who'd abducted her.

Na Murúcha ag Ní a gCeann

Ó thugadar cúl na láimhe glan don uisce
ní féidir leo iad féin a fholcadh.
Glanann siad na háraistí le meascán fuail is luaithe
is *pinch* beag gainimhe tríd
is caithfear a admháil tar éis a bhfaigheann siad dá ndua
gur gléineach a bhíonn siad.

Níonn siad a gcoirp le híle is le rósuisce
is a gceann le seampú tirim,
(ábhar saorga a ghaibheann siad ón bpoitigéir)
nó le púdar talcaim.

An uair fhada fhánach
a fhliuchann siad a gceann
is le huisce bog é.
Caitheann siad é a dhéanamh
roimh dul síos don ngréin,
rud go bhfuil ábhar maith leis.

Do bhí bean fadó ann a bhí ag tuargaint lín
is bhí beirt chailíní aici.
Dúirt sí leothu go nífidíst a gceann
nuair a bheadh an t-airneán déanta.

Siar san oíche a bhí sé sin
is nuair nár thug sí aon bhia dóibh
chuir ceann des na cailíní blúire luaithe ina béal
is an cailín eile roinnt cátha.

Do tháinig an cnag sa doras
san oíche siar
is do labhair an guth ann,
'Luathaigh, luathaigh, bolg luaithe.

The Merfolk and Washing Hair

Since they've put water entirely behind them
they can't as much as take a bath.
They wash their dishes in a mixture of urine and ashes
with a pinch of sand added to it
and you have to admit that with all the hard effort they put
    into it
they really get those dishes gleaming.

Their bodies they bathe with oil and rose water
and they clean their hair with dry shampoo
(an artificial substance that they get at the chemist's)
or even with talcum powder.

The odd time
they do wash their hair
it's with lukewarm water.
This ritual must be performed
before the setting of the sun,
a custom for which there's a very good reason.

There was one female amongst them long ago who was up
    late pounding flax
and she had two girls in working for her.
She told them they should wait to wash their hair
when the late-night work was finished.

That turned out to be very late in the night
and when she didn't as much as give them a bite to eat
one of the girls put a pinch of ashes in her mouth
and the other one a piece of chaff.

The knock came to the door
in the dead of night
and a voice sang out,
'Off you dash, belly full of ash.

Fágaíg', fágaíg', bolg cátha.
Bolg folamh ar an doras seo láithreach.'

Ardaíodh chun siúil bean a' tí agus cailín na luaithe
agus fágadh ar an láthair bean na cátha.

Úsáidtear an scéal seo, fiú sa lá atá inniu ann
chun scanradh an diabhail bhuí
a chur ar na maighdeanacha mara óga.

Stay on my behalf, belly full of chaff.
Let the empty belly evermore
be at this door.'

With that the woman of the house and the girl who had eaten
    the ash were gone
and all that was left was the girl who had eaten the chaff.

This story is still being told, to this very day,
to scare the living daylights
out of the young females of the species.

Na Murúcha i mBun Oibreacha Innealtóireachta

Is dócha toisc an mhéid gur ghaibheadar tríd
is go bhfeacadar an *danger* —
Murchadh nó an tor ba ghoire dho —
go bhfuilid de shíor is choíche ag lorg cosanta is díonadh
is go bhfuilid an-thugtha d'oibreacha innealtóireachta.
Thiar ar an mBóithrín Dorcha, in aice le Lúb a' Chaoil
i gCorca Dhuibhne tá stáisiún draenála
agus é lán suas de chaidéil agus de phumpanna
le húsáid i gcoinne na hanachaine.

Tá tuile mhór á tuar, ó lá go lá.
Pléascfaidh toibreacha uile an duibheagáin mhóir
agus osclóidh comhlaí uisce uile neimhe.
Beidh sé ag fearthain ar an dtalamh ar feadh daichead lá is
   daichead oíche.
Tá cuid acu ag cuimhneamh ar áirc a dhéanamh
de chrann gófar; seomraí a chur inti
agus brat pice uirthi lasmuigh agus laistigh,
a rá is go saorfaidh sé sin iad.

Tá cuid eile acu ag cuimhneamh
ar dhul suas i measc mullach na gcnoc,
mar a dhein Nietzsche i Sils-Maria,
ag súil go dtuirlingeoidh an Tiarna orthu.
Áit nach mbeidh le clos acu, ar mo thuairim,
ach an fiach dubh
is é ag fógairt na ceiste is bunúsaí ar fad,
'Cá? Cá? Cá? Cá?'

Níl an fhaisnéis fhadtéarmach róghléineach.
Má tá tóithín á nochtadh féin le cúpla bliain
i mBá an Daingin

Public Works

I suppose it's because of all they went through
(having seen 'peril' up close and personal
in the shape of Murrough of the Burnings, or the bush nearest
    to him as he swept by),
the merfolk are constantly concerned with safety and security
    issues
and are especially drawn to vast engineering projects.
Back on the Bóithrín Dorcha, near Lúb a' Chaoil,
on the Dingle Peninsula, they have a drainage station
full of water pumps and all sorts of hydraulic systems
in case of emergency.

They prophesy that there'll be a deluge any day now.
All the wells of the deep will burst
and the floodgates of Heaven will open.
A hard rain will fall for forty days
and forty nights.
Some of them are even considering building an ark
from gopher-wood, fitting it out with cabins
and proofing it with bitumen and pitch, inside and out,
in the hope that this will somehow save them.

Yet others are thinking
of heading for the hills,
a bit like Nietzsche did in Sils-Maria,
hoping that the King of Glory will meet them halfway.
Up there, of course, all they will hear
is the raven
asking that most fundamental question of all,
'Whe, oh whe, oh whe, oh where?'

The long-term forecast isn't too bright.
In addition to the dolphin showing up
in Dingle Bay

do tháinig tuairisc chughainn le déanaí
go raibh míol mór le feiscint ar an Maing
agus báid iascaireachta cheana féin ag tabhairt turasóirí
amach ag féachaint air.
Tá na sagairt ó lá go chéile ag cailliúint a sainte
agus iad ag imeacht le hoibreacha sóisialta is le cráifeacht.
Más fíor más ea don seanrá
nach fada go bhfillfidh an fharraige ar bharr Shliabh Mis
de bharr róthruaillithe agus na gásanna úd thigh gloine
n'fheadar ag an bpointe sin cad a dhéanfaidh siad?

Beidh siad titithe i gceart in umar na haimiléise
is i bpoll na hainnise.
Féach ansan, ambaiste, an mbeidh an triail orthu!

over the last few years
it has been reported more recently
that a whale has manifested itself in the river Maine
and fishing boats are already bringing sightseers
out to gape at it.
The priests too, gradually, are losing their tightfistedness
and are all off doing social work and good deeds and acts
   of piety.
So, if the prophesy is to be believed,
and it won't be long until the sea returns to cover Slieve Mish
because of pollution and greenhouse gases,
I wonder, at that point, what stuff they'll be made of.

Then they'll definitely have fallen into the Slough of Despond
and the depths of despair.
That's the time, by cripes, we'll see how they measure up in
   crisis-management.

An Mhurúch agus Naomh Bréanainn

Ar ndóigh, tá stair fhada ag na murúcha in Éirinn
agus mórán scéalta orthu agus ar na rónta.
Luaitear ceann amháin acu fiú i mBeatha Bhréanainn
agus tá dealbh di le fáil ina eaglais i gCluain Fhearta.

'Sé a deireann sé sa Bheatha ná go dtángadar uirthi
díreach tar éis dó bheith ag agallamh leis an nDiabhal Dorcha.
D'inis sé dá mhanaigh cuid des na pianpháiseanna a chonaic sé
díreach mar atá cur síos orthu i seanscríbhinní na ndlíthe ársa.

Ansan 'Ní rófhada ina dhiaidh sin go bhfuaireadar
an iníon mhín, lánfhásta, mhoingbhuí.
Bhí gile sneachta nó cúrán toinne inti
is í marbh de bharr buille gatha a chuaigh isteach
trí lár a gualainne is amach idir a dhá chíoch.
Ba mhórthaibhseach, ambasa, méid na hiníne —
céad troigh ar airde agus bhí naoi dtroithe idir a cíocha
agus seacht dtroigh i bhfaid méire meáin a láimhe.
D'athbheoigh Bréanainn í ar an láthair
is bhaist í is d'fhiafraigh di de cén cineál í.
"D'áitreabhaigh na mara domhsa," a dúirt sí,
"díobh siúd a bhíonn ag guí is ag súil lenár n-aiséirí."
Dh'fhiafraigh Bréanainn ansan di cioca den dá rud ab fhearr léi
"dul láithreach ar neamh, nó thar n-ais go dtína dúthaigh
 athartha."
Do fhreagair an iníon i gcanúint nár aithin ach Bréanainn
 amháin
go mb'fhearr léi dul ar neamh — "mar cluinim cheana féin
guthanna na n-aingeal is iad ag moladh an Choimde
 Chomhachtaigh."

The Merfolk and Saint Brendan

Of course, there's a long history of merfolk in Ireland
and a great tradition of stories about themselves and the seals.
There is even one mentioned in the mediaeval Life of Saint Brendan
and there's a carving of a mermaid in the cathedral at Clonfert.
What it says in the Life is that Brendan came upon the mermaid
just after he had been conversing with the Dark Devil.
He described to his monks all the terrible tortures he saw
and confirmed they were just like what had been described in the old manuscripts.

It wasn't long after that, so, they came upon
the gentle, fully grown, yellow-haired mermaid.
Her skin was as white as snow or the surf on the wave
and she was stone dead because of a harpoon that had entered
her right between the shoulders and was sticking out between her two breasts.
The size of the mermaid was indeed quite extraordinary.
She was a hundred feet in length and there was a span of nine feet between her two breasts
and the length of the middle finger of her hand was seven feet.
Saint Brendan brought her back to life on the spot,
baptised her, and asked her about her kith and kin.
'I am one of the inhabitants of the sea,' she replied,
'one of those who are always praying and hoping for our resurrection.'
Brendan asked her which of the two choices she would prefer,
'to go immediately to Heaven or to return to the territory of her forebears.'
The mermaid answered in a dialect that only Brendan himself could understand
that she would prefer to go to Heaven — 'for I can already hear
the voices of the angels singing the praises of the All-Powerful Creator.'

Ansan do chaith sí Corp Chríost is fuair bás ar an láthair
gan imní ar bith, is do chuir Bréanainn í go honórach.'

Níl aon ní sa mhéid sin a raghadh i gcoinne mo thaithí
pearsanta ar na murúcha, ach amháin ceist seo a méid.
Ar ndóigh d'fhéadfá a rá go raibh smut den áibhéil
i gceist i gcónaí sna seanscéalta, nó rud eile —
gur dócha go raibh an treabh go léir ag dul i minithe
is i mbréagaí, ar nós na héinne eile, ó aois go haois,
mar a mhíníonn na seaniarsmaí ar nós na tuamaí meigi-
   liteacha
go dtabharfá do leabhar gur fathaigh amháin a thógfadh iad.

Then she received the Eucharist and died immediately
without any anxiety or worry, and Brendan had her buried
    with great ceremony.

There is nothing at all in that description that doesn't chime
with my own personal experience of the merfolk, except for
    this matter of her size.
Of course you could always say that a bit of exaggeration
was always a feature of the old stories, or even something
    else —
that it is probable that the whole tribe has gradually been
    getting smaller
and, like everyone else, getting more deceitful from generation
    to generation,
something you'd also surmise from the old relics of antique
    times, such as the megalithic tombs
that you'd swear must indeed have been put in place by a race
    of giants.

An Mhurúch agus Focail Áirithe

Ná luaigh an focal 'uisce' léi
nó aon ní a bhaineann le cúrsaí farraige —
'tonn', 'taoide', 'bóchna', 'muir' nó 'sáile'.
Ní lú léi an sioc samhraidh ná trácht a chlos
ar iascach, báid, saighní trá nó traimile, potaí gliomach.
Tá's aici go maith go bhfuil a leithéidí ann
is go mbíonn gíotáil éigin a bhaineas leo
ar siúl ag daoine eile.

Ceapann sí má dhúnann sí a cluasa is má chasann a ceann
go mbeidh sí saor orthu
is ná cloisfidh sí búir dhúr an eich uisce
ag fógairt gaoil shíoraí léi go doimhin san oíche,
ag cur gráinníní ar a craiceann is brat allais
amach trí lár a codladh uirthi.

Níl aon namhaid eile aici
ach an saol fó-thoinn a chleacht sí
sarar iontaigh sí ar a hathshaol ar an míntír
a chur i gcuimhne dhi. Séanann sí ó bhonn
go raibh oiread is cac snioga de bhaint aici leis
aon am. 'Ní raibh aon tsuim riamh agam
sna piseoga sin, nó in aon sórt seanaimsearachta.
Aer, eolas, solas gléineach na heolaíochta
is ea a shantaíos-sa.'

Ba chuma liom ach go bhfuaireas-sa amach
san éitheach í.

The Mermaid and Certain Words

Whatever you do don't ever mention the word 'water'
or anything else that smacks of the sea —
'wave', 'tide', 'ocean', 'the raging main', 'the briny'.
She'd as soon contemplate the arrival of frost in the middle
   of summer
than hear tell of fishing, boats, seine or trammel nets, lobster
   pots.
She knows that such things exist, of course,
and that other people
have truck with them.

She thinks that if she covers over her ears and turns away
   her head
she'll be free of them
and she'll never hear again the loud neighing of the kelpie or
   water horse
claiming its blood relation with her at the darkest hour of
   night,
causing her to break out in goose pimples and having sweat
   lashing off her
while she's fast asleep.

She hates nothing so much
as being reminded of the underwater life that she led
before she turned over a new leaf on dry land. She totally
   denies
that she had the slightest connection with it
at any time. 'I never had any interest
in those old superstitions, or any of the old traditions.
Fresh air, knowledge, the shining brightness of science
are all I ever hankered after.'

I wouldn't mind one way or the other but I myself have
   found her out
in the deception.

Istigh sa Roinn le Béaloideas Éireann,
tá lámhscríbhinn iomlán de Bhailiúchán na Scol
breactha óna láimh,
scríte in uisce, le clipe de sciathán rotha,
ar scothóg feamainne mar phár.

Tá trí cinn déag de scéalta fada
agus smutaíocha de chinn eile, i dteannta le
horthaí, seanphaidreacha, tomhaiseanna agus aroile
le tabhairt faoi ndeara ann.
Óna hathair is óna máthar chríonna is mó
a thóg sí síos iad.

Diúltaíonn sí glan dó — 'An máistir
a thug mar obair bhaile dhúinn é fadó
thiar sa bhunscoil. Chaitheamair é a dhéanamh.
Ní raibh aon dul as againn.'
Cháithfeadh sí fuil shróine
sara mbeadh sí riamh admhálach ina thionscnamh.

In the Department of Irish Folklore in University College,
    Dublin,
there is a whole manuscript in the Schools' Collection
that was set down by her,
written in water, with the fin of a ray for a pen,
on a long scroll of kelp.

In it can be found thirteen long tales
and odds and ends of other ones, together with
charms, old prayers, riddles and such.
From her father and her grandmother she mostly
took them down.

She refuses to accept its existence, and when she does,
    'It was the master
who gave it to us as homework, way back in the National
    School. We had to do it.
There was no getting out of it.'
She would prefer to suffer a heavy nosebleed
rather than admit she ever had a hand in its composition.

Glór an Uisce

Cuid acu sin a chuaigh amú ar an slí
tagann siad i dtír ar uairibh.

Máire Chathaoir a bhí istigh ina tigh féin
ansúd ar bharr an ché.
Oíche bhreá sa bhfómhar ab ea é
is bhí sé doimhin go maith san oíche.
Bhí sí suite cois na tine, uair mhairbh na hoíche.
Do cnagadh ar an doras is tháinig an t-óganach seo isteach,
an fear ba bhreátha a chonaic a dhá shúil riamh.
Bhí glór an uisce óna bhróga.

Dúirt sé gur bhreá an oíche é
is go mbeadh mórán éisc ar maidin
ag an mbád a bhí ag coraíocht ar an dtráigh.
Loirg sé uisce ansan uirthi chun a chosa a ní
is do nigh is do thriomaigh.
'Dein an t-uisce a chaitheamh an doras amach anois
is ná bain aon úsáid as.'
Bhí sé chun dul isteach go tigh an tsagairt,
a dúirt sé, ach ná ligfeadh an spáinnéirín gadhair
a bhí aige in aice an tí é.
'Cá raghair anois?' ar sí, nuair a bhí sé ag imeacht.
'Raghad 'on seanathalamh.'
'Dia linn,' ar sise.

Chuaigh sí go dtí an sagart
lá arna mháireach ag insint an scéil ar fad dó.
Thug sí a chomharthaí dó.
'Á,' arsan sagart, 'deartháir dom é sin
a bádh ag teacht ó Mheiriceá, i dTalamh an Éisc.'
'Dia linn,' arsa Máire.

Water Voice

Some of those who got lost along the way
do manage to make appearances ashore from time to time.

Máire, the wife of Cathaoir, was sitting in her own house
at the head of the quay.
It was a fine autumn evening
and next thing she knew it was late at night.
She was sitting up by the fire, in the dead of night.
A knock came to the door and this young fellow walked in,
as fine a fellow as she'd ever laid eyes on.
There was the sound of water squelching in his shoes.

He said it was a fine night
and that the boats setting seine-nets near to the strand
would have a fine catch by morning.
He asked her then if she'd a drop of water to wash his feet
and he duly washed them and dried them.
'You must throw the water out the door immediately
without using it for anything else.'
He had been trying to get to the priest's house,
he said, but the little spaniel
near the house wouldn't let him near it.
'Where will you go now?' she asked him as he was leaving.
'I'll go back to the old stomping ground.'
'Mother of Jesus,' said she.

She was off to the priest
the very next day to tell him the whole story.
She described the young man perfectly.
'Sure,' said the priest, 'wasn't it my own brother
who was lost off Newfoundland, on the way back from
    America.'
'Mother of Jesus,' said Máire.

Poltergeist

Bíonn útamáil éigin néaróiseach agus fuarmaíl
le brath i gcónaí
timpeall pé áit go mbíonn siad.

Níor chuir aon ní riamh trí m'úmacha mé
ná níor thug dom a leithéid de dhalladh is tarrac tríd
ná oíche a chaitheas i dtigh lóistín
in aon seomra le duine acu.

Ar dtúis bhí an rapáil is an rapáil
seo le clos i gcoinne phainéil adhmaid an fhalla.
Ansan thosnaigh an trampáil is an trampáil
suas is anuas an staighre.
Ansan mar bharr ar gach mí-ádh
tógadh an stól ó bhun an tseomra
is caitheadh i gcoinne na leapan é.
B'in é an greim is mó a bheir riamh orm.
Cheapas go dtitfeadh an t-anam asam, fuar marbh, tur te
    ar an spota.

Is tá mo dhóthain léitheoireachta déanta agam
ar chúrsaí spioradachais
is ar stair agus teoiricí an 'pholtergeist'
chun a thuiscint láithreach cad a bhí suas.

'An mbíonn an gliothram is an útamáil seo i gcónaí
ins an tigh seo?' arsa mise léi ar maidin.
'Bíonn,' a dúirt sí, gan nath ar bith á chur sa cheist aici.
'Bíonn,' a dúirt sí, 'núthair, tá mo chláirín déanta agam air
faoin am seo.'

Poltergeist

There's always some sort of neurotic vibe and valency
hanging around them
wherever they might be.

Nothing in my whole life has caused me so much grief
or given me such torment and trouble
as the night I spent in a lodging house
in the same room as one of them.

First of all there was this rapping and rapping
against the wooden panelling of the wall.
Then there was this tramping and tramping
up and down the stairs.
And as if that wasn't enough
the stool was lifted up from the far end of the room
and dashed against the bedstead.
That was the worst predicament I was ever in.
I thought that I'd have a heart seizure and fall down dead
    there on the spot.

I'd done enough reading
about spiritualism and the likes
and the case histories and theories behind the phenomenon
    of the 'poltergeist'
to know immediately what was up.

'Is that sort of racket raised all the time
in this house?' says I to herself the following morning.
'Yes,' says she, barely registering my question.
'Yes,' says she, 'it's constant. But sure I'm well used to it
    by now.'

Murúch Linbh gan Baisteadh

Má thagann tú isteach i dtigh
go mbíonn murúch linbh óig ann
is é ag feitheamh lena bhaisteadh
caitheann tú seile ar an leanbh sin.

Is ceart duit an méid sin a dhéanamh
is a rá lena linn,
'Cac is mún is aoileach ort'.
Is é an chiall atá
leis na focail sin ná
'Saol fada chughat'.

An Unbaptised Merchild

If you ever happen to go into a house
in which there is a newly-born merchild
still waiting to be baptized
you absolutely must spit on that child.

You have to do that
and to say while you're doing it,
'May shit and piss and the dunghill be with you.'
What is really meant
by this expression is
'May you enjoy a long life.'

Admháil Shuaithinseach

Aon uair amháin riamh i mo shaol
a fuaireas oiread is an leide is lú ó bhéal
aon duine acu
go raibh saghas éigin cineghlanadh gafa tríd acu
is gur ó áit éigin eile ar fad, i bhfad i gcéin
a thángadar.

A sé déag nó mar sin a bhíos nuair a tharla sé seo.
Mé ag foghlaim bitheolaíochta
is teoiricí ceimice.
Bhíos faoi dhraíocht ag fiseolaíocht agus sláinteachas
is mé lán suas
de théarmaí staidéir gnó is ríomhaireachta.

Thángas de shiúl cos lá trasna an Náth
mo threabhsar fillte suas go dtí mo chromáin
is smut de bhrúscar cladaigh á tharrac i mo dhiaidh agam.
Bhíos fiosrach faoi.
'Cén sórt bric í seo agam, a Thomáis?
Gadhar, ab ea?'

Do leag an seanduine uaidh a rámhainn ar an dtráigh
mar a raibh na luganna á mbaint aige.
Buí, dubhghlas is crón is ea do ghlioscadar
ag snámharnach de shíor sa chróca romhainn.
'Ní haon ghadhar é sin atá agat,' ar sé,
'ach cat. Cat ceannann.'
Do stop sé, thug catshúil thapaidh deas is clé
is chuir cogar-i-leith-chugham.

'Níl aon ainmhí dá bhfuil ar an míntír,' ar sé,
'nach bhfuil a chomh-mhaith d'ainmhí
sa bhfarraige. An cat, an madra, an bhó, an mhuc,

A Remarkable Admission

Only one time ever in my life
did I get as much as the slightest inkling
from one of them
that they had gone through some sort of ethnic cleansing
and that it was to some other place altogether, far, far away,
they really belonged.

I was sixteen or so when it happened.
I was deeply into biology
and chemical equations.
I was enthralled by physiology and hygiene,
up to the eyeballs
in accountancy and computing skills.

I was wading across the Nath one day,
my jeans-legs turned up to my thighs,
trailing a bit of something I'd found on the beach.
I was curious about it.
'What class of a fish is this I have here, Thomas?' I asked,
'Is it a dogfish?'

The old man laid his spade down on the strand
where he had been digging lug worms.
I remember they sparkled yellow, blackish-green and brown
   as they slithered
and seethed in the jam-jar.
'That's no dogfish you have there,' says he,
'but a catfish. A white-faced catfish.'
Then he lowered his voice, glanced left and right
and continued in a whisper.

'There's not a single animal up on dry land
that doesn't have its equivalent
in the sea. The cat, the dog, the cow, the pig.

tá siad go léir ann.
Go dtí an duine féin, agus tá sé sin ann leis.
'Sé ainm atá air siúd ná an mhurúch.'

Ghluais scamall dorcha thar a shúile ar dhath na dtonn
a dhein tiompáin mhara dhíobh.
N'fheadar cad a shnámhaigh anall is anonn
sna duibheagáin doimhne sin
mar sara raibh am agam i gceart
é a bhodhradh le mo chuid cleatrála is le mo chaint
ar cheimic, fisic, is ar fhiosrúcháin mhuireolaíochta
do chas sé ar a shál is d'imigh uaim.

D'fhág sé ar snámh mé idir dhá uisce.

They're all there.
Right up to the human being himself, and he's there too.
The name they call him is the sea-person.'

A dark cloud passed over his sea-green eyes
that made them look like marine trenches.
I'll never know what strange creatures swam around
in their great depths
because, just when I was about to launch into him
and bend his ear
about chemistry, physics and the latest underwater
    explorations
he turned on his heel and disappeared.

He left me hanging there,
like a drowned man between two seams of water.

Leide Beag

Dá gcaithfeá faid do mharthana iomláin'
ag cúléisteacht leis an mhurúch
b'fhéidir go bhfaighfeá leide beag anseo is ansiúd
cárbh as di. Thángas-sa aniar aduaidh
uirthi lá fómhair is a naíonán
á bréagadh faoina seál aici.

'Ní tú éan gorm na mbainirseach,
ní tú gearrcach glas na gcaobach,
ní tú coileán an mhadra uisce,
ní tú lao na maoile caoile,'

an suantraí a bhí á chanadh aici
ach do stop sí suas láithreach bonn
chomh luath is a thuig sí
duine eile a bheith ar an bport.

Tuigeadh dom gur ghlac sí náire
i dtaobh é bheith cloiste agam in aon chor.
Tuigeadh dom chomh maith go raibh blas an-láidir
den bhfarraige air mar shuantraí ar an gcéad scór.

A Tiny Clue

You could spend your entire life
eavesdropping on the mermaid
before you'd pick up the tiniest little clue
about where she was really from. One autumn day
   I happened upon
her and her child
while she was comforting it under her shawl.

'You are not the blue-green pup of the seal.
You are not the grey chick of the greater black-backed gull.
You are not the kit of the otter. Nor are you
the calf of the slender hornless cow.'

This was the lullaby she was singing
but she stopped short
immediately she realized
someone else was in the neighbourhood.

I had the distinct sense she was embarrassed
I'd overheard her in the first place.
I also came away with the impression
the lullaby was, to put it mildly, redolent of the sea.

Leide Beag Eile

Murach go raibh naíonán beag
a tháinig ar an saol róluath
is a bhí i mbaol gairid a bháis
ní bheadh an tarna leide fachta riamh agam,
ach chonac é seo lem' dhá shúil féin.

Bhí an leanbh lagbhríoch báiteach bán
is gan anam ar éigean ann.
Scuab an mhurúch suas ina baclainn é
is thug baisteadh urláir dó.

Chaith sí trí bhraon bheaga
ar chlár éadain an linbh
in ainm an Athar, an Mhic agus an Spioraid Naoimh,
is dúirt sí lena linn:

'Braon beag an Athar
i lár do bhathais bhig, a rún.
Braon beag an Mhic
i gcroí do bhathais bhig, a stór.
Braon an Spioraid Naoimh
ar chlár t'éadain bhig, a ghrá.'

Ansan do nigh sí an bhunóicín
is faid a bhí sí á ní
chaitheadh sí basóg bheag uisce
thar a gualainn aniar
is í á rá mar seo:

'Tonnán dod' chruth.
Tonnán dod' ghuth.
Tonnán dod' chumas cainte.

Another Tiny Clue

Had it not been for the merchild
who came into the world before its time
and who was in serious danger of death
I'd never have taken account of this second clue
only that I saw it with my own two eyes.

The child was so weak and wan
and incapable of any movement
the mermaid swept it up in her arms
and gave it a home baptism.

She put three small drops of water
on the child's forehead
in the name of the Father, the Son and the Holy Spirit,
while intoning at the same time:

'A drop for the Father
on your little brow, my darling.
A drop for the Son
in the middle of your brow, my dear.
A drop for the Holy Spirit
on your little brow, my love.'

Then she washed the newborn infant
and while she was doing so
she threw small handfuls of water
over her shoulder,
chanting all the while:

'A wavelet for your lovely form.
A wavelet for your voice so warm.
A wavelet for the gift of eloquent speech.

Tonnán dod' rath.
Tonnán dod' mhaith.
Tonnán dod' shaol is dod' shláinte.

Tonnán dod' sciúch.
Tonnán dod' lúth.
Tonnán dod' ghrásta.
Naoi dtonnán dod' fhíorghrásta.'

Anois, muna dteaspáineann sé sin
go raibh dúchas na farraige
go leathan láidir inti
dá mhéid a bhí sé ceilte
is curtha faoi chois aici,
ní lá fós é!

In am an ghátair a bhriseann an dúchas.
Cad a dhéanfadh mac an chait nuair is treise dúchas ná
   oiliúint.

A wavelet for good luck.
A wavelet for moral pluck.
A wavelet for a safe haven within your reach.

A wavelet for your throat.
A wavelet to help you float
effortlessly and with ease,
effortlessly and with the greatest ease.'

Now, if you think that doesn't suggest
how firmly implanted in her
was a sense of the sea,
however much she tried to hide it
or how deeply she'd repressed it,
you've another think coming.

When times are hard heredity will out.
What would you expect when nature is stronger than
    nurture?

Baisteadh na Murúch

Bhí cuid acu ar feadh tamaill mhóir
chomh séantach sin ar uisce
gur dhiúltaíodar glan fiú do ghnás an Bhaiste.
Bhí sé ina chlibirt cheart ar feadh i bhfad
idir iad agus cléirigh na Deoise.

Sa deireadh fuaireadar logha speisialta ón Vatacáin
go bhféadfaí fíon a úsáid i gcás na Coisreacan.
Míorúilt Chána droim thar n-ais
a thug lucht seoigh is masla ar an dtarlacan.

The Order of Baptism

There were some of them who had been so long
and so strongly in denial of water
they completely refused its use in the ritual of Baptism.
There was such a racket raised about it
between themselves and the clergy of the Diocese.

In the end they had to get a special dispensation from the Vatican
that wine could be used instead of water during the consecration of the Sacrament.
The Miracle of Cana Backwards
was how the local smart-asses and shit-stirrers termed this phenomenon.

Dúchas Arís

Níl aon teora le dúchas mar a insíonn scéal
ar rud a thit amach do chailín óg de threibh
na farraige láimh le Dún Chaoin.

Do rángaigh sí ag an dtobar ag líonadh canna d'fhíoruisce
nuair a ghaibh an bacach seo an treo. Gaibh sé
Bóthar na Gleidhbe aníos agus Gort na gCearc anoir.
Do nigh sé a lámha is a aghaidh sa séithleán
a bhí ar sileadh síos. 'Mhuise, a chailín mhánla,'
ar seisean, 'arbh aon difear duit t'aprún a thabhairt dom
go dtriomód mo lámha is m'aghaidh ann?'
'Triomaigh is fáilte,' arsa an cailín.

Chuaigh sí abhaile ansan agus níor dhein sí aon ní sa tsaol
ach an canna a bhualadh uaithi is imeacht de gach hop is
  pocléim
siar Bóthar na Lataraí agus an cóngar go Tobar an Chéirín.
Ba chuma léi ach radharc d'fháil arís air. D'oibrigh sí go
  maith na rúitíní
ach ní raibh aon radharc aici air ag Cnocán na bPréachán.
Siúd léi ansan go dtí Mullach an Chlasaigh agus an Clasach
  síos
is gan ag baint na céille di ach go bhfaigheadh sí radharc súl
  air arís.

Do bhí bean ón gCeathrúin ina coinne aníos.
Bean dheas sheanchríonna a thuig go raibh rud éigin suas.
'A Mhuire Mháthair,' arsa an cailín, 'an raibh aon bhuachaill

Second Nature

There really is nothing to compare to the power of heredity
    as is clear from the story
of something that happened to one of the tribe
of merfolk living near Dunquin.

This young one was off to the well one day to fill a can of
    fresh water
when a beggar happened on her. He came
down the Glebe Road and over across the Hens' Acre.
He washed his hands and face in the little stream
that flowed from the well. 'Wisha, my dear,'
he said, 'would you mind lending me your apron
so I might dry my hands and face in it?'
'Dry away to your heart's content,' said the girl.

As she started home the very first thing she did
was put the can down and head off with a hop, step and
    a jump
along Puddle Parade and then the shortcut over to the
    Poultice Well.
All she wanted was another glimpse of him. Though she
    moved at quite a lick
there was no sign of him at Ravens' Rock.
Then off she went to the crown of the Clasach and down
    the Clasach itself
with nothing on her mind but the possibility she might see
    him again.

There was a woman from Ferriter's Quarter coming up the
    road towards her.
She was an experienced woman who knew immediately
    something was up.
'Mother of God,' said the girl, 'was there by any chance
    a young man

id' choinne aníos?' 'N'fheaca cailín ná buachaill
ná beithíoch ná préachán, ach tusa amháin.'
D'fhéach sí ina deilbh agus ina haghaidh istigh
is d'aithin go raibh athrú uirthi.
Fuair sí an scéal ar fad ó thús uaithi.

An diabhal rud a dhein an tseanbhean ach a lámh a chur
san aprún is é a stolladh anuas den gcailín.
Ansan dhein sí líathróidín de idir a dhá láimh istigh
is dhein é a rúideadh síos Gleann an Chlasaigh.
Tá leagan eile leis den scéal a chuala á rá
gur thóg sí sisiúirín as a póca is ghearr sí lásaí
an aprúin; gur thit an cailín siar ina baclainn
ach gur lean an aprún ag gluaiseacht síos an bóthar
i ndiaidh mo stumpa bacaigh de shodar.
Bhí sé seo caite, is dócha, idir dhá thoirtín
ag fanacht lena sheans go ngeobhadh sé chúichi.
Chuaigh an cailín abhaile go Baile Bhiocáire
is níor fhan aon rian de chuimhne an bhacaigh aici
ó baineadh di an t-aprún.

Mianach na farraige a bhí sa bhacach
is mura mbeadh an tseanbhean a bheith chomh tuisceanach
bhí sí imithe leis de seait.
Sin dúchas duit!

on the road?' 'No, I saw neither girl nor boy
nor beast nor crow,' said the woman, 'but only yourself
   until now.'
She looked closely at her countenance
and recognized at once that a change had come over the girl.
Soon she got the whole story out of her.

What did the old one do then but reach
for the apron and rip it straight off the girl.
Then she gathered it up into a ball between her two hands
and fired it down the length of the Clasach Trench.
There's another version doing the rounds,
that she took a pair of scissors out of her pocket
and cut the apron strings. With that the girl fell back straight
   into her arms
and the apron went down the road on its own
in search of that fine lump of a beggar.
He had hidden himself, sure enough, between two bushes,
waiting for his chance when she caught up with him.
The girl went home to Vicarstown,
retaining not the slightest trace of a memory of the beggar
once the apron was taken off her.

That beggar had merfolk written all over him
and if the old woman hadn't been so quick on the uptake
the young girl would have been away with him in a flash.
That's the power of heredity for you!

Na Murúcha agus an Ceol

Aon rud amháin eile a bhí le tabhairt faoi ndeara orthu
a d'fhág aisteach go leor iad.
'Sé sin nach raibh nóta ceoil acu.

Ní raibh cluais ar bith ag oiread is duine acu
ná aon chumas ar aer a aithint ná é a thabhairt leo ina gceann
ná ansan é a rá thar n-ais leat. Bhíodar chomh dall ar fhonn
le bonn mo bhróige nó smut de gheansaí.
Chuaigh sé seo go mór ina gcoinne is iad ag cur isteach
ar phoist áirithe, mar shampla, múinteoireacht náisiúnta
agus cuid acu a chuaigh leis an eaglais, is ar dhein sagairt
    díobh,
bhíodh deacaireachtaí i gconaí acu le ceiliúradh na searmanas.
Ní hamháin go ndéarfá ina dtaobh gur phíobairí an aon phoirt
    iad,
ach níos measa ná san go mór, lucht cantaireachta an aon nóta.

B'ait leat go mór é seo is tá sé róshimplí a rá
gurb é an saol a chleachtadar fó thoinn is cúis leis
nó tá sé curtha in iúl go mór ag lucht eolaíochta
ar nós Jacques Cousteau gur féidir fuaimeanna a chlos
go doimhin faoi uisce is go mbíonn
cantaireacht chaoin ar siúl ag míolta móra
gan trácht ar 'chlic cleaic' cuideachtúil
na ndeilfeanna is na dtóithíní muca mara.

Ba chuma liom ach go bhfuil a fhios ag an saol
gur ó bhean acu a fuair Mhuintir Dhálaigh Inis 'icileáin
an chéad lá an ceol draíochtúil dúrúnta úd
go dtugtar Port na bPúcaí air.
Bhíodar ina gcodladh sa tigín ar an Inis tráth
nuair a tháinig an bhean lasmuigh de dhoras is í ag amhrán.

The Merfolk and Music

There was one other thing that was quite remarkable about
     the merfolk
that left them oddly out of the swim.
They didn't have as much as a note of music between them.

For not a single one of them had an ear for music
nor could catch a tune, never mind carry it
and give it back to you. They were all as tone-deaf
as the sole of my shoe or the snood of a hoodie.
This condition went against them when they were applying
for certain jobs — National schoolteachers being a case in
     point —
while for those of them who went into the Church, and were
     ordained priests,
it was always hard for them when it came to conducting the
     ceremonies.
Not only could it be said of them that they were pipers with
     only one tune
but, even worse, psalm-singers with only one note.

However strange it might seem, it's too easy to say
that it all went back to the type of life they lived under water
when it's well established by marine specialists
like Jacques Cousteau that you can hear very distant sounds
deep under water, what with the whales
singing their lovely songs
and the interactive clicking
of dolphins and porpoises.

I wouldn't mind if the very dogs in the street didn't know
that it was from a mermaid that the Dalys of Inishvickillane
first got that otherworldly tune
known as 'Port na bPúcaí'.
Once they were asleep out in the tiny cabin on the Inish
when a woman arrived at the door and she singing.

Bhí sí ag tabhairt an phoirt uaithi go fada bog binn
í ag déanamh a gearáin, ag olagón is ag éagaoin.
Bhí fear éigin istigh go raibh cluais mhaith air
a thug leis é go cruinn is d'éirigh sé ar maidin
is sheinm sé é ar an veidhlín.

Bhí focail fiú ag dul leis:
'Is bean ón slua sí mé, a tháinig thar toinn
agus gur goideadh san oíche mé tamall thar lear
is go bhfuilim sa ríocht, faoi gheasa mná sí
is ní bheadsa ar an saol seo ach go nglaofaidh an coileach.
Caithfeadsa tabhairt faoin lios isteach.
Is a bhfuil ar an saol seo go gcaithfidh imeacht as.'

Ach fágfaimíd an scéal sin mar sin
mar ní mhíníonn sé aon ní dúinn
i dtaobh a n-iontaithe i gcoinne an cheoil
nó an fuath a ghlacadar ina leith.
Is cuimhin liom an mhurúch seo 'gainne
lá go rabhamair ag tiomáint bóthar fada ó áit amháin
go dtí áit eile, bhí téip le Nat King Cole
ar siúl age mo Dhaid, é ag gabháilt de 'Georgia On My
    Mind'
is sinn go léir ag canadh leis 'Georgia, Oh Georgia . . .'
'Múch an diabhal rud sin,' arsa an mhurúch gan choinne.
Bhí iontas orainn go léir. 'Canathaobh?' arsa duine
roinnt deiliúsach inár measc. (De ghnáth ní chuirtí aon
    cheist.)
'Múch an diabhal rud sin,' a dúirt sí arís.
'Sin é an sórt ceoil a dheineann daoine díomhaoin!'

She was giving forth the tune in a long-drawn-out and
    melodious wail
as if keening, all ochones and ullagones.
One of the Dalys had such a particularly good ear for a tune
that he got it down exactly, and when he got up in the
    morning
he played it on the fiddle.

There were even words going with it:
'Who am I but a woman from the shee
who's come from far across the sea?
It's been ages since the night I was spirited away
and, in my present form, held under the sway
of an unearthly power, unable to show
my back to this world till the great cock crow.
Then I'll be off into the fairy mound
just as one and all must go to ground.'

But let's leave that story for the moment
because it doesn't at all explain
why they turned so vehemently against music
and hated it so profoundly.
I well remember our own mermaid
one day when we were driving a long distance from one place
to another, my Dad had Nat King Cole
on the tape-player, singing so sweetly 'Georgia On My Mind',
and we were all singing along with him 'Georgia, Oh
    Georgia . . .'
'Turn that bloody thing off,' said the mermaid, out of
    nowhere.
We were all very taken aback. 'Why?' ventured one of us
who was a bit more impudent than the rest. (Usually you
    didn't ask questions.)
'Turn that bloody thing off,' she repeated.
'That's the kind of music that turns people into layabouts.'

Mo chráiteacht, an créatúr bocht!
Is dócha go raibh an saol róchruaidh orthu
nuair a thángadar aníos as ucht
na bóchna. Gur chaitheadar oibriú ar dalladh
ó dhubh dubh, Domhnach is dálach
inniu is amárach, chun a gcosa a thabhairt leothu.
Chaitheadar uathu amhráin, ceol is rince
imirt chártaí, spórt is cuideachta —
aon ní ná féadfá do bhuilín a dhéanamh air láithreach,
is éirí sa tsaol is ar an gcuma san bheith ó bhaol.

'Sé bunús an scéil go léir, ar ndóigh, ná tráma a dtriomaithe.

Alas, the poor thing!
I suppose it was that life had been too hard for them
when they were flung up from the warm bosom
of the ocean. They had to work
from before dawn till after dusk, Sundays and weekdays both,
day after day, just to keep up with themselves.
They put away from them all songs, music, dancing,
card-playing, sports and pastimes —
anything on which you couldn't make a quick profit
and get on in the world and have some sense of security.

What lies at the bottom of all of this, of course, is the trauma
   of their being left high and dry.

An Mhurúch agus an Sagart Paróiste

Toisc go raibh sí cliste do scrígh sí sár-aiste
ar 'Éanlaithe' i gcomhair scrúdú an Bhun-Teastais.
Bhí mórán den eolas bailithe aici ón *National Geographic*
is ó leabhartha tagartha a bhí sa tigh acu.
Bhí sí fiain i ndiaidh éanlaithe, toisc gur rudaí chomh nua aici
    iad.
Sórt éisc gan uisce, ag snámh san aer mar neacha neamhshaolta.
Ní haon ionadh go raibh éileamh an diabhail aici orthu.

Tháinig an sagart paróiste isteach lá an scrúdaithe.
Do léigh sé an aiste is bhí sé an-thógta leis.
Seachtain ina dhiaidh sin d'iarr sé ar an mbean rialta
teachtaireacht a chur anall go dtí tigh an tsagairt léi.

Ní dhearmhadfaidh sí go deo boladh a sheomra staidéir.
Na leabhartha ina sraithe, is an mus aisteach a bhí san aer.
Labhair sé as Gaeilge léi. Theaspáin sé Bíobla *Bhedell* di.
Ansan chuir sé ina suí isteach ina bhaclainn í
is a cosa ar scaradh gabhail timpeall air.
Do bhrúigh sé ina coinne arís is arís eile
is tháinig saothar obann air is allas amach tríd.
Do dhubhaigh sé is do dheargaigh is do bhánaigh ar a aghaidh
is do bhraith sí rud éigin ag fliuchadh i gcoinne a bhríste.

Thuig sí go raibh rud éigin suas, ach níor thuig sí aon ní as.
(Ní raibh sí ach a haon déag, is í fós dall ar na himeachtaí sin.)
Ach nuair a tharla an rud céanna, arís is arís di
ar bhonn rialta seachtainiúil, bhraith sí múisc is míobhán.
Sa deireadh, dhiúltaigh sí glan dul ann.
Is rud a bhí an-ait, ní dúirt an bhean rialta faic
is cuireadh íobartach beag eile chuige thar a ceann.

Mermaid with Parish Priest

Because she was so clever she wrote a brilliant essay
on 'Birds' for the Primary Cert Exam.
She had collected her knowledge from old copies of *National Geographic*
and other reference books she found at home.
She was crazy about birds, partly because they were so
    newfangled to her.
They were like fish, swimming in air like supernatural things.
It is small wonder that she lost the head over them.

The parish priest came into the school in the middle of the
    exam.
He picked up her essay and read it and was very taken with it.
A week later he asked the nun in charge of the class
to send the mermaid with a message of some kind to the
    Parochial House.

She would never forget the smell of his study.
The long lines of books and the musky smell in the air.
He spoke to her in Irish. He showed her Bedell's Bible.
Then he put her sitting on his lap
with her legs astride him on either side.
He pushed against her again and again
and he began to huff and puff and break out in a sweat.
His face went from dark to red to white
and then she felt something wet about his trousers.

She knew something was up but she couldn't make out what.
(She was only eleven and still totally ignorant of such things.)
But when the same thing began to happen again and again
on a weekly basis, she felt nausea and self-loathing.
In the end she refused point-blank to go over there again.
To her astonishment the nun made no comment whatsoever,
and another little victim was sent over in her stead.

Aon uair amháin eile a thug sé fúithi,
nuair a chuaigh a hiarratas do scrúdú
Scoláireachta na Comhairle Contae amú
is a máthair tar éis foláireamh dóite a thabhairt di
gan dearmhad é a chur sa phost. Chaith sí dul
is ceann eile a sholáthar, is a shíniú siúd a fháil
ar bhun na bileoige. Chuaigh sí suas go tigh an tsagairt
is a croí beag ina béal, is na glúine ar crith uirthi.
Bhraith sí díreach mar Íosác is adhmad na híobartha dóite
á iompar ar a mhuin aige. Is ní raibh aon reithe ar an láthair
is a adharca in achrann sa tor chun í a shaoradh.

Dhein sé a chúram léi, ach fuair sí an síniú.
Ach do bhraith sí mar a bheadh sí tar éis í féin a dhíol air.
As san amach níor thug sí aon iontaoibh le daoine fásta
is leathbhliain ina dhiaidh sin nuair a fuair sí
an chéad áit sa Chontae sa scrúdú Scoláireachta
ba bhua folamh aici é. Bhí smál na haithrí air.
Go háirithe nuair a chíodh sí an fear céanna sa sáipéal
gach Domhnach is é ag bualadh na puilpide le buillí bagartha,
ag tabhairt amach ar dalladh i gcoinne rincí mímhórálacha
(an *Twist* a bhí i gceist aige). É ag strampáil ar nós tairbh.
Thug sí faoi ndeara rud gur chuimhin léi go dearfa é
conas a dubhaigh sé is do dheargaigh sé is do bhánaigh sé.

B'in deireadh leis an Aifreann di.
Aon uair a théadh sí ina ghaobhar
do thiteadh sí síos fuar marbh le lagachar is fanntaisí.
Blianta fada ina dhiadh sin, tar éis di cónaí i bhfad thar lear
nuair a chuala sí ar deireadh gur thit an t-anam as an bhfear
ag cluiche Craobh Chontae iománaíochta, in Inis, Contae an
    Chláir
níor chuir sí paidir lena anam, ach díreach a mhalairt glan.

There was only one other time he came on to her
when her application form
for the County Council Scholarship had gone missing
after her mother had warned her in no uncertain terms
not to forget to mail it. So she had to go
and pick up another one, which needed his signature
at the bottom of the form. She went up to the Parochial
    House
with her tiny little heart in her mouth, and her knees knocking
    against each other.
She felt just like Isaac must have felt with the sacrificial wood
round his neck. And this time there was no convenient ram
with its horns caught in the bushes to let her off the hook.

He did his business, and she got the signature.
But she felt as if she had prostituted herself for it.
From that day on she lost complete faith in all adults
and six months later, when she took
first place in the county in the Scholarship exam,
it was a Pyrrhic victory. It was tainted with misery.
Especially when she could see that same man in the chapel
every Sunday where he thumped the pulpit
and fulminated against 'immodest dances'.
(He meant the Twist.) He was pawing and stamping like a
    bull.
She noticed something she remembered all too well,
how his face went from black to red to white.

That was the end of Mass for her.
Any time she went next nor near the church
she would fall down in a fainting fit.
Years later, after she'd lived abroad for a long time,
when she heard he'd died
at a County Hurling Championship, in Ennis, County Clare,
she didn't say a prayer for his soul but cursed him roundly.

Ní bheadh sí réidh leis go ceann i bhfad
ach é ag teacht chúichi i dtaibhrimh ar chuma vaimpíre
nó deamhan fola; é amuigh ar an mbalcón
lasmuigh d'fhuinneog na seomra leapan
is é de shíor ag iarraidh cead slí
chun teacht isteach ann. Dhúisíodh sí faoi imní
is go minic í ag cáitheadh allais le líonrith is anbhá
í sceimhlithe ina beathaidh go dtí go ritheadh sé ina ceann,
an seomra leapan ina raibh sí nach raibh air aon bhalcón.

Níl iontas ar bith ina dhiaidh sin gur thug sí cúl na láimhe leis
    an nGaeilge.
Ní lú ná mar a leag sí súil arís ar chóip do Bhíobla *Bhedell*.
Is níor stad an damáiste ansan. Nuair d'éirigh léi é insint
blianta ina dhiaidh sin dona máthair, 'sé an freagra
a fuair sí uaithi ná 'An sagart bocht, nach fear
é siúd chomh maith le duine.' 'Sé a dúirt sí ina bolg ná 'Bhuel,
sin é an rud deireanach a déarfad riamh leat.'
Agus mar a tharla, b'in mar ab ea.

But she wasn't free of him for a long time after
for he'd appear to her in dreams as a vampire
or bloodsucking fiend. He'd be standing on the balcony
outside the window of her bedroom
always asking leave
to come in. She used to wake up in a state of anxiety,
sweating profusely, her heart in her mouth,
terrified out of her wits, till she gradually realized
the bedroom she was in didn't have a balcony.

Little wonder that shortly afterwards she renounced the Irish language.
Never again did she set eyes on Bedell's Bible.
But the damage didn't just stop there. When she finally plucked up the courage,
years later, to tell her mother what had happened, the response
she got from her was 'Oh, the poor priest, isn't he a man
like any other?' 'Well,' said the mermaid inwardly,
'that's the last thing I'll ever tell you.'
And, as it happens, it was.

Bás agus Aiséirí na Murúiche

Máthair an-mhallaithe is cruaidh bhí ag an mhurúch
is ní scaoilfeadh sí a hiníon amach as an dtigh ón dtús.
Éad is formad a bhí aici léi
go háirithe lena cúl fada gruaige ar dhath na feamnaí
a bhí ar nós scuaibe mhada rua ag rith faoi chith báistí.
Ní ligfeadh sí di é a chíoradh céad uair mar ba ghá
nó ní ligfeadh sí in aon ghaobhar í do scáthán.

Chaith an mhurúch a háilleacht féin a fheiscint ar dtúis
sa sruthán a bhí ag gluaiseacht síos feadh an tí ón gcnoc
nó níos minicí, ins an trach uisce thíos sa chuaisín
mar a dtugtaí na ba chun uisce lá beirfin.

Bhí aoire ar an mbaile darb ainm Mícheál,
is ní fada ina dhiaidh sin gur chuir sé in iúl
di chomh hálainn is a bhí sí.
Nuair a chuala a máthair go raibh a leithéid ar siúl
do thóg sí eachlasc ruaimní is do bhuail timpeall an bhuaile í
is tá finnéithe ann ón lá san a thabharfadh an leabhar
gur bhris sí cos leapan aniar thar a drom.

An oíche sin, chuir an mhurúch íle le lúndracha an dorais
chun ná déanfaidíst gíoscán. Ansan thug turas
thar an abhainn ar Mhícheál. Do shuíodar faoi naomhóg
istigh cois na faille. Timpeall orthu bhí rabháin
agus boladh géar na sáile. Is ansan a tharla
an rud a tharla. Dhein bean den mhurúch
nach raibh go dtí san ach ina cailín óg.

Nuair a d'fhill sí ar maidin níor dhein an doras aon ghioscán
ach ba leor lena máthair go raibh bláth den rabhán
fós i lámh na mná óige. Níor ghoil is níor dhein olagón

The Death and Rebirth of the Mermaid

The mermaid had a very spiteful and hardhearted mother
who from the start would hardly let her daughter out of the house.
She was eaten up with envy and jealousy towards her,
especially with her long head of hair the colour of seaweed
that resembled nothing so much as a fox's tail in a shower of rain.
She wouldn't let her brush it the usual hundred times
nor would she let her anywhere next or near a mirror.

The mermaid first became aware of her own beauty
in the little stream that ran down from the hill beside the house
or, more frequently, in the trough near the strand
where she used to bring the cows to drink on a hot day.

There was a shepherd in the village whose name was Mícheál
and it wasn't long till he made her even more aware
of just how beautiful she was.
When her mother heard what was going on
she took a horsewhip of horsehair and beat her round the
   dunghill with it
and there are witnesses to that day who would swear on the Bible
she broke the leg of a bed on her back.

That night the mermaid oiled the hinges of the door
so that they wouldn't squeak. Then she made her way
over the stream to Mícheál. They hunkered down under a currach
by the brow of the cliff. All about them were sea pinks
and the tang of the tide. That was when
what happened happened. The mermaid became a woman,
the mermaid who had until then been only a young girl.

When the mermaid returned home early in the morning the door
   may not have squeaked
but her mother did notice the sea pink
still blossoming in the girl's hand. She didn't immediately raise
   a ruckus

ach théigh sí dabhach mhór copair is d'iarr sí cabhair
na Maighdine Muire ar an rud a chuir sí roimpi.

Ghaibh an mhurúch thar bráid is d'fhéach isteach sa dabhach
chun radharc beag eile d'fháil ar a háilleacht.
Ach cad a bhí i gcroí na daibhche, thíos ina bun
ach bláth úd an rabháin, is é dubh dóite go tóin.
Thapaigh an mháthair a seans is sháigh í isteach san uisce
    fliuchaidh
is fágadh an mhurúch gan áilleacht is fiú gan beatha.

Bhí a huaigh fós úr nuair a tháinig Mícheál.
Dhein sé corpán na murúiche a thochailt as an bpoll
is chuir amach ar an bhféar í. Ansan in ainm na ndeamhan,
i dteannta Aingil an Uabhair, is clann Á is É, na mairbh,
thóg sé aniar arís leis í, is í ina *zombie* balbh
is thug sé leis as an áit sin í. Chuala go n-imíodar go Gaillimh
áit ar tháinig a caint chuici arís, de réir a chéile
cé go raibh luaithbhéalaíocht éigin ag roinnt de shíor léi.
Dheineadar saol nua dóibh féin ann. Mar sin féin
ó am go chéile, bhí dúire mar a bheadh croí crainn
le braith ar a ceannaithe is ar a ballaibh beatha
is easpa aicillíochta, is gan aon chumas rince
chun gur dhóigh leat óna geáitsíocht gur i gcónra a bhí sí.
Is b'fhéidir go raibh leis. Mar déanta na fírinne
bhí oiread sin tarlaithe di ná samhlófaí dár leithéidne
ach an céatadán is lú de. Ní lú ná mar a luadh é
go dtí an lá atá inniu fiú. Níor le héinne a cúram.
Dhein sí siúráil de. Bhí sí chomh ceanndána le miúil faoi.

but calmly prepared a copper bath of boiling water and asked
   the help
of the Virgin Mother to carry out what she had planned.

As the young mermaid went by she glanced into the bath
to get another glimpse of her own beauty.
But what did she see in the depths of the bath
but the blossom of the sea pink, all frizzled and frazzled.
Her mother seized the opportunity and tipped her into the bath
and the mermaid was left without her beauty or indeed her life.

Her grave was still fresh when Mícheál arrived.
He took the mermaid's corpse from the grave
and laid her out on the grass. Then by the devil,
in the name of Satan, the children of Adam and Eve,
didn't he raise her from the dead, like a zombie,
and quickly spirit her away. I heard that they went to Galway,
where her speech returned to her, though slowly at first,
and there was always a certain impediment that always stayed
   with her.
They made a new life for themselves there. All the same,
from time to time a hardness came over her as if she were made
   of wood,
a hardness that completely transformed her
so that her stiffness was quite noticeable, so she wasn't able to
   dance a step
and one might have deduced from her strange movements that
   she was stuck in a coffin.
And maybe she was for, let's face it,
she'd been through far more than most of us can even imagine,
except perhaps to some minor degree. Nor did she ever allude
   to it
right up to the present day. It was nobody else's business.
Of that she was sure. She dug her heels in on that one.

Briseadh an Tí

Chuaigh an mhurúch suas oíche go tigh Khatie Shea,
seanbhean ar an mbaile a bhí lán de cheol is spraoi.
Ní raibh bailithe isteach le chéile ach na cailíní óga
ach bhí oíche go maidin acu, ag déanamh ceapairí le bulóga
breátha builín, le caint is cuideachta, is b'fhéidir fo-ghloine
   fíona.

'An dtáinig Rhyno fós?' arsa an bhean óg eile sa tigh ar
   maidin
ag tagairt do dhiopsamáineach clúiteach a bhí ar an mbaile
go raibh sé de cháil air, is roinnt deoch istigh aige
go mbíodh sé ag spalpadh carraigreacha Béarla soir siar ar
   dalladh.
'There is no erosion without sedimentation'
nó 'The Rhynosérus is a bésht of the Néygro kind.'

Mar mhagadh ar ndóigh, is ea a dúirt sí é.
Ach ní mar sin a thóg máthair na murúiche é.
D'imigh sí ina ruaill nimhe ar fuaid an tí.
Níor fhág sí thíos ná thuas acu é.
Chlabhtáil sí a raibh istigh.
Dhein sí stán díobh.
'Bhris sí an tigh,'

nó is mar sin a dúradh é, blianta ina dhiaidh sin, ag tórramh
an t-aon uair riamh a chuala an scéal sin á áireamh.
Nuair a labhradh na focail sin
do thit tost obann ar a raibh i láthair.
Thom gach uile dhuine den gcomhluadar
isteach i nduibheagán fomhuireach ná féadfainn fiú a
   thomhas
is dá mhéid lapadaíle atá déanta agam thart fán scéal seo
ní dóigh liom go bhfaighead amach go deo ó éinne acu é
cad a bhí i gceist, go díreach
le 'Do bhris sí an tigh'.

Wrecking the House

The mermaid went up one evening to the house of Katie Shea,
an old woman in the village who was full of music and mischief.
Only the young girls from the village were gathered in her house
but they still managed to sit up all night, making sandwiches
from the finest store-bought bread, with plenty of chitchat and
maybe even the odd glass of sherry.

'Has Rhino come home yet?' said the other young woman in
    the house next morning,
referring to a distinguished dipsomaniac in the village
who was notorious, when he was three sheets to the wind,
for bursting out with huge boulder-size English words:
'There is no erosion without sedimentation'
or 'The Rhinoceros is a baste of the Negro persuasion'.

She'd said it only in jest, of course,
but that's not how it was taken up by the mother of the
    mermaid.
She took a mad rush through the house.
She left no stone unturned,
but gave them a sound hiding.
She beat the tar out of them.
'She wrecked the house,'

as it would be described, years later, at a wake,
the one time ever I heard mention of this episode.
When that phrase was used
a sudden silence fell on everyone who was in attendance.
Every member of the company
dove into a deep underwater abyss which I couldn't plumb
and no matter how much fancy footwork I've done around
    this issue
I don't suppose I'll ever find out from any of them
what really happened or what is meant, exactly,
by the phrase 'She wrecked the house'.

An Mhurúch ina hAthbhreith

Is cuimhin léi go minic thar aon ní eile
méid an dlúis a bhí inti ar dtúis.
Bíonn sí chomh beag, chomh beag, le haingeal i measc cór
dá macasamhail ag plódaíocht ar bharr bioráin,
nó le duine éigin d'anamnacha na marbh
a bhíonn chomh tiubh
ag míogarnach is ag foluain inár dtimpeall
leis na míolta corra; scata acu ag fáil bheith istigh
ar na braonaíocha drúchta ar an aon ribe féir amháin.

Ansan de phreib ruthaig bíonn sí MÓR MÓR
is í ag siúl gan dua tré hallaí arda marmair
i dtreo an tsolais; boghaisíní áthais is creathaí aitis
ag gabháilt stealladh di gach re sea.
Ina matáin is mó a bhraitheann sí é seo
is ní ina ceann. Cuimhne chorpartha is ea é
seachas ceann intleachtúil. Tosnaíonn an codladh grifín
ag bun na méar agus snámhann drithlíní sámhnais
is eagla i dteannta a chéile aníos a corp
go mbuaileann siad sa cheann í.
Bíonn sí líonraithe ansan.
Gaibheann uaigneas leis mar bhraistint.
Níl sé nádúrtha, nó bainteach leis an saol seo.
Osréalta, b'fhéidir, an focal a d'fhéadfá a lua leis.
'Unheimlich' a thabharfá leis air.

Ní gá dhi seisiúin d'aon tsórt teiripe holagrafach
chun teacht go furasta ar an gcuimhne bhunaidh seo.
Tá sé go feillbhinn cheana aici ina hanam agus ina corp.

The Born-again Mermaid

She remembers more than anything else
just how compact she was at first.
She was so small, as small as an angel in a troop
of angels congregating on the top of a pin,
or one of the souls of the dead
who are known to be as thickly
and droopingly hovering in our midst
like midges, scads of them fitting
into the drops of dew that cling to a single blade of grass.

Then all of a sudden she was BIG, BIG,
walking effortlessly through high marble halls
in the direction of the light; shuffles of pleasure and
   shudders of apprehension
were hitting her in alternating waves.
She remembers this is her actual physical makeup
and not in her head. It's a muscle memory
rather than a mental one. The pins and needles start
in her fingers and toes and twinges of pleasure
and fear together sweep up through her body
till they hit her in the head.
She's very agitated.
There's something very unearthly about this sensation.
It's not natural, not connected with this world.
Surreal, perhaps, is the best term for it.
'Unheimlich,' as the Germans would say.

She doesn't need to take part in holographic therapy sessions
to summon this basic primal memory.
She already feels it through and through, in her soul as much
   as her body.

An Mhurúch ag Coigilt na Tine

Coiglíonn sí an tine,
ní mar a choiglíonn Críost cách,
Muire i gceann an tí agus Bríd ina lár,
an dáréag aingeal is fearr i gcathair na ngrást
ag gardáil an tí aici, agus a muintir go lá . . .

Coiglíonn sise an tine
in ainm Chroim agus lucht a pháirte,
ag súil go dtriomóidh sé gach aon bhraon uisce atá
   ar an láthair.

The Mermaid Smooring the Fire

She smoors the fire
not as Christ covers every spark,
with Our Lady at the head of the house, Saint Brigid
   at the heart,
the twelve most glorious angels from the City of Grace
keeping the house and everyone in it safe . . .

She smoors the fire
in the name of the great Crom and his race,
in the hope that he'll dry every drop of water in those parts.

An Mhurúch is a Tigh

Toisc nach bhfuil sonas i ndán di amuigh nó istigh
cuireann sí a fuinneamh go léir isteach ina tigh —
bungaló leathscoite ina ghairdín féin.
An phlásóg féir atá lasmuigh de, gearrann sí é le sisiúirín.

Tuigtear di gur ábhar mór mórtais is laochais
é bheith sciomartha glan ó bhun go barr buacais.
Tá sé mar a bheadh músaem aici, is i gcuntais Dé,
tá cairpéad fada bán aici sa seomra suite féin.
Tá cosc ar chuairteoirí bróga nó fiú slipéirí
a iompar. Caitheann siad gabháil timpeall ina mbuimpéisí.
Sin é an béas atá aici.

Ba chuma liom ach nach í féin a dheineann an obair throm.
Agrann sí a cuid straidhneach go léir ar a clann.
Imríonn sí a dúlaithe orthu, ceann ar cheann
is níl éinne chun lámh chabhartha a thabhairt dóibh
mar ní chreidfeadh éinne an scéal dá neosfaí dóibh é —

go n-ordaíonn sí as an leaba iad ar maidin go moch
le ramsach den mbruis: 'seo, bígí amuigh';
go gcaitheann siad fuinneoga an tí a ní amuigh is istigh
gach uile lá den bhliain, is cuma conas a bhíonn an síon;
gur minic a reoigh a méireanta des na pánaí gloine
is iad ag cuimilt leo ar dalladh aimsir doininne is seaca;
go bhfuil duine acu gur cuimhin leis an seomra folctha
a sciúradh cúig n-uaire in aon lá amháin, de réir a horduithe.

Ní féidir aon chothrom a bhaint di. 'Is ann a dhéanfaidh sé
maitheas dóibh,' an mana a bhíonn aici féin.
'Nach mar sin a tógadh mise, is féach cén díobháil a dhein sé?
Díomhaointeas máthair an oilc, is muna gcoimeádann tú
ag obair de shíor iad, beidh drochbheart á thaibhreamh dóibh.'

The Mermaid and Her House

Since happiness is not destined to be her lot, in- or out-of-doors,
she puts all her energy into her house,
a semi-detached bungalow with its own garden.
The front lawn she trims with scissors.

According to her it's a source of bragging and boastfulness
that a house be spick and span from bottom to top.
You'd swear it was a museum, for Christ's sake,
what with the white shag carpet in the very living room.
Visitors are forbidden to wear shoes
or even slippers. They have to go around in their stockinged feet.
That's how it is with her.

I wouldn't mind but it isn't herself who does any of the heavy
    work.
She takes out her bad temper on her family.
She gives them hell, one after the other,
and when all is done there is no one to whom they can turn
and even if they did, who on earth would believe them,

how she orders them out of bed at the scrake of dawn
with a swipe of the floor brush and an 'Up you get',
how they have to wash the windows inside and out
every day of the year, no matter what the weather is like,
how their fingers have often frozen to the panes of glass
as they wiped and wiped in times of snow and frost,
how one of them remembers scouring the bathroom
five times in a single day, as she'd been ordered.

And nobody can put her on notice. 'Sure, isn't it only good
it'll do them?' is her eternal refrain.
'Isn't that how I was brought up, and did it do me a damn bit
    of harm?
Idleness is the root of all evil and if you don't keep
their noses to the grindstone they'll be up to no good.'

Is ní deireann na leanaí faic, táid ina leathamadáin
ag an mburdáil is an chlabhtáil atá fachta acu cheana féin.

Is san áit a mbíonn ag daoine eile fógraí ar an bhfalla
mar 'Home Sweet Home' nó 'Céad Míle Fáilte'
nó fiú 'Má tá Gaeilge agat labhair í' ag lucht dílseachta teangan
is é a bhíonn in airde aici féin, ina peannaireacht bhreá mná
   rialta
ná 'Laborare est orare', nó leithéidí eile mar
'Ní bhíonn an rath ach mar a mbíonn an smacht,'
is os cionn fardorais an tseomra suite
an ceann is aistí acu amuigh, gur dhóigh leat le ceart
gur sórt magaidh dóite é, ach faraoir, ní hea:
'Arbeit macht frei'. Rud a chreideann sí chomh maith.

The poor children say nothing, being already half-crazed
from the thrashing and thumping they've all got.

And where others have mottoes on the walls
such as 'Home Sweet Home' or 'A Hundred Thousand
   Welcomes'
or even the 'If you have Irish, speak it' of the language lobby,
what she has up on hers, in her handwriting like a nun's
   handwriting,
is 'Laborare est orare', or the likes of
'Spare the cane and spoil the child',
and over the lintel of the living room
the strangest one of all, so strange you'd think
it must be some kind of gallows humour, though
   unfortunately it's not:
'Arbeit macht frei'. Which she believes, to boot.

Teoranna

Ón méid a thuigimíd i dtaobh teanga na murúch
ó bhloghtracha fánacha den 'Ursprache'
is ó leideanna eile atá ar fáil againn,
is féidir a aithint go raibh sé difriúil ar fad
leis na teangacha Ind-Eorpacha
nó, déanta na fírinne,
le gach uile ghrúpa teangan eile atá ar aithne go dtí seo.
Níor mhór rangú ar leith a sholáthar dó,
ceann ar a dtabharfaí 'peiligeach' b'fhéidir
nó go dtreasnaíonn sé na seacht mbóchna.

Is féidir linn a thabhairt faoi ndeara gan stró
go ritheann gach uile rud isteach ina chéile ann,
is nach bhfuil teoranna dochta i gceist idir rud ar bith.
Ní hionann, mar shampla, aimsirí na mbriathar
is an córas atá i bhfeidhm ins na teangacha seo 'gainne.
Tóg, mar shampla, an gnáthréimniú, an chéad phearsa uatha,
d'fhéadfadh sé an Aimsir Chaite, nó an Aimsir Láithreach
nó an Aimsir Fháistineach a chiallú
ag brath go hiomlán ar aois an chainteora.

Is léir chomh maith nach bhfuil a leithéid de rud acu
agus ainmfhocal,
nó go dtuigeann siad an coincheap, fiú,
ach gur le cabhair na n-ainm briathartha
a chuirtear gach ciall in iúl.
Is dála na teangan aduaine úd 'Tlön' sa ghearrscéal úd
de chuid Bhorges, 'sé an tslí a déarfá
'd'éirigh an ghealach os cionn na habhann'
ná 'aníos laisteas den umshruthlú do ghealaigh sé'.

Boundaries

From what we can make out about the merfolk's language
based on the odd snatches of the 'Ursprache' that remain
and such other clues as are available to us
it's immediately obvious it's absolutely different
from the Indo-European languages
or, if the truth be told,
from any other previously known language group.
It deserves a special category all of its own,
one that might be dubbed 'pelagic', perhaps,
since it covers the seven seas.

We can recognize at once, without any difficulty,
that everything in the language runs into everything else,
that there are no strict boundaries between one thing and
    another.
For instance, the system of tenses of the verbs
is quite unlike the system that obtains in our languages.
Take, for example, the ordinary conjugation, first person
    singular.
It could mean the Past Tense, the Present Tense,
or even the Future Tense,
depending entirely on the age of the speaker.

It's obvious as well they didn't have such a thing
as a noun,
or didn't even understand the concept,
but only by gerunds and participles — by verbal nouns —
was meaning expressed.
And rather like that strange language 'Tlön' in the short story
by Borges, the way you would say
'the moon rose above the river'
would be 'up over the upstreaming it mooned'.

Is dócha gurb iad cúinsí speisialta an tsaoil fó-thoinn
faoi ndeara na nithe suaithinseacha seo.
D'fhéadfá a shamhlú go furaist gurb iad a luigh
laistair des na deacaireachtaí faoi leith
a bhí ag an mhurúch seo 'gainne.
Bhí trioblóidí speisialta aici i gcónaí i dtaobh teoranna.
Níor fhéad sí a aithint riamh, mar shampla, go rabhamair
  go léir
aonaránach is discréideach, inár nduine is inár nduine.
Ritheamair go léir isteach ina chéile, ba dhóigh leat uaithi,
faoi mar a bheadh na dathanna ó smearadh íle
ar an mbóthar tar éis cith báistí.

Níor thuig sí riamh ach chomh beag
nach cuid bhunúsach di féin gach uile dhuine dhínn.
Bhí deacaireachtaí nach beag ag roinnt leis seo, chomh maith.
Dá ndéanfá rud ar bith nár thaithn léi
nó dá ndéarfá do mhian go neamhbhalbh suas lena béal
ba mhar a chéile léi é is dá bhfaigheadh sí clabhta sa phus
óna deasláimh féin.
Níorbh fhéidir léi é a sheasamh.
Níor chuir sí suas leis.
Sin é an fáth, sa deireadh, ní foláir
gur tharla gach ar tharla.

It's most probable the particular circumstances of their
　　underwater existence
would explain these remarkable facts.
It's also easy to imagine these circumstances are what lay
　　behind
the particular difficulties of our own mermaid.
She always had a real difficulty with boundaries.
She could never understand, for instance, that we were all
separate and discrete, each and every one of us.
We all ran into each other, you'd swear to listen to her,
like the different colours in an oily puddle
after a shower of rain.

She could barely take on board
we were not all fundamental parts of herself but separate
　　people.
This caused quite a few difficulties.
If you did anything she didn't like
or if you stated your own wishes straight to her face
it was as if she'd just given herself a slap in the puss
with her own right hand.
She couldn't stand for it.
She simply wouldn't put up with it.
That's why, I expect, in the end
things turned out as they did.

An Mhurúch is a hIníon

Nuair a d'fhás a hiníon suas ina cailín óg
bhí sí dathúil
go háirithe tar éis di teacht ar an bhfionnachtain ba mhó —
rud ba thábhachtaí léi go mór ná cúrsaí gnéis —
is é sin mascara.
Nuair a chimil sí é dá fabhraí fada bána
thug sé súile móra breátha di.
Chuir san an mhurúch le báiní.
'Bain an stuif sin anuas ded' phus,'
ar sise léi de sceamh
ag tabhairt leiceadair sa dá chluais thall is abhus di.

Roinnt blianta níosa dhéanaí
nuair a fuair sí ag dul amach le buachaillí í
is gur thuig sí go raibh sí ag luí leo
is go raibh sí istigh léi féin ina thaobh —
'bien dans sa peau' — mar a déarfá
chuir an méid sin as a meabhair ar fad í.
'Toice bheag ghránna' a thug sí uirthi,
'leadhbóg, calbóiseas mná, straoille, striapach',
is ar eagla na míthuisceana dúirt sí an athuair é
sa tarna teanga oifigiúil
'you filthy little prostitute'.

I lár na hargóna istigh
is an chlann go léir trí chéile
leis an díth céille is an tarrac tríd
dúirt duine éigin, chun í a mhaolú, gurb é toil Dé é.
'Ní hé,' a dúirt sí de shnap thar n-ais,
'ach toil an diabhail'.

The Mermaid and Her Daughter

When her daughter grew up to be a young woman
she was very attractive,
especially after she had stumbled across the greatest
   discovery of all —
something even more profound than sex —
by which I mean mascara.
When she brushed it on her long pale lashes
it made her eyes look big and discerning.
The mermaid lost it completely.
'Take that stuff off your dirty puss,'
she barked at her,
all the while boxing her ears
left and right.

A few years later,
when the mermaid found her going out with boys,
and even sleeping with some of them
in a fairly easy-going way —
'bien dans sa peau' as the French have it —
the mermaid went entirely round the twist.
'You wanton wench,' she called her,
not to mention 'slattern, a big fat lump, a slut, a harlot',
and just so that there would be no misunderstanding
   she repeated it
in the second official language,
'you filthy little prostitute'.

In the heat of the debate,
when the whole family was discombobulated
by the craziness and commotion,
one of them said, to mollify her, that it was the will of God.
'Indeed it is not,' she snapped back at them.
'It's the devil's doing.'

Blianta fada ina dhiaidh sin
nuair a bhí sí ag druidim chun deireadh a saoil
is an scéal ar fad is iliomad scéalta eile mar é
imithe chun sámhnais,
'An t-aon rud a shábháil mé riamh,' a dúirt sí
'ná go raibh eagla orm roimh fhearaibh.'

N'fheadarsa.
Deinim amach gurb é díreach a mhalairt ghlan é.

Years later again,
when she was coming to the end of her life
and that particular chapter, along with many others like it,
was long since closed,
'The only thing that ever saved me,' she announced,
'was that I was terrified of men.'

Maybe so.
But I'm inclined to think it was the other way around.

Melusine

Is léi i gcónaí
an tigh ina mairim
is gach a bhfuil ann —
caisleán uaigneach cois locha
is dabhach mór folctha
i lár mo sheomra leapan.

Caitheann sí an lá go léir ann
gach aon Dé Sathairn, ar a sáimhín
só, ar a cúilín seamhrach,
ag meidhréis is ag gleáchas
san uisce alabhog, ag tomadh ann
is á scaoileadh thairsti anall.

'Má tá iomard nó máchail
ar gach uile dhuine clainne agam
bíodh sé amhlaidh. Is cuma liom.
Ní mór liom dóibh iad
ach is mór an t-iontas liom
iad a bheith ann in aon chor.'

Is fíor di. Ba mhaith an mhaise dhúinn
nár cheistíomair í níos crua.
B'fholláin dúinn nár bhuail an smaoineamh sinn
silence ar bith a bhualadh uirthi
is sinn ar thóir na fírinne.

Laistiar den gceist
tá fiosracht. Laistiar den bhfios
tá éitheach. Laistíos den urlár
tá na mairbh
ag osnaíl is ag éagaoin.

Is cá bhfios dúinn cad a dh'imigh orthu?
Nó cá bhfios dúinn cad a d'éiligh?

Melusine

She still owns
the house I live in
and all its bits and pieces.
A lonely castle beside a lake
complete with a huge bathtub
in the middle of the bedroom.

She spends the whole day in it
every Saturday, taking her ease
and kicking back and playing
in the lukewarm water, diving deep
and having it break over her again.

'If there is a blemish or deformity
on every single one of my children,
it is what it is. I'm good with it.
I don't begrudge them anything
but it's still a source of great amazement to me
they managed to get born at all.'

She was right. I think we were wise
not to question her more closely.
It was lucky for us it didn't occur to any of us
to probe more deeply
for the sake of truth.

Behind each point to be solved
lies some prying impulse. Behind the fact
is some falsehood. Beneath the floorboards
lie the ancestors,
wailing and gnashing their teeth.

And who are we to know what really happened to them?
How are we to know what pressures they were under?

Nó cá bhfios dúinn an gníomh gaile groí
a thionscnaigh sí chun éaló?

How are we ever to understand what heroic feat it took for her to struggle free of them?

Fáidhiúlacht na Murúiche

Tá smaoineamh éigin fós ina ceann
cé nach féidir léi é a chur i bhfoclaibh.
'An leaid óg sin arís — ní féidir liom
cuimhneamh ar a ainm — tá sé —'
(sos beag anseo agus creathán ina láimh)
'tá sé — tá sé —
tá sé in áit dhorcha.'

Cé tá i gceist aici? Mo mhac?
M'fhear céile? Nó duine éigin eile den gclann?
Nó an bhfuil sí, ar leibhéal éigin
ag trácht uirthi féin?

Bhí sí riamh domhain.
Ach anois tá sí ag labhairt aníos chughainn
as tobar gan tóin.

The Mermaid's Gift of Prophecy

There's some idea at the back of her mind
she just can't put into words.
'That young fellow out there — I don't seem
to be able to recall his name — he's — he's —
(a small break here while her hand shakes)
he's in a dark place.'

Who does she mean? My son?
My husband? Or some other member of the family?
Or is she, at some other level,
referring to herself?

She was always deep.
But now she seems to be talking up to us
from a bottomless well.

Filleadh na Murúiche ar an dTír-fó-Thoinn

Sa deireadh
is dóigh liom gurb é a tharla
don mhurúch seo 'gainne
ná gur fhill sí thar n-ais faoi loch
ar an áit aisteach úd arb as di.

Bhí sé mar a bheadh an cochall draíochta
a bhí curtha i bhfolach le cianta sa chúl-lochta
aimsithe aici de bharr a síorphóirseála.
Cé go raibh sí fós inár bhfianaise go corpartha
bhí sé mar a bheadh seithe róin
fillte go cúramach aici uimpi
is í ag snámh amach in aigéan éigin fo-intinneach
nárbh fhéidir le héinne againn í a leanúint ann.

Bhíodh sí de shíor á suathadh ag feachtaí inmheánacha
a thagadh aníos ón duibheagán
is ag cuilithíní mara is guairneáin stoirme
gurb eagal le mairnéalach ar bith,
dá éifeachtaí, é féin a fháil ina measc
fiú dá mbeadh coileach Márta is caipín an tsonais
ar bord aige.

Lá do chuas á féachaint
is níor labhair sí focal liom
go ceann trí huaire a' chloig.
Bhíos siúráilte dhe nár aithnigh sí
in aon chor mé.
Thugas 'n Aifreann í, ghearras a cuid bídh di
is le cabhair na banaltran chuir isteach 'n leaba í
i gcóir sraite.

The Mermaid Returns to Land-Under-Wave

In the end
I think what actually happened
with our own mermaid
is that she slipped back under the sea
to the place she'd come from.

It was as if
she'd one day stumbled upon the magical hood
that had been hidden for ages up in the back loft
simply because of her endless poking and pottering about.
Even though she was still physically in our presence
it was as though she had wrapped a layer of sealskin
carefully around herself
and was swimming off in some deep subconscious ocean
where none of us could follow her.

She was being continually buffeted by inner currents
that rose up out of some abyss,
by whirlpools and eddies and maelstroms
in which any sailor, however seasoned, would be afraid to
   find himself
even if he had such charms as a March cock and the caul of
   a newborn infant
on board with him.

One day I went to see her
and she didn't say a word to me
for a good three hours.
I was sure I wasn't in the least
familiar to her.
I brought her to Mass, cut up her food
and, with the help of the nurse, got her back into bed
so she could have a nap.

D'fhanas suite taobh na leapan
faid is a bhí sí ag titim ina codladh
is d'osclaíodh sí leathshúil anois
is ansan an leathshúil eile
am' sheiceáil, féachaint an rabhas fós ann.
Go hobann, d'oscail sí an dá shúil le chéile
is d'fhéach orm go cúramach
is gan aon oidhre eile uirthi
ach rón a chuirfeadh a ceann aníos ón bhfarraige
is a d'fhéachadh ort go fiosrach.

'Níl tú leath chomh rua agus a bhís,'
a dúirt sí liom, ag tabhairt le fios
go raibh a fhios aici go maith cé bhí aici.
Bhí an chloch fós sa mhuinchille aici
is ní dhéanfainn dabht ar bith di i dtaobh
an ropadh beag scine a ghortódh.
'Táim ag liachtaint, a bhean, ag liachtaint,'
adúrtsa thar n-ais léi.
'Nach bhfuil sé i bhfad thar am agam
is mé geall le leathchéad bliain d'aois.'

Dhún sí an dá shúil ansan go mall is go maorga
ag fógairt go raibh an t-agallamh thart
is an comhrá críochnaithe.
Táim fós ag iarraidh a dhéanamh amach
ab ann ab amhlaidh gur aithin sí an lá ar fad mé
is ná labhródh liom le teann pusa is mioscaise
nó arbh é a bhí san abairt obann aonair úd amháin
ná mar a bheadh bréitseáil míl mhóir os cionn an uisce.

I waited beside the bed
while she fell asleep.
All the time she would half-open one eye,
then the other,
by way of checking me out, just so see if I was still
   in the vicinity.
Suddenly, she opened both her eyes together
and stared at me very intently,
looking for all the world
like a seal putting its head out of the water
with a very knowing look.

'Your hair's nowhere near as red as it used to be,'
she announced, giving me to understand
she knew exactly who I was.
She still kept a stone up the sleeve
and I didn't doubt her still
being able to give the knife a little twist.
'Sure I'm going grey, woman dear,' I shot back,
'finally going grey.
And isn't it about time
now that I'm almost hitting the half-century?'

She closed her two eyes then, slowly and surely,
letting me know the colloquy was over
and our discussion at an end.
I'm still trying to figure out
if she knew all along who I was
but wouldn't speak to me out of sheer malice
or if that single, sudden sentence
was like a whale leaping and launching itself out
   over the ocean.

An Mhurúch i nDeireadh a Saoil Thiar

Luíonn sí sa leaba ospidéil
pus is breill uirthi roimh gach éinne.
Tá sí namhaidmhear leis an saol
is nimhneach i dtaobh gach aon ní.

Tá sí sroiste, i ndiaidh a marthana,
go ceann scríbe, go deireadh a ré.
Tá sí titithe isteach sa bhíoma ábhalmhór
atá i súilibh Dé.

Dar léi nach bhfuil inti
ach mála fuail is caca.

Dála na coda eile againn.

The Mermaid Nears the End

She lies in the hospital bed
curling her lip and sneering at everyone.
She is hostile towards the whole world,
bitter about everything.

She has reached the end of her life,
run her course, come to the end of her allotted span.
She has fallen on to the huge beam
that's lodged in the eye of God.

According to her she's no more
than a bag of shit and piss.

She's finally just like the rest of us.

An Mhurúch Seo 'gainne fó Thoinn Arís

Ba chuma liom
nuair a d'fhill thar n-ais ar an dTír-fó-Thoinn
dá mbeadh sí sona a dóthain ann.

Ach ní raibh ná í.
Bean nár labhair puinn riamh
amach ós ard i measc an phobail i rith a saoil,
is nár dhein, le mo chuimhne-se ar a laghad,
ach trí gháire riamh faid is a bhí sí ar an míntír
is gach ceann acu ina gháire dóite —

lá gur gháir sí agus í ag gabháilt thar dhuine ins an tsráid
a bhí ag tabhairt amach i dtaobh na mbróga nua
a bhí ceannaithe aige — go raibh na sála orthu i bhfad
   ró-thanaí.
Gháir sí sa phus air, á rá go mbeidís reamhar go leor dá
   chúram.
Is ann a bhí a fhios aici go mbeadh sé caillte curtha i gceann
   trí lá.

Ansan lá eile gur ghaibh sí thar fhear eile i lár an bhóthair
a bhí ag mallachtú dubh domhain is ó thalamh
ar chloch go raibh sé tar éis ordóg mór a choise clé
a ghortú ina coinne. Níor thug sí aon phioc eolais dó-san
ach dúirt liomsa ina dhiaidh sin dá mb'áil leis féin é
   thógaint bog
is an chloch a thaighde, go bhfaigheadh sé órchiste ag
   fanacht do
ar an dtaobh eile.

Is an tríú gáire — bhuel, ní cuimhin liom é a thuilleadh.
Ach seo anois í is chloisfeá ó cheann ceann an tí altranais í.
Ag gabháil fhoinn de shíor nach bhfuil aon fhocail leis.
Níl ann ach 'ech, ech, ech, ech' gach uair den lá
is den oíche, ag líonadh is ag dul i dtrá

Our Mermaid Goes Under Again

I wouldn't mind so much
had she returned to the Land-Under-Wave
and found her share of happiness.

But she didn't.
Here was a woman who hardly ever
spoke out in her natural life
and who laughed, so far as I can remember,
three times only when she was on dry land,
each of those a somewhat uneasy laugh.

One day she laughed as she passed a man in the street
who was giving out about the shoes
he'd just bought, how the soles on them were too thin.
She laughed right in his face, saying they'd be thick enough
    for his needs.
She knew rightly he'd be dead and buried within three days.

Another time she laughed when she passed a man in the
    middle of the road
who was cursing and swearing
at a stone on which he'd stubbed the big toe of his left foot.
She didn't give this one any information
but later on told me that if he'd only got a grip on himself
and dug up that stone he'd find a pot of gold waiting for him
    underneath it.

As for the third laugh, I can't remember it anymore.
But now there's this woman whom you can hear throughout
    the hospice.
She's forever singing, but singing a song that has no words.
There's this perpetual 'ech, ech, ech, ech' throughout the day
and the night as well, coming and going

de réir mar a bhuaileann na tonnaíocha líonrith is anbhá
i gcoinne a hintinne, is go mbraitheann sí céim níos cóngaraí
do chiumhais an duibheagáin.

Níl sí anseo nó ansúd.
Ní hiasc is ní feoil í.
Uaireanta searann sí polláirí a sróine
i slí is go dtuigfeá go b'ann a bhíonn sí
a bá san aer
faoi mar a bheadh breac go mbeirfeá air le slat
is go leagfá aniar ar an bport é.

Ar a shon san, níl sí sásta bheith faoi loch.
Anois, nuair a thagann na focail chúiche in aon chor
is 'olagón ó' a síorphort.

with the great waves of panic and consternation
breaking against her mind as she feels herself draw closer
to the edge of the abyss.

She's neither here nor there.
She's neither fish nor flesh.
Sometimes she has a sharp intake of breath through her
    nostrils
that would make you think she's
drowning in air,
like a trout you'd caught with a rod
and taken to the bank.

All the same, she's not happy to be in this submerged state.
Now, the odd time she does have anything to say,
you can take it to the bank it's some version of 'Woe is me'.

Spléachanna Fánacha ar an dTír-fó-Thoinn

Tá fianaise láidir ann, dar le daoine áirithe
gur thriomaigh an limistéar go léir sin, An Tír-fó-Thoinn
i ngiorracht cúpla céad míle den Mhol Thuaidh.

Ar ndóigh,
ón uair go mairimíd i ré na ngréasán satailíte
is ós na seascaidí i leith go bhfuil spásairí mórán tíortha
ag timpeallú na cruinne uair amháin gach ceithre uaire fichead
níor tugadh puinn aird ar na scéalta úd
a ríomhadh ó am go chéile ar oileán aisteach aduain
á nochtadh ins an Mhuir Thuaidh.
Bhí mórán a chuir ar chomhchéim iad leis na seanscéalta
i dtaobh ollphéisteanna mara nó na dragain úd
nó na hochtapais ábhalmhóra a bhíodh á lua ag mairnéalaigh
na seanré. Nó an scéal sin a insíonn Naomh Bréanainn féin
i dtaobh tine á lasadh ag a mhanaigh ar charraig aonair,
sarar thuigeadar, óna shearradh fíochmhar, gurb é a bhí fúthu
ná an Míol Mór é féin, ris a ráitear Leibhiatan.
(Tá pictiúr dó seo ríofa ag an mairnéalach Moslamach Piri Réis
ina léarscáil cáiliúil domhanda ón gcúigdéagú haois.)
I mbeagán focal, dhein na húdaráis spior spear ar fad díobh
   mar scéalta.

Ach tá mórán daoine a chonaic an áit, nó samhailt éigin mar é.
Loingseoirí is mairnéalaigh go raibh a mbárcanna beaga
ag coraíocht go cruaidh in aghaidh oighearshruthanna
na hoíche Artaice,

Some Observations on Land-Under-Wave

There's ample evidence, according to some people,
that the whole region of Land-Under-Wave
emerged from the waters within a couple of hundred miles
   of the North Pole.

Of course,
since we live in the era of the satellite network
and, since the seventies, astronauts of every nationality
have been circumnavigating the globe at least once every
   twenty-four hours,
these are stories in which no one puts a lot of store,
stories that themselves surfaced from time to time about some
strange and wonderful island
appearing in the Northern Sea.
Most people put them on a par with the legends
about sea monsters and dragons
or gigantic octopuses recounted by mariners
in olden times. Or even that legend that Saint Brendan
   himself sets down
of how his monks had lit a fire on this far-flung smooth rock
before they realized, by its fierce shaking and shuddering,
   what lay under them
was the Great Whale itself, the one known as Leviathan.
(There's even an illustration of this by the Muslim
   cartographer Piri Reis
on his famous fifteenth-century map of the world.)
In a word or two, the authorities dismiss these reports as
   being inconsequential.

Still, quite a number of people have seen the place or some
   version of it.
Seamen and sailors whose small barques
have been contending with the glaciers
in the Arctic night

mhaíodar gur cuireadh an croí trasna orthu
go minic nuair a nochtaí go hobann
faoi mar a bheadh i bhfís aislingeach
dún is pálás lonrach is é go léir faoi bharr lasrach.

D'áirigh cuid acu gurb é an rud a chonaiceadar
ná túr ard criostail ar fhaill do-shroiste
nach raibh fáil air ó aon taobh.
Dúirt a thuilleadh acu go raibh fuinneoga ina sraithibh
gearrtha sa charraig, is solas ag sceitheadh astu.
Bhí an fhaill go léir pollta sa tslí is gur dhóigh leat
gurb é a bhí ann ná cruiceog bheach.

Do dheineas féin iniúchadh doimhin
agus miontaighde nach beag ar na tuairiscí seo
toisc suim fé leith a bheith agam i gcinniúint na murúch.
Is ní mór a admháil go mbíonn eithne éigin den bhfírinne
le fáil ins gach aon scéal scéil.
'Sé an rud is mó ar fad a chuir ag cuimhneamh mé
nach bhfaighfeá píolóit eitleáin ar bith
ar ór ná ar airgead
a eitleodh thar an limistéar áirithe seo.
Sheachnaídís é ar chuma an bháis,
de bharr a raibh d'eitleáin a chuaigh ar lár ann,
gan tuairisc orthu ná tásc.

Caithfidh mé a admháil go bhfuilim go mór faoi dhraíocht
ag íomhá an oileáin seo.
Tá go leor tagairtí dó i litríocht na seanteangan,
is ainmneacha difriúla air san mbéaloideas comhaimseartha.
Orthu seo tá 'An Bhreasaíl', 'Tír Hiúdaí' lámh le Dún na
    nGall,
'Beag-Ára', 'Cill Stuithín', 'Teach Doinn' is 'Dún idir Dhá
    Dhrol'.

have sworn their hearts were in their mouths
often enough when, suddenly, there would hove into view
as if in a vision or a mirage,
a palace or strong fortress and it all ablaze with lights.

Some of them have suggested that what they saw
was a tall tower of crystal on an imposing cliff
that couldn't be scaled from any side.
Others said there were rows of windows
cut into the rock itself, with light streaming out of them.
The whole cliff-face was so honeycombed
it resembled nothing so much as a beehive.

I've made a detailed inspection of,
and made painstaking research into, these reports
because of the special interest I have in the fate of the merfolk.
I have to admit there's a kernel of truth
in even the most outlandish of these yarns.
The one thing that's given me cause for reflection
is that you'd never get any pilot,
never mind how much you might offer him by way of money,
to fly over that particular area.
They avoid it like the plague
because of the number of planes that have gone down there,
disappearing without trace.

I also have to admit I'm spellbound
by the image of this island.
There are many references to it in the literature of Old Irish,
along with many variant names for it in contemporary
   folklore.
Among these are 'Hy-Breasil', 'Tír Hiúdaí' (hard by Donegal),
'Beag-Ára', 'Cill Swithin', 'The House of Donn', and 'The
   Fortress-between-Two-Cauldrons'.

Ach ón méid a thuigim
ní raibh aon cheann acu seo róchóngarach don Mhol.

D'fhéadfá a shamhlú go raibh murúch éigin a dhein lab
is a d'éirigh chomh saibhir le Croesus nó le Crassus,
fear lán de chomhacht, a chruthaigh sórt 'buen retiro'
dó féin in áit chomh sceirdiúil.
Fear neamheaglach go raibh a dhúil
i gcodarsnachtaí aeráide.
Shéidfeadh stoirmeacha fiaine is gálaí fíochmhara
is bheadh glafarnach gaoithe de shíor ina chluasa.
Bheadh an t-aigéan lán de bhloghtracha leac oighir
is de ghrúm a bheadh á raideadh ag an fharraige cháite
i gcoinne na cloiche basáilte.

Ní raibh fearann riamh chomh fuar leis
ins an domhan iomlán.
Is laistigh, a mhalairt glan — teas folcadán
agus gairdíní geimhridh, ceol uirlise i hallaí arda
is thar gach aon rud eile,
an uaillmhian is an saibhreas,
an rachmas seo gan teora.
San áit seo
éiríonn gan chuimse le gach aon rud.
Chualathas trácht go minic ar an gCaor Aduaidh,
ag titim mar chuirtíní ar oícheanta spéirghealaí.
Lasmuigh, seolann cnoic oighir thar bráid is iad go
   mómharach.
Titeann na stoirmeacha móra chun síochána.
Tá sámhnas ann.
Tá cothromaíocht sheasmhach i bhfeidhm,
faoi mar a bheadh fórsaí dochreidte ar foluain
faoi dhromchla na dtonn.

From what I understand, though,
none of these is anywhere near the North Pole.

You could easily imagine a merman who'd made a lump
    of money
and become as rich as Croesus or Crassus,
a very powerful merman, might build some class of
    'buen retiro'
for himself in this godforsaken place.
He'd need to be a fearless soul, one who enjoyed
the extremes of climate,
given the wild storms and fierce gales
and the constant howling of the wind in his ears,
the ocean full of slabs of broken ice
and ice floes dashed and dashed by the choppy seas
against the basalt.

There was never a region so cold
in the whole wide world.
And inside, the direct opposite — hot springs
and winter gardens, stringed music heard in high halls
and, above all,
the overvaulting ambition and riches,
the unimaginable wealth.
In this place
everything exceeds all expectations.
It's said the Northern Lights
hang over it like curtains on moonless nights.
Outside, icebergs gracefully glide by.
The great storms blow themselves out.
There's a period of calm.
There's a constant balancing act,
as if incredible forces were heaving
just underneath the waves.

Bímíd ag tnúth go mífhoighneach le rud mór éigin
ag tarlú amach anseo ach idir an dá linn
táimid suaimhneasach, gan uamhan,
gan anbhá, gan líonrith.

Tá's ag an mhurúch seo 'gainne cá bhfuil an t-oileán seo.
Sin rud amháin go bhfuilim nach mór siúráilte dhe.
Labhair sí tráth dá saol ar an bpríomhbhealach isteach ann,
go raibh sé cosúil le Cabhsa na bhFomhórach nó Uaimh
   Fingal.
Níor luaigh sí riamh níos mó ná san, ná níor labhair
smid ar na fleánna is féastaí a chleachtadar
ar chiumhais an duibheagáin; an tine ghealáin
ag rince ar fhaobhar maol an neamhní, an bearna baol
nach luaitear san Amhrán Náisiúnta.
Cé gur mó rud dorcha duairc a chonaic sí,
táim cinnte de, bíonn sí anois,
is í ag athbhreithniú, tostach i gcónaí.
Tá sí tugtha go mór do mhórfheabhas niamhrach an chiúinis
is í ag leathchuimhneamh i gcónaí
ar na hoícheanta gealaí spéiriúla.

Is tá an ré sin go léir thart, ar aon nós.
Éinne a dhéanfadh a shlí, ar ais nó ar éigean,
isteach sa dún am éigin anaithnid amach anseo
cad a chífidh sé roimis
ach sraitheanna fada de sheomraí folmha
ceann i ndiaidh an chinn eile?
Cuirfidh troist trom a bhróga féin,
ag macallú faoi bhíomaí coincréite an díona,
uamhan is ceann faoi air.
Leanfaidh sé leis, ar feadh i bhfad,
ag siúl go dtí ceann scríbe

We are waiting impatiently for some earth-shattering event
to occur at any moment but in the interim
we are at peace, free of dread,
terror- and panic-free.

Our own mermaid knows where this island lies.
That's one thing I'm definitely sure of.
At one stage in her life she even described its entranceway,
how it was like the Giant's Causeway or, more precisely,
　Fingal's Cave.
That's all she ever mentioned about it, nor did she ever discuss
the junketing and jollification engaged in there
on the brink of the abyss. Like St Elmo's fire
dancing on the bare edge of nothingness, at a 'gap of danger'
that's not mentioned in our National Anthem.
Though she was probably a witness to many dark deeds —
of that I'm pretty sure — she's now
completely mum about them.
She's much more given to propose just how splendid a thing
　is silence,
to perpetually ponder as she does
those cloudless, moonless nights.

Besides which, anyway, those days are long gone.
Anyone who might make his way
sometime in the future
into that fortress
would find there
only row upon row of empty rooms,
one leading into the next.
The heavy tread of his own shoes
echoing up to the concrete beams of the roof
would at once startle and shame him.
He would follow on, for a long time,
to the bitter end

go dtí go dtiocfadh sé i ndeireadh báire,
thíos i siléar íochtarach na cruinne,
ar iarsmaí deireanacha an domhain úd
atá imithe as cuimhne — ar chualaí móra d'fhiacla óir,
d'fháinní cluaise is de spéaclaí,
ar na mílte is na mílte
de bhallaibh éadaigh ina gcarnáin smúiteacha,
ar chomhaid is innéacsaí iomadúla
clúdaithe faoi líontáin damhán alla,
ar stórais stoc earraí tirime,
go háirithe mórán Éireann drochghallúnach.

where he would at length,
in the deepest cellar under the earth,
stumble upon the last remnants of a complete world
which has disappeared from memory, its heaps of gold teeth
and earrings and eyeglasses,
thousands and thousands
of old garments in garment-piles,
a filing system with its innumerable indexes
covered in cobwebs,
a huge amount of dry goods
including a mountain of low-grade soap.

Acknowledgement is due to An Sagart, An Daingean, for poems by Nuala Ní Dhomhnaill which were published first in *Cead Aighnis* (1998).

The publishers acknowledge the assistance of Liam Mac Cóil with the Irish.